MAN ON THE MOVE

ERRATA

P 149 — Caption 4 should read *The Model "T" Ford, 1910*

Caption 5 should read *Citroen,* 1922

Caption 7 should read *White Steamer,* 1904

Credits: 4 and 7 Firestone Archives

P 212 — Caption at top-right page should read Jan. 17, 1955

Line 13 should read Jan. 17, 1955

MAN ON THE MOVE by Harvey S. Firestone, Jr.

G. P. PUTNAM'S SONS, New York

MAN
ON
THE MOVE

The Story of Transportation

by HARVEY S. FIRESTONE, Jr.

G. P. PUTNAM'S SONS, *New York*

ACKNOWLEDGMENTS

The author and publisher acknowledge with thanks the co-operation of the following for the illustrations reproduced in this work: American Trucking Associations, Inc.; Association of American Railroads; The Boeing Company; The Cunard Steam-Ship Company Limited; The Firestone Tire & Rubber Company; Ford Motor Company, Educational Affairs Department; General Dynamics Corporation; General Motors Corporation; Italian Line; Lockheed Aircraft Company; National Aeronautics and Space Administration, Audio-Visual Division; New York Public Library, Picture Collection; North American Aviation, Inc., Columbus Division; Mr. Donald Robinson; Sikorsky Aircraft (Division of United Aircraft Corporation); The Smithsonian Institution; Standard Oil Company (New Jersey); Mr. Edwin Tunis and The World Publishing Company for six illustrations from *Wheels*, © 1955, by Edwin Tunis; and Wide World Photos, Inc.

The quotation on page 53 is from *Satires and Epistles of Horace*. Translated by Smith Palmer Bovie. Copyright, 1959, 1963, The University of Chicago Press. Reprinted by permission.

Library of Congress Catalog Card
Number: 66–25866

To my wife, Betty

Contents

Preface

The United States government's Space Defense Center in Colorado Springs has just reported that 1,094 satellites—American, British, Russian, Canadian and French—are orbiting the earth today. Some will remain in space for another hundred years or more. Before reentering the atmosphere of earth, many of them will have traveled tens of billions of miles.

If these facts were not so scientifically documented, they would be nearly unbelievable. Even in the relatively short span of time between the turn of the century, shortly after I was born, and today, there has been such an evolution in transportation and man's use of it that any single word describing its progress, no matter how superlative, would be inadequate.

My family has been identified with transportation since August 3, 1900, when my father founded The Firestone Tire & Rubber Company. When I was a youngster in Akron, Ohio, the horse and buggy were still the principal means of local transportation. And the horseless carriage, chugging along the dusty street, was stared at with an uncertain combination of derision and wonder.

Even as late as 1916, when I was on a camping trip with Thomas Alva Edison, John Burroughs, Henry Ford, and my father, most of the people along the rutted dirt roads were more impressed by the sight of the automobile in action than by eminent Americans in it.

When I ride in a jet plane today at close to the speed of sound, I hearken back to 1918 when I was learning to fly for the U.S. Navy. The open-cockpit biplane with rickety wings could sometimes hit ninety miles an hour provided the wind was blowing the right way.

Even in the middle 1920's, when Mrs. Firestone and I arrived by ship in Liberia, we had to go ashore in dugout canoes.

And today, less than half a century later, astronauts are on the verge of rocketing through space at 25,000 miles an hour, heading for the moon and the planets beyond it.

What giant strides have been made in transportation in our own century! Much of this progress in modern times, however, stems from what has gone before in centuries past.

Ever since my student days at Princeton, I have had a constant awareness of the transportation industry because it was about then I began my career in the management of the Firestone company which has now spanned nearly fifty years. I've traveled to virtually every part of the world, going from place to place on everything from jackasses to jets, from tractors to tramp steamers.

I have always had the hope that I could one day tell the story of the evolvement of transportation and the involvement of man in it: how the human race always has wanted to go farther, higher, faster; how we always have had men of vision to devise the means of going, and brave men willing to push the frontiers of distance and space out a little further than they were before.

The essence of the story, of course, is that those who dreamed and those who dared have together made this a better, richer, and happier world.

From the beginning of recorded time, transportation has helped to mold the social, economic, military, and political history of the world. Those whose accomplishments broadened the horizons of transportation through the ages have helped shape the course of civilization, and this will continue to be true.

Writing the history in one brief volume represented a sizable problem of planning and editing, particularly in the light of the mountains of material that I had gathered over the years. However, it seemed to me that it was worth trying.

The time spent in researching, editing, and writing this book has been rewarding. Meeting the challenge of being a historian was different from but as fulfilling as meeting the challenge of business.

Lucian, the Greek writer, in his essay "On How To Write History" urged the ideal historian to be "fearless, incorruptible and free; outspoken and a friend of truth . . . uninfluenced by likes or dislikes . . . a fair and impartial judge who will never give one side more than its due." In this book I have tried to follow Lucian's advice.

My thanks are due to many: to Dr. Mohammed El Zayyat, former Professor, University of Cairo, for his knowledgeable interpretation of early Egyptian history; to David A. Titus of Wesleyan University for his guidance through the labyrinths of the Oriental past; to J. Frank Diggs of *U.S. News & World Report* for his insight into Latin American road transport; to Rose Benes, editor of *Airworld* magazine, for her files on air transport; to Scott Bailey, editor of *Automobile Quarterly,* for his automotive data; to Robert J. Fitzpatrick, Texas Eastern Transmission Corporation, for his collection of facts about pipelines; to Tom Mahoney, author, for his help on the history of early automobile days; and to Michael Harwood for both his taste and his scholarship in conducting overall research.

The staffs of the Library of Congress, the New York Public Library, and the Columbia University Library have been cooperative far beyond the call of bibliographical duty.

Dr. William D. Overman, founder and past president of the Society of American Archivists, has aided appreciably in solving research problems. Bernard Frazier has given encouragement and good counsel. Eve Jackson has performed splendidly at her typewriter in readying the manuscript for publication, and William Targ of Putnam's has been a fine editor, rich in ideas.

I owe my special gratitude to Donald Robinson for his invaluable editorial assistance. He has long known and understood my eagerness to go exploring through the yesteryears of transportation.

Harvey S. Firestone, Jr.

AKRON, OHIO
Summer, 1966

MAN ON THE MOVE

I

The Road to Rome

THERE IS A HAZE OVER the beginning of man's travels, but this much seems sure. Manlike creatures were traveling through the trackless jungles, deserts, primeval forests, and plains in Africa, western parts of Asia, and Europe 500,000 years ago. They were recognizable as men. They walked erect, they wore clothing of a sort, and they carried weapons. They lived in caves, a family to a cave. Little communities of them were scattered about the countryside. Transient communities, because these manlike creatures were constantly on the move. They were hunters and when the wild game on which they fed—deer, bison, elephants, tigers, and the like—wandered on, they had to follow for hundreds of miles. During the ice ages, they had to go still farther in order to escape the cold that swept down from the north. And to return northward as the cold relented.

Just one means of land transportation existed—man's own feet.

This was true even after *homo sapiens* with his bigger brain evolved 50,000 years ago. Man continued to move by foot only. No one had discovered how to ride on an animal's back. The wheel was undreamed of.

Then men began to imitate nature. A swift stream was crossed by chopping down a tree so that it formed a bridge. A gorge was spanned by vines. Soon men went nature one better. Game that

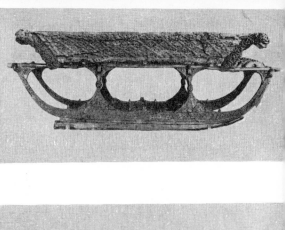

Sleighs with runners, found in Norse ships, Oseberg, Norway.

used to be dragged home by its horns was slung from a pole and carried between two men. Hides were fashioned into sacks to tote belongings. The seeds of progress were being planted.

Toward the end of the last ice age, certainly by 8000 B.C., trade was underway. Seashells were being bartered hundreds of miles inland. Apparently they were all the rage for necklaces, bracelets, and anklets.

Trade was just the impetus man needed to improve his tools and his transport. He started to make better implements out of stone, bone, wood, and reindeer antlers, and with them he was able to construct conveyances to help him carry things.

The first great development along these lines came around 7000 B.C. It was a sledge with runners, and it originated in the ice-covered regions of northern Europe. Women pulled it with thongs made of hide. The men had to keep their arms free for fighting.

The sledge was to be invented again, in other parts of the world, from the Mediterranean to China. Through history it's been like that. The same good idea has occurred independently to many different persons, in different areas, at different times.

In the north, sledges ran smoothly on the ice and snow. People in the south used them on dry land. They poured water on the ground in front of the runners. Or, later, milk. The butterfat content in the milk proved to be a most effective lubricant.

Civilization was germinating faster now. Here and there, permanent little villages and towns were springing up in the Near East. (One of the first of them was named Jericho, its population got to be 3,000, and its famous stone walls, the ones that came tumbling down at Joshua's behest, were built around 7000 B.C.) Men began to domesticate animals and reap wild grain. Between 7000 and 5000 B.C., they learned to sow their own grain and to irrigate their farm land. They started to make baskets and pottery. And in Iran and Asia Minor, metalworking was introduced.

By the fourth millennium, the metalsmiths had discovered that copper and other metals could be softened under high heat and shaped. It was a vast stride forward, right out of the stone age. Weapons and tools could be made of copper rather than clumsy, hard-to-handle stone. The whole way of life was changed. As one scholar wrote:

"Think what the impact of copper must have been on a community that had only stone weapons—especially if a rival village had equipped itself with metal weapons!"

Communities that once had been completely self-sufficient had to trade in order to obtain the new copper weapons and utensils.

Meanwhile, another industry was spreading. Pottery was beginning to be traded beyond the boundaries of the towns in which it was made.

The need for better land transport was growing.

The use of animals was the next big advance. Somewhere, somehow, men learned to pack goods on the backs of asses.

It is known that asses were carrying goods in Egypt in 3500 B.C. Jokes were circulating even then about the obstinacy of donkeys. A bas-relief in one Egyptian tomb pictures three exasperated men trying to get a stubborn ass to move. The first man is tugging the beast by a front hoof and an ear, the second man is pushing it from behind, and the third is about to hit it with a stick—hard.

Before long, men learned to ride their donkeys. Then came a

bigger advance. Some time in the fourth millennium, farmers learned to yoke oxen to their plows and sledges. For the first time, man had at his disposal a power other than his own muscles to pull loads. And in the second half of the fourth millennium, somebody had an idea for one of the greatest inventions in the entire history

Edwin Tunis

Solid wheels on fixed axle.

of mankind. He thought of applying rotary motion to a vehicle and created the wheel.

There are conflicting theories about the origin of this brilliant device. Some authorities believe that it evolved from the roller. Centuries earlier, they say, men had conceived the notion of cutting a tree into small logs and placing the logs under a heavily loaded sledge. The men then pushed the sledge forward until it rolled off the logs. Thereupon they moved the logs ahead, set the sledge on them again, and repeated the process. It eased their hauling problems immeasurably. After a while, the theory goes, other men cut grooves in the rollers and fitted them into projections on the bottom of the sledge to keep them in place. From these "captive rollers," so it is thought, evolved the wheel.

Another widely held theory is that potters first developed the wheel for use in their trade and it was later adapted to vehicles.

The best thinking seems to be that the vehicular wheel was a separate invention. Probably it was born in the land of the Garden of Eden, or Iraq, as the atlases label it now. Here, in the Tigris-Euphrates Valley, from the fifth millennium B.C. to 2000 B.C., or thereabouts, lived a fascinating people. They were the Sumerians and their accomplishments were nothing short of amazing. They created the world's first method of writing, and much more. They composed the first histories, erected the first churches, produced literature, art, music, and architecture, plus spectacular new ideas in government. They built a flourishing commerce, and, sad to record, an exorbitant system of taxation. In Sumer everything was highly taxed, including death.

The first hints of the wheeled vehicles are those we get from the records which the Sumerians so carefully kept. On clay tablets dated about 3000 B.C. appear symbols for two-wheel carts and four-wheel wagons. They show that the Sumerians had perched their sledges, curved runners and all, on wheels.

Even in the twentieth century, oxen continue to pull loads. Photo taken in Scott County, Miss., 1912.

Standard Oil Co., (N. J.) photo.

It was in a Sumerian cemetery that the earliest remains of vehicular wheels were found. The distinquished British archeologist, Sir Leonard Wooley, discovered them when he was digging in the tombs of the monarchs of Ur. Inside the tomb of a King Abargi, who ruled around 2800 B.C., Professor Wooley came upon the remnants of two wagons together with the bones of seventy-four servants (six men and sixty-eight women) who had been buried alive so that they could serve His Majesty in the next world. Each wagon had four wheels and was pulled by three oxen.

These remains of wheels were little more than impressions, merely stained earth and some metallic fittings. But enough was left to indicate what the wheels had looked like. Each was made of three pieces of wood held together by bands of copper across the face of the circle. Archeologists think there was probably a leather tire around the rim, tacked down by copper nails.

The evidence implies that the use of the wheel spread out of Sumer in all directions, like ripples following the splash of a stone in a pond. The Indus Valley, in present-day Pakistan, saw wheeled transport around 2500 B.C.; Crete, Turkey, and southern Russia about 2000 B.C.; Palestine and Egypt about 1600 B.C. It got to mainland Greece about 1500 B.C.; to China during the Shang Dynasty in the fourteenth century B.C. Slowly but surely, it continued its spread, to northern Italy somewhere before 1000 B.C., to central Europe and north to Scandinavia between the thirteenth and ninth centuries B.C.; across the channel to Britain around 500 B.C. In most places, spoked wheels soon coexisted with the solid wheels.

One cannot overestimate the wheel's significance. Virtually every iota of progress man has made in land transport has depended upon it.

Inevitably, the wheel was adapted for warfare. By 2700 B.C. or thereabouts, the versatile Sumerians had come up with a devastating new weapon—the chariot.

Down in the tombs of the same kings of Ur, Professor Wooley uncovered the evidence that war had taken to wheels. He found a sumptuous wooden box (the so-called Royal Standard of Ur), about one and one-half feet long, adorned with figures made out of shell and limestone set against a background of lapis lazuli. In the various scenes are portrayed four-wheel chariots, each pulled by four onagers, donkeylike cousins of the horse. The chariots were apparently made of hide stretched over a wooden frame. Their shape may best be imagined by visualizing an old-fashioned, high-backed armchair—the back of the chair being the front of the chariot. One man drove and another, a spearman, stood behind him on a sort of tailgate, ready to leap off into action.

Naturally, the chariots are shown riding mercilessly over hapless, bleeding victims.

Not that there weren't many other uses for vehicular wheels. We know from clay models that covered wagons were rolling across the northern steppes as early as 2000 B.C. and we learn of more imaginative functions yet from the Greek historian Herodotus.

A certain kind of sheep, Herodotus wrote, had "such long tails—not less than four and a half feet—that if they were allowed to trail on the ground, they would develop sores from the constant friction; so to obviate this, the shepherds [made] little [wheeled] carts and [fixed] one of them under the tail of each sheep, to keep it clear of the ground."

Although they had learned to utilize animals to do some of their work, men long remained beasts of burden themselves.

Men alone supplied the motive power when Pharaoh Cheops of Egypt decided to build a gigantic sepulcher in the twenty-eighth century B.C. Slaves lifted blocks of stone that weighed as much as fifteen tons apiece onto sledges and dragged them from quarries in the Arabian hills to the Nile where they were ferried across on barges and agonizingly hauled the rest of the way to a forbidding desert spot at Giza. In the course of thirty years, they moved more than 2,300,000 of the immense stone blocks and erected a structure that was to become one of the seven wonders of the world—the Great Pyramid, which covered nearly thirteen acres and rose as high as a forty-story skyscraper.

Those straining, sweating slaves did have one enormous advantage—a paved road.

Before work on the pyramid was begun, Cheops' engineers spent ten years constructing a raised road, paved with limestone blocks, that was sixty feet wide and ran five-eighths of a mile from the Nile's high-water mark to the construction site. This wasn't man's first paved road. One was built on the island of Cyprus perhaps as early as 5500 B.C. But it unquestionably was the first big road construction job.

There were more innovations that helped to expedite transportation, such as tunnels. The scene: Babylon, capital of the empire that supplanted Sumer. The time: the twenty-second century, B.C., at the peak of Babylonia's early power.

Through the middle of the city flowed the Euphrates, a principal artery of transport and at the same time an annoying hindrance to the citizens with business to conduct on both sides. Among those discommoded by the river was the mighty King Nimrod. His palace was on the wrong side of the water from his favorite temple of Jupiter. In 2180 B.C., he commanded that a tunnel be dug under the 600-foot-wide stream.

Twenty years' work went into the project. Vast walls of brick were put up to divert the river into a temporary channel during the dry seasons. Under the muddy riverbed, a tunnel was dug that was more than 3,000 feet long. Arched with brick, it was 15 feet wide and 12 feet high, big enough for a modern-day subway train to run through.

As the means of transportation improved, travel increased. By the start of the second millennium, the movement of people and goods over long distances was well-established. Trade routes linked India, Afghanistan, all of Mesopotamia, Iran, and Anatolia. The Assyrians were shipping textiles by donkey train to Kanesh on the plateau of eastern Anatolia. From there, the donkey caravans brought back amber that had originated on the shores of the Baltic Sea and metals like iron that cost five times as much as gold.

Travel by caravan was laboriously slow. Despite the wheel and the pack animal, the average caravan went only as fast as a man could walk. Even the kings' couriers didn't go very fast. King Khannurabi of Babylon once sent a command to an official 125 miles away to return home posthaste. "Day and night you shall travel, so that you may arrive at Babylon within two days," His Majesty decreed.

That came to the breakneck speed of approximately two and one-half miles per hour.

Something new and revolutionary was about to develop in land transport, though, that was to give men mobility beyond their most extravagent dreams and a speed that was not to be exceeded for 3,800 years. It was the horse.

It seems odd to think of the horse as a new development like the automobile and the jet plane. Yet that is precisely what it was, and its effects were as dramatic. It was to topple empires and create new ones.

According to all findings, the horse originated 45,000,000 to 50,000,000 years ago in what was to become known as North America. For some mysterious reason, the entire North American species died out and no horse was seen on that continent until the Spanish arrived in the New World in the early part of the sixteenth century A.D. Luckily, before their extinction, the North American horses had spread to South America and on to Africa, Europe, and Asia. There they roamed through the forests and plains, from France all the way to Mongolia.

These early horses were small and hairy, a mere 4 feet high at the shoulder, with startlingly big heads. In Asia they were a reddish-brown color. Those in Russia and western Europe were a dull gray.

They were a hard lot to tame. Oxen had been domesticated more than 1,000 years before men were able to domesticate horses. The first men to do it were probably nomads in Mesopotamia and China, and the time was probably somewhere between 2500 and 2000 B.C. After that, the use of the horse spread rapidly. By 2000 B.C., the Sumerians were riding horseback. A little fable indicates it.

"If my burden is always to be this," a Sumerian horse loudly laments, "I shall become weak."

The Greeks were using horses by 1700 B.C., the Egyptians by 1600 B.C., the Indians by 1500 B.C., the Swedes by 1300 B.C. In 1000 BC., the horse was in use up and down Europe, Asia, and North Africa.

Men could go twenty miles per hour on a horse. A week's travels could be reckoned in hundreds of miles. Governments could exert control over much larger territories. And military operations could encompass vast distances, so war took on a whole new dimension. The day of the great conquests was at hand. Between 1900 and 1500 B.C., the Hittites with their horses subjugated horseless Babylon and eastern Turkey. The Achaeans conquered Greece. The Aryans poured into the Indus Valley, and the Hyksos took over Egypt. The horseless Egyptians adopted the equine weapon of their

conquerors, expelled them, and forged an empire for themselves
that reached to the mountains of northern Syria and the upper
Euphrates.

Since they were too small to bear men in armor, horses were
primarily employed to draw chariots. They gave them speed and
deadliness such as chariots had never before known. No force of
infantrymen could stand up against them.

Edwin Tunis

Greek traveling cart, about 250 B. C.

Chariotry became so pivotal that a warring power was identified
as "a state of 300 (400, 500, etc.) chariots." The chariots came in
all shapes and sizes, and were drawn by one to four horses. Some
nations made them nastier by attaching curved knives to the hubs
of the wheels.

Horse-drawn chariots were equally valuable for peaceful transportation. They were employed in traveling, hunting, racing, carrying the mails. Sang an ancient Chinese poet:

> Shu has gone hunting,
> Mounted in his chariot and four.
> The reins are in his grasp like ribbons
> While the two outside horses move as dancers do.

There is a vivid passage in the *Odyssey* describing travel by
chariot. Homer has Nestor command:

"Lo now, my sons, yoke for Telemachus horses with flowing

mane and lead them beneath the car, that he may get forward on his way.

"Quickly, they yoked the swift horses beneath the chariot," Homer goes on. "And the dames that kept the stores placed therein corn and wine and dainties, such as princes eat. . . . So Telemachus stept up into the goodly car, and with him Peisistratus, son of Nesyot. . . . (He) grasped the reins in his hands, and he touched the horses with the whip to start them, and nothing loth the pair flew toward the plain. . . . All day long they swayed the yoke they bore upon their necks."

It was a lot better going places this way than in the slow old oxcarts.

The variety of chariots and other horse-drawn vehicles became myriad. Among others, the Greeks had the two-horse *biga*, which women often drove; the three-horse *triga*; and the four-horse *quadriga*. All of them were chariots equipped with seats. The Romans rode in such vehicles as the *reda* which looked like a bathtub on wheels and could carry six people; the *cisium*, a light two-wheeled cart; the *carruca*, a traveling conveyance which sometimes contained a bed; and the *birotum* which was an ancestor of today's trotting sulky.

Like many Roman vehicles, the *birotum* could be rented. A sort of a drive-it-yourself chariot.

Kings of China during the Chou Dynasty, between 1027 and 221 B.C., had five different kinds of chariots: the *Kin Loo* for state occasions; the *Seang Loo* for driving to audiences; the *Kih Loo*, a leather-bound affair for military expeditions; the *Muh Loo* for hunting jaunts; and the *Yah Loo*, a magnificent, bejeweled equipage which they utilized when they went to make sacrifices. Queens had four kinds of conveyances, including one for visiting the king and another for picking mulberries.

Vehicle-pulling was rough on the horses. The ancients harnessed them in the same manner they did oxen, with wooden yokes over their necks that were held in place by straps around the horses' throats. If the unfortunate animal pulled too hard, he choked himself and had to halt. Consequently, horses achieved one-fourth of the power in those days that they develop now. The horse collar which lets horses breathe normally wasn't invented until the fourth century A.D.

For all its effectiveness, the chariot went out of fashion in war, replaced by the armored rider on a new, larger type of horse.

In western Iran, a tribe named the Medes spent generations breeding horses for size and finally developed horses that were as big as those we know today, and large and strong enough to carry men equipped for battle.

With mounts like that at their disposal, the Medes, the Persians and other Irani peoples were able to build invincible cavalry forces. Chariots, which were restricted to comparatively smooth terrain, couldn't possibly cope with them. By the end of the fourth century B.C., the chariot had practically vanished from the battlefield.

Riding horseback was no joy at first for the rider or the horse. Stirrups were not invented until the first century B.C., and the true saddle didn't come until the fourth century A.D. Cavalrymen had to ride bareback, balancing themselves and their armor without the benefit of stirrup support. They made quite a clatter when they fell. Which was often. As for the horse, it was not until the fourth century B.C. that the first horseshoe was invented, and it was a skimpy concoction of leather merely tied on to the horse's foot. Iron horseshoes didn't arrive for 300 more years.

Some other animals were also making their bow on the transportation scene. The mule was one. That ingeniously contrived offspring of the horse and the ass seems to have been bred as early as 1700 B.C. It was mentioned in a fable of that period.

"Oh mule, will your sire recognize you, or will your dam recognize you?" the fabulist rhetorically inquired.

The answer clearly was no.

The mule's strength, nimbleness, and evil temper rapidly became legendary. So much so that the Roman historian Pliny the Elder felt it necessary to record the popular preventative for the mule's propensity to kick.

"A mule can be checked from kicking," he wrote, "by rather frequent drinks of wine."

The camel, another beast with a bad disposition, was in use as a pack animal at the beginning of the first millennium. Or before. Many of the early imports from China, the fine silks and spices, were delivered by camel caravan. The elephant had been domesticated in China by 1000 B.C., too. The elder Pliny waxed quite rhapsodic about pachyderms:

> The largest land animal is the elephant, and it is the nearest to man in intelligence. It understands the language of its country and obeys orders, remembers duties that it has been taught, is pleased by affection and by marks of honor, nay, more, it possesses virtues rare even in man, honesty, wisdom, justice also respect for the stars and reverence for the sun and moon. . . .

There were other inventions such as skis. They came into use in northern Europe about 2000 B.C. and gave the northerners wings on snow and ice.

There was the first map, at least the first that is known. It was drawn on a clay tablet around 1800 B.C., in Mesopotamia, and charted the sacred city of Nippur, with its river harbor, piers, two big canals, and imposing temples to the omnipotent god En-lil. There was the first map done on papyrus, dated about 1200 B.C., in Egypt. It showed the hills that had gold in them. There was the first map of all the inhabited portions of the earth. The Greek astronomer Anaximander of Miletus drew it around 550 B.C.

Another Mesopotamian innovation should be noted—the paved city street. The Hittite city of Hattusas had one in 1200 B.C. By the sixth century B.C. when King Nebuchadnezzar II carried the Jews off into captivity, the city of Babylon had an elegant thoroughfare paved with yard-square red and white stone tiles. Its name was The Street On Which May No Enemy Ever Tread.

Mesopotamia had to its credit the first No Parking sign. King Sennacherib, a tough warrior who ruled Assyria with an iron hand from 705 to 681 B.C., ordered signs posted along the main processional way in Nineveh stating: *Royal Road. Let No Man Lessen It.* By royal edict anyone who parked a chariot or other conveyance on this avenue was executed and his head stuck on a stake in front of his house.

Mesopotamia gets credit for history's first great bridge as well. Old King Nebuchadnezzar II built it in the sixth century. It spanned the Euphrates, in Babylon, at a point where the river was more than 3,000 feet wide. The bridge was built of timbers resting on 1,000 stone piers. Each night, the roadbed was taken up to prevent people from crossing in the dark and robbing each other.

The construction of the first pipeline deserves attention, and here the Chinese get the praise. About 940 B.C., they drilled wells hundreds of feet down into the ground and piped the natural gas there to salt plants through pipes made of hollow bamboo poles. They used the gas to dehydrate brine. The same bamboo pipelines are still in operation today.

Edwin Tunis

Chinese wheelbarrow.

Several other Chinese inventions might be mentioned, such as the kite and the wheelbarrow. A general named Jugo Lyang invented the wheelbarrow in the third century A.D. The backward Occident didn't contrive one until the thirteenth century A.D.

Step by awkward step now, we have witnessed the origins of the art of transportation. We have watched the beginnings of various means of land transport, from the footsore hiker to the ripsnorting horseback rider, from the clumsy sledge to the dashing chariot, and we have observed their impact upon the life of early man. Government has grown more powerful, trade has spread, and cultures have been cross-fertilized through the help of transportation. Empire has become plausible and big-scale war has gotten to be technically feasible.

Fast, convenient land transport for large numbers of people was stymied, however, until the development of a strong, central government willing to spend the energy and the money necessary to construct a reliable, countrywide road system.

This finally happened about 1000 B.C. and again China led the way, as it did in so many areas of transportation.

Under the potent Chou Dynasty, the Chinese embarked on an intensive program of road construction that included the building of inns and the planting of shade trees along the new highways. Admittedly, some of the roads didn't wear well. It was not for nothing that the ancient Chinese had a saying roads are good for seven years and bad for 4,000. Still the Chou Dynasty created history's first national road network. A road commissioner was appointed and all roads, from footpaths to broad highways, were meticulously classified according to their size and use.

Furthermore, the Chinese under the Chous enacted the first traffic laws. These regulated a variety of travel matters, from the dimensions of vehicles and the speed they could move to traffic control at intersections.

The Persians were the next pace-setters. By the sixth century B.C., their empire reached from the Indus to the Mediterranean and they built an impressive network of roads to facilitate the governing of this territory.

The foremost of these was the Royal Road which ran 1,600 miles from the capital at Susa, north of the Persian Gulf, to Sardis, near the western shore of Turkey. Herodotus traveled it and found it a splendid highway with excellent inns at regular intervals. "The road itself is safe to travel by, as it never leaves inhabited country," he reassuringly reported.

To handle official mail, the Persian government instituted an extraordinary courier system along this road that covered the 1,600 miles in nine days.

"Nothing mortal travels so fast as these Persian messengers," wrote Herodotus. "The entire plan is a Persian invention; and this is the method of it. Along the whole line of road there are men, stationed with horses, equal to the number of days which the journey takes . . . a man and a horse to each day. . . . The first rider delivers his dispatch to the second, and the second passes it to the third; and so it is borne from hand to hand along the whole line.

"Nothing stops these couriers from covering their allotted stage in the quickest possible time," he declared, "neither snow, rain, heat, nor darkness."

It was the Persians who created the pontoon bridge. King Xerxes was responsible for the most celebrated of these, the one he built across the Hellespont in preparation for his invasion of Greece in 480 B.C. It was seven-eighths of a mile long.

During the construction, a violent storm blew up and the partially built bridge was wrecked by pounding waves. Xerxes, enraged, had his engineers beheaded, and commanded that the Hellespont be verbally insulted, branded, and given 300 lashes. A second team of bridge builders headed by a Tenedos school teacher named Harpales was more successful.

Although the Greeks ruled a substantial empire from the fourth to the second centuries B.C., they contributed little new to the techniques of land transport. They were better at abstract scientific theory than at workaday practicalities. The one interesting thing they did was to build roads with grooves for wagon wheels to roll in, somewhat like a railroad, and the idea was not new with them. The Hittites had done something similar centuries before.

A civilization was growing to the west of Greece, though, that was to advance transportation on land more than any other nation before or since. Already it had begun to construct a magnificent road system that was destined to remain unsurpassed for 2,000 years. This was Rome the resplendent.

Mark the year 295 B.C. This was the date when the small city-state of Rome achieved supremacy over all Italy. Now mark the year A.D. 117. By then Rome ruled all Europe up to the Rhine and the Danube, as well as Britain, North Africa, Egypt, the Middle East, Mesopotamia, and Asia Minor to the Caspian Sea. She had 100,000,000 subjects, and wealth and power beyond compare.

Rome's roads made this possible. They let the rugged Roman legions and their supply trains move swiftly wherever they were needed, and they let through the traders that bound the empire together.

At the peak of Rome's glory, A.D. 117, 372 important roads traversed the Empire. They covered nearly 50,000 miles. No less than 29 major roads radiated out from the city of Rome. And such roads! Many of them have remained continuously in service to this day.

Appius Claudius Crassus, a politician out to impress the masses, started the most famous of them, the *Via Appia*, in 312 B.C. It eventually reached from Rome to Brindisi in the heel of Italy, and all 366 miles of it were paved for all-weather use. You can ride on the original stones, coming into Rome today. The popular *Via Flaminia,* named for another publicity-hungry politician, was built around 220 B.C. It cut across the whole of Italy, northeast from Rome to Rimini.

The most remote provinces boasted fine roads. The soldier-emperor Trajan constructed a divided highway from the Red Sea port of Aqabah to Bostra in Arabia. A row of stones separated the two lanes. Trajan's nephew, Hadrian, constructed a road from Berenice to Atinoöpolis in Egypt which was as fine. You can still read the modest inscription on the mileposts. It says:

> The Emperor Caesar Trajanus Hadrian Augusta, son of the deified Trajan Parthicus and grandson of the deified Nerva, *pontifex maximus imperator,* holding the tribunican power for the twenty-first year, twice acclaimed *imperator,* three times consul, father of his country, built from Berenice to Antinoöpolis through secure and level country the new Hadrian Way, with copious cisterns, resting stations, and garrisons at intervals along the route.

A typical Roman paved road—the *via lapide strata*—was 14 to 18 feet wide. It had a base of hard earth or sand, 3 feet deep. Above that were four layers of rock, gravel, cement, concrete and mortar. The surfacing was of heavy stone, usually six-sided like modern bathroom floor tiles. Often a sidewalk ran alongside, and sometimes, one or two soft strips for horseback riders.

Normally, the roads went straight as a die because they were primarily designed for military purposes and the Roman infantry was in a hurry to get there first. Marshy valleys were filled in or spanned by viaducts. Hills were not circled. The Roman engineers generally went straight up and down them regardless of how steep they were. It made it embarrassing for the Roman wagon driver who had no such thing as brakes. The most he could do was to tie off one wheel with a rope to keep it from rotating.

When engineers came to rivers, they threw across stone arch bridges or bridges made of stone with wooden superstructures. Great tunnels and cuttings were hewed. One tunnel for a road between Naples and Pozzuoli extended 3,000 feet through a mountain! The entrances were 75 feet high to let in light. To go through the rock, the Roman engineers had to heat it with fire, dowse the rock with water to make it split, and hack away with hand tools.

Engineers rated high in the Roman culture. Under the Empire, they were exempted from paying certain taxes. The Roman government didn't have much respect for bridge builders, though. Each bridge builder had to put up a deposit on every bridge he erected, and he got it back only after the bridge had stood for forty years.

These superb Roman roads were more and more thronged. In the second and third centuries A.D., column after column of legionnaires would go swinging down them. Traders went by with wine from Gaul and Spain, leather and pork from Britain, metals from central Europe, wool from Asia Minor, and stupendous quantities of grain from all over to be made into bread for the Roman multitudes. People came along walking, on horseback, or riding in conveyances of every description. Light two-wheelers, covered and uncovered, rolled up, pulled by horses, mules or donkeys. Four-wheelers lumbered along behind as many as ten horses or oxen. One saw farmers' oxcarts and nobles' horse-drawn chariots and wagons carrying gold and silver, baggage, mail. The Roman government operated the official mail service, with relay stations every ten to twelve miles for changing horses, and, every thirty to forty miles, larger stopping places called *mansiones* where one could find inns, doctors, and blacksmiths.

The private traveler rode in his own vehicle, if he could afford one. Or he might hire a carriage in one town and drive it to the next big town, where he switched to another carriage. Late in the Empire he could buy a first- or second-class ticket on the Imperial post. If he was going any distance, he brought along his food, cushions to ease the jouncing, and blankets for sleeping out under the stars. The inns of the Empire had poor reputations. One could buy bread and wine at an inn for a penny, enough hay for a mule for two cents, and lodgings were reasonable. But the company was rough, and most of the inns were fleabags where guests and horses rested for the night in stench and proximity.

Steadily, travel got to be more rapid. Midway in the first century B.C., Julius Caesar did one-hundred miles a day and Cicero wrote admiringly to his brother, Quintus, in England, "Just as I was folding up this epistle, letter-carriers arrived from you and Caesar (from Britain) after a journey of twenty days." A century later, Emperor Tiberius made 184 miles in a day as he hurried to the bedside of his ill brother in Germany. Messengers brought the news of Nero's death to Emperor Galba, his successor, 332 miles away in Spain, in thirty-six hours.

Getting around Rome itself wasn't as easy. At the height of its ancient glory, the city had a population of perhaps 1,000,000 and the traffic jams were appalling. The main avenues were continually packed with people of innumerable nationalities, colors, and costumes. Most of them walked, some rode horses or donkeys, some drove in carts and chariots. The very rich were carried in begemmed litters by four sturdy bearers wearing luxurious liveries. The traffic got to be so bad that the consuls had to ban all wheeled vehicles from the streets in the daytime unless they were making a delivery to a public building.

"Rome is clean, Rome respects her roads, her forums, her splendid gardens. The circulation of the people should not be hindered by . . . noisy chariots," a consular edict declared.

Transportation had come a long, good way on land. It was a tragedy that the Roman Empire was to break up soon.

II

Mare Nostrum

A LONG TIME PASSED before man felt skilled enough to brave the open sea, and he had to work up to it gradually. He served most of his boatman's apprenticeship inland, on the rivers and the lakes.

The archeologists tell us that this began hundreds of thousands of years ago when some manlike creature first learned to cross a stream by straddling a log and paddling with his hands. He also learned to cross in an emergency by hanging on to the swollen corpses of animals. They made fine water wings.

As man became more knowledgeable, he learned to fasten several logs side by side, or to tie bundles of sticks or reeds together into rafts. To increase his speed, he shaped wooden paddles bigger than his hands and he cut poles for pushing. The progression from floats to boats followed naturally, and in many places.

Just what kind of a boat came first, the scholars are unable to say. It might have been a dugout—a length of log with a cockpit in the middle, hollowed out by fire and ax. It might have been a bark boat. It might have been a skiff made of tightly bound reeds, or a bowl-shaped boat with hides stretched over a light wooden frame. In any case, men were using real boats by 6000 B.C.

By the middle of the fourth millennium B.C., dugouts and probably bark boats were plying the inland waterways of Europe and making short trips over salt water. The Nile was swarming with crescent-shaped boats made of papyrus reeds and propelled by paddles. Traffic was heavy on the Tigris and Euphrates. Men had discovered that boats were valuable means for trade and travel, fishing and fighting.

At about this time man made the greatest advance in the history of water transport.

The evidence of it was found in the ruins of ancient Eridu, the chief seaport of Sumer. It is a small clay model of a boat which the Sumerians are thought to have used around 3400 B.C.

Dugout Canoe. Model from Smithsonian Institution collection.

Something about this little model is of far greater importance, though, than the mere fact that the Sumerians had boats. There is a socket in the bottom which could have held a mast, and there are two holes in the rim on either side of the boat which could have held the stays.

A mast means a sail.

After all those ages of pushing and paddling, man had learned to harness the winds. It was a discovery that immeasurably changed travel habits on water. It multiplied tenfold the distance he could travel on water in a day if the wind held fair. It let him leave the rivers and dare the broad seas.

Some authorities think that the first sails were freshly cut tree branches set on board ships. Early Egyptian drawings depict ships with branches standing in them, and evidence abounds that the Northern peoples employed them. The finding at Eridu argues that the ever-versatile Sumerians probably had sails as far back as 3400 B.C. They definitely used sails in 3200 B.C. In fact, they may have been sailing their cocky little ships to Egypt. There are indications of a Sumerian invasion of the upper Nile in this period. It required a phenomenal journey for the attackers. Either they sailed 3,500 miles via the Persian Gulf and the Red Sea, and portaged their slim, high-prowed ships to the Nile, or they built a naval base on the eastern Mediterranean shore near the upper reaches of the Euphrates and launched the assault from there. One route or the other, the inferences are exciting. Sailing ships were traveling whopping distances along the seacoasts before the turn of the third millennium. The sailor's know-how was far enough advanced to challenge the winds and the waves, and his knowledge of navigation and geography was sufficiently developed to get him where he wanted to go.

The pace of nautical progress quickens now.

By 3000 B.C., men had begun to construct their boats of wooden planks instead of digging them out of logs. They replaced their paddles with oars, and they made big sails of linen or papyrus which hung down from a pole fastened crosswise to the mast. Western sailors depended exclusively on this one type of sail for more than three millennia. It was called the square sail although it actually was rectangular in shape.

In the northeastern corner of the Mediterranean, a style of boat building emerged that was to be the foundation of marine architecture in the West to the present day.

If a boat has the wind directly behind it—"running before the wind" is the expression—it asks nothing more than a steering oar and the sail to keep it more or less on course. On the Nile, where the wind blew fairly steadily from the north, a spoon-shaped sailing ship riding rather high in the water was perfectly satisfactory. The Egyptians sailed upriver with the wind at their back and rowed, paddled, or drifted downstream.

But if a sailor wants to sail in a direction other than the one the wind is blowing toward, he needs a differently shaped boat. In order for the sail to drive it forward, the boat has to have lateral resistance to the wind which can only be provided by a keel or by having much of the hull below the surface of the water.

The shipwrights of the northeastern Mediterranean discovered this vital principle.

When they began to build planked ships around 3000 B.C., they designed ships with long, strong frames sitting deep in the water.

Forty-eight hundred years later, the designers of sailing ships in Europe and America hewed to the same good theory.

(The Egyptians were not as wise. The craft they turned out looked rather like a pyramid sitting on top of the water, and it had its two-legged mast set up forward. It would run before the wind at sea no matter what its crew desired it to do. Consequently, it had to be rowed much of the time. To make matters worse, the Egyptians built their ships without frames. They were so weak that the Egyptians had to wrap ropes around the hulls to prevent them from breaking up in rough seas.)

With sailing ships men could search the other side of the seas for the things they needed.

Ancient records show Phoenician freighters putting to sea as early as 2650 B.C. with cargoes destined for Egypt. Pharaoh Snefru, so these records state, ordered "the bringing of forty ships filled with cedar logs." Most probably, the logs were shipped from the busy Phoenician port of Byblos at the foot of the Lebanese mountains. The Cretans were unquestionably in contact with Egypt by the middle of the third millenium. They also traded with Greece and the islands of the Aegean.

Year by year, sea trade increased. Pharaoh Sahure dispatched a big fleet to the land of Punt—modern Somaliland and Aden— about 2550 B.C. and it came back with 80,000 measures of myrrh, at least 6,000 weights of an exotic alloy of gold and silver named electrum, and more than 2,500 pieces of an expensive wood, ebony no doubt. By 2400 B.C., the Egypt-Byblos traffic was so heavy that a special type of seagoing vessel was produced to handle it. This was known as the byblos-ship.

The Mesopotamians dealt with the port of Oman in Arabia for copper, timber, and the stunning building stone, diorite. From India they got chank shells for jewelry. Through the Persian Gulf their ships returned with wool, cloth, leather, and olive oil.

In his delightfully written, erudite book *The Ancient Mariners,* the classicist, Lionel Casson, tells of the earliest letter extant from a dissatisfied customer for seaborne commerce. Apparently, Ea-nasir, a merchant of Ur, had delivered a shipment of poor-grade copper from the island of Telmun to one of his customers. The customer was furious. He wrote Ea-nasir an indignant letter on a clay tablet that has been dated somewhere between 2000 and 1750 B.C.

"Who am I that you treat me in this manner and offend me?" he sizzled. "That this could happen between gentlemen as we both are! Who is there among the traders of Telmun who has ever acted this way?"

No reply from Ea-nasir has survived.

Inland water trade and travel expanded. Canals stretched through the countryside. Man was digging waterways where none had been before—an outgrowth of the irrigation ditch.

In Egypt, canal building was so important that the first title of a district governor was Digger of Canals. One district governor, Nuri, who presided over Upper Egypt sometime between 2300 and 2180 B.C. dug five canals in a year. Achtoy IV, an unpleasant pharaoh around 2000 B.C. who has been denounced by Egyptian historians as "more terrifying than any before him," had a canal dug that was fifty-five miles long, from Heracleopolis to Memphis.

And in the twentieth century B.C. the first "Suez Canal" was dug.

The trade with Punt had always presented problems to Egypt. Every time the temples ran low on myrrh, the pharaoh had to equip an elaborate expedition to cross the desert, build a ship, sail down the Red Sea to Punt, get the incense, sail back up the Red Sea, and trudge home across the desert. It was either that or buy in a seller's market at the end of a long line of middlemen, trading overland.

With this in mind, Pharaoh Sesostris I ordered that a 75-mile canal be dug from the Mediterranean, at the southeastern edge of the Nile delta, to the Red Sea. It was a Gargantuan accomplishment. Not only did it open a waterborne trade route to the south, it also eased the grueling journey to and from the Egyptian copper mines in the Sinai peninsula.

During the next 500 years, the pharaohs lost interest and the canal to the Red Sea silted up. When Queen Hatshepsut, the first female monarch to make a name for herself in history, came to power about 1500 B.C., the canal was impassable.

Never underestimate the power of a woman. Hatschepsut had a vision.

Temple inscriptions record that the great god Amon spoke to the queen in his shrine, saying that he wanted her "to establish for him a Punt in his house." By "house," he meant his shrine.

"[Punt] is a glorious region of God's land," Amon explained, "it is indeed my place of delight; I have made it for myself in order to divert my heart."

The queen obliged. The canal was dug open and a fleet of five transports made its way down into the Red Sea, down to Punt, where they took on a rich cargo: myrrh trees with their roots bundled in earth to keep them fresh for replanting, gold, ivory, ebony, and baboons.

"It was done," Hatshepsut concluded. "I have for him a Punt in his garden, just as he commanded me. . . . It is large enough for him to walk abroad in."

Thanks to the survival of bas-reliefs in Amon's temple, pictures of the ships that took part in the expedition are available. They were beautiful craft with their curved sternposts terminating in lotus flowers, their paired steering oars, their long, curved spars, their spread sails that were almost as wide as the ships were long. But they were not very seaworthy. They still rode too high out of water, and ropes were still necessary to hold them together. The baboons from Punt found the ropes a handy perch on the return trip to Egypt.

Although the Egyptians had a big empire and a rich foreign trade through most of the second millennium, the best sailors and traders were to be found elsewhere.

An advanced civilization flourished in Crete for three centuries, from 1800 to 1500 B.C. We call the people the Minoans from the name of their great King Minos. According to the Greek historian Thucydides, King Minos was "the earliest ruler we know of who possessed a navy."

Minos, wrote Thucydides, "made himself master of a great part of what is now termed the Hellenic Sea; he conquered the isles of the Aegean and was the first colonizer of most of them, installing his own sons as governors. . . . He cleared the sea of pirates, so far as he could. . . ."

These Minoans had fine ships and crews, and they sailed long and wide. They traded as far off as Sicily, possibly Sardinia, and Libya. They may have gotten to Spain in a quest for tin.

Regrettably, the chief clues we have as to what their ships looked like are only crude scratchings on third-millennium vases and some later seals with which Minoan shipowners marked their property. The former are so crude that marine historians won't say for sure which end is the bow and which the stern. Nor are the latter much of an improvement. Nevertheless, we can tell that the Minoans used rowed boats and sailing ships constructed with keel-and-rib skeletons. They may have had ships with two masts.

Then there's Phoenicia. Its sailors and ships were superlative. Century after century, they carried much of the seagoing trade in the Mediterranean.

The Egyptologist, James H. Breasted, has described some of the goods that Phoenician ships sailed to Thebes in Egypt:

> . . . . Gold and silver vessels of magnificent workmanship, from the cunning hand of the Tyrian artificer or the workshops of distant Asia Minor, Cyprus, Crete and the Aegean islands; exquisite furniture of carved ivory, delicately wrought ebony, chariots mounted with gold and electrum, and bronze instruments of war; besides these, fine horses for the Pharaoh's stables and untold quantities of the best that the fields, vineyards, orchards and pastures of Asia produced. . . . the annual tribute of gold and silver in large commercial rings, some of which weighed as much as twelve pounds each. . . ,

An Egyptian mural, now ruined by damp, contains pictures of some typical Phoenician merchantmen. They had bows and sterns rising well above the water and were driven by short, extremely broad sails. Rough fences of brushwork ran along their decks to protect the deck cargo.

Like the Minoans, the Phoenicians may have been trading as far as Spain by the middle of the second millennium. They long prospered as the Mediterranean's most successful traders. We shall meet them again.

Not the Minoans. The end came quickly for them. From the mainland north of Crete an invasion was launched in the fifteenth century B.C. that terminated Crete's glory. When it was over, the backward Greeks ruled all of the northeastern Mediterranean.

Initially, the Greeks were not a major trading power. They were much more interested in piracy.

In his epics, the *Iliad* and the *Odyssey,* Homer was describing the exploits of a horde of pirates. The first thing Odysseus and his fleet did on their return journey to Ithaca from Troy was to raid an innocent city: "The wind that bare me from Ilios brought me nigh to the Cicones, even to Ismarus, whereupon I sacked their city and slew the people. And from out of the city we took their wives and much substances, and divided them amongst us. . . ."

The Greek raiders knifed along the coasts in sleek, low-riding craft. These ships were undecked except for a platform in the stern for the skipper and steersman, and one for the lookout in the prow. The masts they carried could be taken down when the wind was unfavorable. From twenty to fifty oarsmen would man the benches and "smite the gray sea water with their oars" until the wind was fair again.

Because they were so open, the raiding ships were not well suited for the high seas. Moreover, they couldn't carry much in the way of supplies and had no room for the crew to lie down. Hence the pirates stayed near land. In the evening they would run their ships up onto a beach, steal a few animals for supper, and get a good night's sleep.

Piracy "was a life-long pursuit," wrote Thucydides, "one that hadn't as yet received any stigma but was even considered an honorable profession."

Piracy was not limited to the Aegean. Sailors from the southern coast of Asia Minor and the Levant also dealt in goods and slaves plucked violently from sleepy coastal towns. Free looting became so rife that Amenhotep III (he who styled himself Ikhnaton) created a coast guard to patrol the sea and keep unauthorized ships out of the Nile. If a city did not have such protection or could not join together with others in defensive measures, it had only one other

course to safety. Thucydides noted that "because of piracy cities
. . . , both in the islands and along the coast of the mainland, were
preferably built far in from the sea."

At the close of the thirteenth century B.C., the pirates banded
together into a monster armada for an assault on all Egypt. Re-
pelled, they attacked twice more, by land and sea, in 1194 and
1190 B.C. and they were defeated twice more. Not that it cured
them. They continued to maraud for centuries. The Old Testa-
ment is full of their doings.

So much for the Mediterranean. At the same time, sailors of
another sort were engaged in spectacular voyages some 8,000 miles
to the east. In a very different type of ship, Polynesians were defying the unknown expanses of the Pacific, hunting for new island
homes.

Our knowledge of Polynesian history is fuzzy. Archeological
study is not easy in scattered islands where the natives object fero-
ciously to people digging in their past. Nonetheless, we have scientific reason to believe that the Polynesians used three kinds of
boats: a simple dugout with an outrigger; a plank canoe; and, for
lengthy trips, an extraordinary double canoe. The last-named consisted of two canoes set parallel to each other, supporting a platform that had little shacklike cabins on it. The mast was usually
placed amidships and it displayed a triangular sail—the world's
first.

The triangular sail hung with its two leading edges attached to
wood spars, and the foremost point of the triangle projected beyond
the line of the mast. Potentially this was excellent for sailing into
the wind. Beating to windward, the boatman described a zigzag
course, pointing the bow of his ship as close to the source of the
wind as he could. In the Mediterranean where seagoing vessels
traditionally had a defined bow and stern, the early triangular sail
was to cause considerable difficulty. The sail had to be switched
from one side of the mast to the other whenever the tack was
changed. On Polynesian ships, this shifting was unnecessary. The
Polynesians merely put steering oars at both ends. As they changed
course, they changed the bow to the stern.

What sailors these ancient Polynesians must have been. They

explored hundreds of thousands of square miles in the Pacific and colonized islands within an enormous triangle whose points were New Zealand, Hawaii, and Easter Island. They seem to have navigated by the sun, moon, and stars, by wind and ocean currents, by cloud formations, by flights of birds, by the smell of land, and by memory.

Their staple food during extended sea journeys was a fermented fruit paste. On an expedition to a new home, seed plants were packed in the double canoes so that the colonists could start farming when they arrived. Pigs and chickens came along, although some of the animals might be eaten en route if the other food ran out and the fishing was poor.

In this manner they covered on some single voyages as much as 1,500 miles without sighting land.

They were a daring people.

Back in the Mediterranean brave skippers were also widening the horizons of man's world.

Legend has it that the first great explorer was a Greek named Jason who went off in quest of the Golden Fleece 3,000 years ago. He is said to have sailed his ship, *Argo,* to the country of Aea on the east side of the Black Sea. There he successfully stole the fleece and a bride by the name of Medea, and brought them back to Greece. The poets say that he and Medea lived unhappily ever after—until he left her for another woman.

What induced the urge to explore?

Since the inception of time, some men have itched to break with the familiar and take to the open road. They had to know what lay beyond that island, what was over the edge of that sea.

Appropriately enough, the first great ocean exploration of which there is a definitely written record was made in the spirit of simply wanting to know. In the sixth century B.C., Pharaoh Necho II of Egypt sent off an expedition of Pheonicians to circumnavigate the continent of Africa. He wanted to learn if Africa was surrounded by water.

The Phoenicians sailed out of the Red Sea in their high-prowed, high-tailed, little ships, down through the Indian Ocean, around the Cape of Good Hope, up the Atlantic to the Straits of Gibraltar, and back through the Mediterranean to Egypt. It took them three years. As Herodotus reported it, "every autumn [they] put in at some convenient spot on the [African] coast, sowed a patch of ground, and waited for next year's harvest. Then, having got in their grain, they put to sea again, and after two full years rounded the Pillars of Hercules [the Straits of Gibraltar] in the course of the third, and returned to Egypt."

Yet, while much exploring may have been done for the sake of knowledge alone, commerce and colonization were responsible for most of man's earliest geographical discoveries.

The Egyptians helped to colonize Crete about 3000 B.C. The Minoans colonized parts of Greece, Sicily, and the shores of Syria as well as the Aegean Islands. The Phoenicians established settlements along the shores of Africa and Spain. Carthage was one of these, Cadiz another. (Carthage's lovesick Queen Dido was a Phoenician.) The Greeks spread to the old Minoan colonies, to Asia Minor, Italy, North Africa, Spain, the southern coast of France, eventually creating some 250 different outposts of Greece.

The drive for trade led men still farther abroad. The seven-league strides of Pytheas are an example.

Sometime in the fourth century B.C., a ship raised anchor in the harbor of Marseilles, then a Greek colony-port called Masillia, and set a course for Gibraltar. It was skippered by the foremost navigator of the age, a man known as Pytheas of Marseilles. His expedition may have been sponsored by Greek merchants looking for a way to break the monopoly which the Phoenicia-Carthage-Cadiz axis had over sea trade with England. To protect the monopoly, Carthaginian sailors had been blockading the Straits of Gibraltar since 480 B.C.

Pytheas ran this blockade, sailed up the coast of Europe to Brittany, and then headed across the channel to England. He went ashore to visit the tin mines in Cornwall, and then embarked again for a circumnavigation of England. Recrossing the channel, he coasted northeastward to the mouth of the Elbe River. He may have sailed around Denmark to gain the Baltic; the evidence is contradictory on this point. At last, he set sail for home, ran the Gibraltar blockade once more, and ended a journey that had carried him a minimum of 7,000 miles.

Ancient sailors owed Pytheas much. He was the first to discover that the moon affected the rise and fall of the tides, and that the North Star did not mark the exact spot of the pole. "For centuries," Casson informs us, "whatever was known of the northern regions—Brittany, Ireland, the British Isles, and the North Sea—was derived from [Pytheas'] observations." It was he who named Britain.

So, very early, at least one expedition had sailed around Africa. Another had circled Britain. Phoenician ships had touched the Azores. Some researchers suggest that the intrepid Phoenicians reached South America.

They were unlocking the world.

Ships grew better, and deadlier.

There were historic battles as nations fought for control of the seas and of the lands that went with them. There was the epochal Battle of Salamis in 480 B.C. where 366 Greek ships routed a fleet of 700 Persian ships, and saved Greece from Xerxes. There were the many naval conflicts in the Peloponnesian War between Athens and Sparta. There was the Battle of Amorgos in 322 B.C. when Athens' naval power was smashed forever.

Up to the seventh century B.C., the average warship had fifty oars, twenty-five to a side, plus two steering ones. Between 705 and 681 B.C., the Mediterranean shipwrights grew more ambitious. They designed a war galley with double rows of oars, the bireme. It had a long, heavy keel that ended in an ugly ram, sharply pointed or tipped with a bronze head, that was utilized to smash gaping holes in enemy vessels. The bireme's sides were built outward and up from the keel. In the first version we know about, Phoenician in design, a narrow, fenced-in deck ran along the center of the craft from the stern almost to the bow. It was much higher than the sides. Somewhat modified, this upper deck appeared again in later Greek galleys. The rowers sat along or near the waterline, some under the raised center deck, others near the sides. As a rule, they were not slaves. In the ancient world, rowers usually were highly trained, paid specialists.

To counter the Persian strike at Greece in 480 B.C., Themistocles, the Athenian admiral in command, persuaded his fellow-citizens to build bigger—a warship with three banks of oars. After the Greeks trounced the Persians with it, the trireme became the standard galley for most of the Mediterranean. In the Greek navy, it measured 140 feet long and 20 feet wide, and it carried a crew of 200 including 170 oarsmen, and a contingent of scrappy marines.

Dionysius, the dictator of Syracuse, had more original ideas yet. He staged a revolution in naval design by ending the system by which one man pulled one oar. In 398 B.C., he built ships in which four and five rowers pulled at each long sweep. They could go a lot faster. Quadriremes ("fours") and quinqueremes (fives"), these were called. (In later years, "sixes," "sevens," "sixteens," "thirties," and a "forty" were built. Such names had nothing to do with the number of banks of oars. They pertained to the number of men pulling each sweep.)

These war galleys weren't meant to be long-distance ocean sailors: they couldn't carry enough provisions for that. Open water sailing was the job of the wider-beamed merchant ships.

From vase decorations we know what some merchantmen in this period looked like. They were squat and deep-drawing, without oars, relying on sails for propulsion. We also know that some merchantmen were combination traders and warships. Rowed as well as sailed, they had bows that slanted down and forward toward the waterline as if to end in a submerged ram. The bows were decorated with goggling, oversized eyes.

Navigating from one port to another, the ancient sailors customarily kept close to shore and steered by prominent land features like cliffs, hills, and river mouths. A Persian reconnaissance force prepared for Darius' invasion of Greece, for example, by cruising along the Greek coast scouting the characteristics of the shoreline.

By the first century B.C., this method was beginning to be augmented by the use of maps drawn with parallels of latitude and longitudinal meridians, some of them quite accurate. Mediterranean sailors were even utilizing a forerunner of the sextant. A lodestone spoon spinning on a bronze plate was in experimental use in China in the first century B.C. The magnetic compass did not appear anywhere before the twelfth century A.D., though.

Many seaports built elaborate breakwaters, anchorages, and docks to provide havens for shipping. One harbor, Alexandria in

Egypt, erected the first lighthouse around 280 B.C. Its light, a wood fire burning nearly 300 feet above the waves, was beamed thirty-five miles by mammoth metal mirrors.

With all these improvements in shipping, sea trade boomed. By the latter half of the millennium, India was trading with Burma, Malay, and Ceylon. Athens was doing business from Marseilles to southern Russia. (A round trip by sea from Greece to Russia lasted three weeks.) Little Rhodes was selling millions of gallons of its cheap wine abroad, and its big merchant marine was moving cargoes for countless nations. The city of Rhodes was one of the world's busiest seaports; it earned a million drachmas a year in harbor fees. For a time, Egyptian trade ebbed, but it revived. Farther west, the Carthaginians were doing very well. Until the Romans decided to eliminate Carthage, that is.

The sea was still a mean, frightening adversary, of course. The annals are full of tense tales.

"No sooner were we in the Tuscan Sea," wrote Publius Aelius Aristides of Smyrna around A.D. 175, "when there arose surf, darkness, a hurricane, and an uncontrollable turmoil of the sea. The helmsman dropped the tiller, the captain and the sailors threw dust on their heads, and kept bemoaning their own and the ship's fate."

A Chinese traveler, Fa-Hian, had a grisly time on a voyage from Ceylon. He was aboard a big merchant ship which was towing a smaller one for use in case of shipwreck. As the ancient *Chinese Accounts of India* relates it:

> They sailed eastward for two days when suddenly a tempest arose, and the ship sprung a leak. The merchants then desired to haul up the smaller vessel, but the crew of that ship, fearing that a crowd of men would rush aboard and sink her, cut the towing cable and she fell off. The merchantmen were greatly terrified, expecting their death momentarily. Then dreading lest the leak should gain upon them, they forthwith took their heavy goods and merchandise and cast them overboard. Fa-Hian also flung overboard his water pitcher and his washing basin, and also other portions of his property. . . .

For thirteen terror-ridden days the hurricane blew the ship before it until it found haven at a small island. There the crew fixed the leak and embarked again. Much the worse for wear, Fa-Hian ultimately reached Java or Sumatra. The report is vague as to which.

One Roman grain ship was blown seventy sailing days off its course on a brief trip from Alexandria to Italy.

Men kept going to sea anyway.

The city of Carthage was long the supreme naval power in the western Mediterranean. By the sixth century B.C. it had a population of 750,000 and a fleet that was nearly invincible. Across the sea to the north another power was on the rise, but those Romans shied away from water. And after all there was nothing to attract them to it until the interests of their growing republic clashed with those of Carthage. Inevitably this happened and in 264 B.C. began the First Punic War between the two powers.

After four years of unsuccessful campaigning, the Romans became convinced that they had to have a navy in order to eliminate Carthage's Sicilian seaports. How to build it was the question.

The Romans approached the problem with typical energy and single-mindedness. They developed a style of quinquereme based on a Carthaginian ship that had gone aground on a Roman shore. In two months they built one hundred of them and twenty triremes, trained 30,000 sailors, and put to sea. Very likely this amateur fleet would have been obliterated by the crack Carthaginian navy had not somebody had an idea that changed the whole nature of the battle. What the Romans needed was something that would enable them to use their land tactics at sea, and they got it: a gangplank hinged to the deck and equipped with a long spike at the outer end. The Romans sailed into the fray with the gangplanks—called ravens—raised. As the enemy ships confidently rushed in to ram, the ravens went down, their spikes imbedding themselves in the Carthaginian decks, and the Roman marines poured into action. The first eager Carthaginian pass cost them thirty-one galleys. When the battle was over, Carthage had lost forty-four ships and 10,000 men.

Subsequently, the Roman tyros managed to wreck practically all of their fleet in storms—twice. However, through the use of the tested method of capture, copy, and conquer, and by maintaining superior numbers, they ended the war on the sea in 241 B.C. with the crushing defeat of a Punic flotilla that was merely a shadow of its predecessors.

For 500 years thereafter the Mediterranean was a Roman lake, *mare nostrum*. Occasionally, Rome became smug, let its naval forces dwindle, and rivals would arise. Rome soon put them down. In the first century B.C., the Romans even allowed pirates to run rampant for a while. One band of pirates kidnaped the youthful Julius Caesar on a journey he was making to Rhodes. (When the pirates fixed his ransom at twenty talents, young Caesar objected. He claimed he was worth fifty, so they raised the ante.) Pirates got so bold that they raided the Italian mainland itself and dragged off noble Roman women into slavery. The Appian Way became unsafe to ride on and Roman ships didn't dare go to sea. The Roman government got fed up with the situation, and in 67 B.C. it sent Pompey to chase the pirates out of business permanently. He did it in forty days.

The Romans did considerable fighting among themselves in this period. One of their internecine sea struggles, at Actium in 31 B.C. ranks among the decisive battles of history. It was here that Octavius sent Antony and Antony's Egyptian mistress Cleopatra fleeing for their lives.

The victory at Actium made Octavius Rome's first emperor and established the famed *Pax Romana* throughout the civilized world.

Trade was never better. Aristides, said in a speech before Marcus Aurelius, "What could be better or more profitable than the present state of affairs? Now any man can go whither he pleases with absolute confidence, the harbors all over the empire are full of business, even the mountains are as safe for those who journey over them as the cities are to those who dwell in them."

To Rome came silks from China, jewels, rare woods, and pepper from India, cosmetics from Arabia, incense and ivory from Africa, glassware from Syria, wine from Sicily, art works from Greece, copper and silver from Spain, beautiful girl and boy slaves from everywhere. Out from Rome went oil, wine, pottery, metal goods, and marble. The trade in grain was immense. Rome imported 150,000 tons a year from Egypt alone. All told, it needed 450,000 tons a year to feed its populace.

Of necessity, ships grew bigger. One Roman grain ship in the second century A.D., the *Isis*, was 180 feet long, displaced 1,200 tons, and had a crew of 1,000 men. She held three times as much cargo as any merchant vessel that plied between Europe and America before 1820! It was not until 1845 that the North Atlantic saw a vessel of her dimensions.

Lucian, the Greek writer, saw the *Isis* once when she was blown off course into Peiraeus, the harbor for Athens. He couldn't get over the sight of her. He gaped at the height of the mast, at the fiery red topsail, at the gilded goosehead on the stern, at the cabins aft. He wrote:

> Everything was incredible, The crew was like an army. They told me she carried enough grain to feed every mouth in Athens for a year. And it all depends for its safety on one little old man who turns those great steering oars with a tiller that's no more than a stick. They pointed him out to me; woolly-haired little fellow, half-bald; Heron was his name, I think.

Big ships such as the *Isis* made their way almost completely under sail. They had a mainmast with a big square sail, sometimes topped by a pair of triangular topsails, and a second mast which leaned sharply over the bow and flew a small sail called the *artemon*. Some ships had another small sail hung from a mast aft of the mainsail.

It made a boundless difference when the fore-and-aft rig appeared in the second century A.D. (from where no one knows). Ships could now sail close to the wind.

Sea travel was not exactly convenient. There were few regularly scheduled ship lines. If you wished to go somewhere by sea and you were rich enough, you chartered a ship. Otherwise, you just waited at a seaport until you heard of a ship that was going where you wanted to go.

Sooner or later, you usually got there.

Goods bound from Rome had to be unloaded at Pozzuoli, the port of Naples, or at Rome's harbor, Ostia, at the mouth of the Tiber. Bustling, crowded ports these were—so jammed that in A.D. 42, Emperor Claudius built a new artificial harbor to the north which he called Portus. It was connected with the Tiber by a canal along which barges were hauled by teams of oxen.

Travel by canal was common. But not always much fun. Wrote Horace about the overnight trip between Tarracina and the Appian Way:

Never take a night boat, reader. You spend the first hour
Paying fares and hitching up the mule. Then fearless mosquitoes
And resonant swamp frogs keep sleep safely at bay.
A sailor and a passenger, soused with cheap wine, compete
In songs to their absent girl friends. The mule driver finally
Drops off to sleep: the lazy driver lets the mule browse,
Fastens the rope to a rock, stretches out, and snores.
Dawn was already at hand before we observed
That the boat hadn't budged an inch.

Emperor Caligula enjoyed somewhat more comfort with his barge transportation. He used a pair of pleasure barges on Lake Nemi; each was 240 feet long and nearly 70 feet wide. Their decks were paved with mosaics and fitted out with ponds surrounded by lovely gardens.

By sea and by land, man had come far. But he had to halt, for the civilization that he knew was about to die.

III

Out of the Ashes

THE REPORTS of the death of the Roman Empire in the middle of the fifth century A.D. were not exaggerated.

It was a brutal death, and the Romans brought it upon themselves. Generation after generation, they had let their freedoms and strength be corroded. By the year 400, the Senate had relinquished its last powers to a government that had become a full tyranny. The middle classes had been all but eliminated, and the majority of farmers had sunk to the level of serfs. Decadence was everywhere, together with the most dangerous of national sins, complacency. So few citizens would serve in the army that it had to fill up its ranks with untrustworthy foreigners. The navy was allowed to rot away and no one gave it a second thought.

The barbarians saw all this and moved. Alaric and his Visigoth hordes poured over the Julian Alps, and in 409 forced Rome to pay a large ransom for its safety. A year later, they returned, slashed their way into the city one night, and pillaged it dry, the first time in 800 years that an enemy had sacked potent Rome. Worse was to come. In 455, a Vandal fleet led by the awesome Gaiseric sailed unmolested up the Tiber into the heart of Rome. Bloody slaughter, rape, and looting went on for two weeks. Temples were denuded of their relics, homes were stripped of their furniture. The Vandals carried 30,000 inhabitants of the city back to North Africa with them as slaves.

Rome never recovered from the blow. In 476 the Empire broke in two and proud Rome became just another small barbarian monarchy. Most of Europe and North Africa, so long ruled by a single, powerful government, split into helpless little kingdoms.

There also died the magnificent system of transportation the Romans had so lovingly built. Untended, the splendid Roman roads fell to pieces, and wheeled transport practically vanished from the continent of Europe. Most interurban roads shriveled to narrow tracks, no broader than footpaths. The few people that traveled them had to go by horse, ass, or mule. Those that were too old or infirm to ride astride an animal could move by litter, but the litters had to be hung between two horses walking single file. At sea, it was equally bleak. The number of ships that put into or out of European ports steadily dwindled.

The rise of Islam in the seventh century made the scene grimmer. With no Roman legions to fend them off, the Moslem armies made a crescent of power for the Arabs from the Pyrenees around the northern coast of Africa through the Levant to the Caucasus Mountains and east to the Indus and the borders of China, thereby cutting Europe off from almost all the Eastern sources of silk, spices, and gems. This by 732.

As if the enemies in the south weren't enough for the Europeans to cope with, late in the eighth century new harassment arrived from the opposite quarter: the Northmen of Scandinavia, of whom the most infamous were the Vikings.

They sailed in long, low, brightly painted ships with many-colored square sails and horrific dragons' heads on their bows. They attacked without warning, plundered, laid waste, and fled. They struck seacoast towns and river ports from England to northern Russia. The very name *Russia* came from the Slavic word for the Vikings—the rowers, or Russ. Some went as far south as the Mediterranean. One band tried to attack Rome. Confused by poor directions, it looted Pisa by mistake.

As time passed, the Vikings settled down among their victims, creating bases for further robbery and conquest. They were such a plague that the Christians included in their church service a prayer that asked, "From the fury of the Northmen, good Lord, deliver us."

Fragmented, tortured by pirates, shut off from its lucrative trade with the East, Europe went stagnant. The growth of feudalism accentuated the trend. Cities deteriorated into puny towns. Few knew or cared what was going on in the next province. Save for a brief period under Charlemagne, travel over long distances shrank almost to zero.

Viking ship from the ninth century.

As the historians Wallace K. Ferguson and Geoffrey Bruun have well written, the isolation of most communities in the Middle Ages was such that "a Norman peasant had probably a clearer mental picture of the topography, climate, and general living conditions of hell than of those of Burgundy or Aquitane."

The darkness wasn't everywhere.

Inside the Moslem world and beyond its borders to the east, trade prospered. Ships from India, China, and Arabia dotted the Indian Ocean and crowded the seaports on India's shores. Overland, the camel caravans provided other links in a chain that stretched from Russia to Africa.

China embarked on a herculean canal-building program in the seventh century. An ancient Chinese account says that Emperor Yang Ti of the Sui Dynasty drafted more than 5,430,000 people to labor on the Grand Canal. Then, "When the work was done, the Emperor . . . ordered the various prefectures . . . to construct with the speed of fire 500 large boats. . . . Those who refused to work on the boats were punished by flogging and neck weights."

The account continues: "At last, the dragon boats were completed and . . . lined up one beside another, and when their silken sails passed, their perfume could be smelled for a thousand *li*." About 333 miles that would be.

This Grand Canal was 120 feet wide and 1,200 miles long, and it was just one of thousands of canals that were dug. It's the reason that Communist China has 200,000 miles of good canals today.

The Chinese were as active on dry land. By A.D. 522 they had developed carriages that were propelled—when the wind blew from the right direction—by sails. Between 617 and 916, they laid out an excellent system of post roads, many of them surfaced with stone slabs. Some were wide enough for three wagons abreast!

Things were happening in South America, too. Beginning A.D. 900 the exotic Incas of Peru built a stone-paved road with superb bridges that is one of the engineering miracles of the world. It stretched 3,250 miles over the Andes from Ecuador to central Chile and was the longest continuous highway built before the nineteenth century. All told, the Incas built over 10,000 miles of fine paved roads

One of the ironies of history is that these highly civilized Incas had no wheeled vehicles to run on their roads. Not a wheel was used for transport in the Americas until Europeans introduced it.

What you viewed on the imperial Incan road network were armies marching on foot on their way to conquest; trains of llamas, sometimes as many as 25,000 together, with goods on their backs; Incan nobles riding in curtained man-borne litters; and, twenty-four hours a day, couriers racing in relays that sped messages 250 miles a day.

The couriers went on foot. In the Incan empire nobody rode on animals except cripples.

Europe had little cognizance of these activities. Turned inward on itself, it stayed in the stultifying dark.

It was the rugged, blond Vikings who first let in a breath of fresh, outside air to dormant Europe.

Hungry for adventure, a Norwegian sailor named Eric the Red sailed westward from Iceland in 982 and discovered a capacious island which he called Greenland. He passed three years exploring its southwestern coast and founded a colony in 986. Eric's son, Leif Ericson, couldn't wait to emulate his father. About A.D. 1000, he went to see a Viking sailor by the name of Bjarni Herjulfson, bought a ship from him, hired a crew of thirty-five men, and set sail. Twice he touched land but neither place pleased him, so he sailed on.

The Flatey Book, a collection of Icelandic sagas written by a pair of priests between 1380 and 1395, relates the story of Leif's voyage as it was handed down through the ages:

> They sailed . . . in the open sea with a north-east wind, and were out two days before they saw land, towards which they sailed, and having come to an island which lay to the north of the mainland they landed on it, the weather being fine, and looked around; and they perceived that there was a dew on the grass, and . . . they put their hands in the dew, and carried it to their mouths, and thought that they had never known anything so sweet as that was. . . .

The mainland was lovelier yet. They found it full of vines and grapes, so much so that Leif named it for them. "In spring," it is recorded in *The Flatey Book,* "they made ready and sailed away, and Leif gave the country a name according to its resources, and called it Wineland."

Some experts hold that Leif landed on the coast of Labrador, some say Newfoundland, others maintain that it was New England. At any rate, other Vikings are believed to have come soon after Leif, reaching south to Cape Cod and perhaps Long Island, planting short-lived colonies along the New England coast. Some historians believe they explored inland to Minnesota, via the Great Lakes.

In Europe itself, the Vikings began to think more of peaceful pursuits than of piracy. With their encouragement, trade and travel slowly started to revive.

Another stimulant was the enterprise and avarice of the merchants in cities like Venice, Genoa, and Pisa. They built themselves a rich commerce with Constantinople.

Then commenced the Crusades. A culture that could not protect or speed travel on its own highways was able, through religious fervor and desire for loot, to transport hundreds of thousands of soldiers by ship, by horseback, and on foot to the Holy Land. It was the most vital factor in the revival of European trade and travel from the eleventh century on.

The First Crusade, beginning in 1096, far exceeded the expectations of Pope Urban II who issued the call to free the Holy Land from the infidels. A quarter of a million men made the long trek. In 1099, they climaxed three years of southward conquest by capturing Jerusalem.

With the Levantine coast once more in the hands of Europeans, a busy trade with the East began. And as Europe felt the influx of new goods, its own commerce increased.

There were nine Crusades altogether to the Holy Land. Edward Gibbon wrote of one that sailed from Venice:

> A similar armament, for ages, had not rode upon the Adriatic. It was composed of 120 flat-bottomed vessels or *palanders* for the horses; 240 transports filled with men and arms; seventy store-ships laden with provisions; and fifty stout galleys, well-prepared for the encounter of an enemy. While the wind was favorable, the sky serene, and the water smooth, every eye was fixed with wonder and delight on the scene of military and naval pomp which overspread the sea. The shields of the knights and squires, at once an ornament and a defense, were arranged on either side of the ships; the banners of the nations and families were displayed from the stern; our modern artillery was supplied by 300 engines for casting stones and darts; the fatigues of the way were cheered with the sound of music; and the spirits of the adventurers were raised by the mutual assurances that 40,000 Christian heroes were equal to the conquest of the world.

Some of the Crusades were idealistic, and some were tawdry, like the time, early in the thirteenth century, when the Crusaders overthrew a Byzantine emperor, Alexius III, strictly for Venetian cash. The Venetians wanted the emperor deposed because he'd been favoring their business rivals in Pisa. But even if they did have their squalid aspects, each one of the Crusades helped to reawaken Europe to the worth of trade and travel.

Religion also helped to restore commerce in another, more pacific way. During the tenth and eleventh centuries, the Church at Rome promoted two reforms for Europe: the Peace of God, and the Truce of God. The Peace restricted feudal nobles to attacking military personnel and objectives exclusively. The Truce declared Lent and all Fridays, Saturdays, and Sundays as intermissions in fighting. Later it was enlarged to include the harvest season, and in the other months, fighting was sanctioned solely on Mondays after dawn, Tuesdays, and Wednesdays until sunset.

Both reforms made life more secure for the merchant, pilgrim, and friar trudging along the rutted roads.

Now started out the greatest traveler and travel writer the world has known. His name was Marco Polo, and he introduced the West to the mysterious wonders of the Far East. He was the only source of information the West had on some far-off parts of the Orient until the nineteenth century.

At the age of seventeen, Marco went with his father and uncle, two veteran Venetian traders, on a trip from Acre to Baghdad, across the dread Gobi Desert and on to the Forbidden City of Peiping where, in 1275, he met Kublai Khan, the most powerful ruler on earth. The great Khan liked the boy, showered him with presents, and sent him on diplomatic missions that took him to provinces of China, Tibet, and Burma which no European had ever visited. Probably to India, too. He made him governor of a large Chinese city. For seventeen thrilling years Messer Marco lived a life of exoticism.

The sights he saw! Towering, snow-clad mountains, burning deserts, rivers that carried jade, sea beds studded with pearls. The lustrous court of the Khan who dressed his nobles in jewel-strewn gowns and his 5,000 elephants in robes of pure gold. The biggest city in the world—Hangchow with its 2,000,000 inhabitants. Paper money. Black stones, splendidly abundant and cheap, that burned all night and gave off wonderful heat, geysers of a marvelous liquid that also burned hot, and a strange material that wouldn't burn at all. Coal, petroleum, and asbestos, they were. People who had themselves tattooed, others who had their teeth covered with gold. Sumatra where cannibals feasted on human meat, and India where widows were expected to burn themselves alive on their husbands'

Courtesy N. Y. Public Library
Picture Collection

funeral pyres. A land where merchants wouldn't tell a lie to save their lives or to make a sale.

Marco saw many fascinating items on the Oriental transportation scene: the traveling conveyance of the Khan, a mammoth wooden palace borne on the backs of four elephants; the stags that were used for transport; the dog sleds; the admirable post road system which spoked out from the capital and had posthouses at stated intervals with luxuriously furnished, silk-draped apartments for travelers of importance; the tens of thousands of beautiful trees that were planted to shade the roads; the imperial messenger service with relay runners who sprinted three-mile stretches bearing news, dispatches, and fresh fruit for the Khan; the amazing bridges, including a covered toll bridge in the city of Cheng-tu which was lined with busy shops; the traffic on the Kiang River. "Incredible to anyone who had not seen it," Marco said. Once he was in the port of Sinu on the Kiang River and "saw there no less than 15,000 vessels." The boats were propelled by teams of ten and twelve horses hauling from the banks.

At sea, he came upon something still more astonishing—Indian merchant ships with four masts, sixty cabins, and thirteen water-tight compartments in the hold. (European ships didn't get water-tight compartments for another 450 years.)

One road hazard that Marco encountered in China was unique and unpleasant. If any descendant of Genghis Khan died, it was best to stay off the roads until after the funeral. It seemed that any traveler who met the funeral train on its trip to the ancestral burial grounds at Mount Altai was summarily killed. "Depart for the next world, and there attend upon your deceased Lord," the funeral escorts would say. Marco related that "when the corpse of Mangu Khan was transported to this mountain, the horsemen who accom-panied it slew upwards of 20,000 persons who fell in their path."

When the three Polos finally left for home in 1292, Kublai Khan gave them a gold *laissez-passer* (passport) to ensure their safe voy-age. Without it, they never would have made it alive past the ban-dits. With it, the Polos took three years to get back to Venice.

The book that Marco wrote about his seventeen-year trip, *The Travels of Marco Polo,* was read widely and set many a man to dreaming of a voyage to the Orient. A Latin edition of the book got into the hands of an Italian sailor named Christopher Columbus who jotted seventy notes in its margins.

With the Vikings and the Crusaders leading the way, Europeans began to travel more and farther. They started giving thought to bettering their modes of transport, and the Age of Discovery was born.

You saw more businessmen traveling: merchants on horseback, selling cloth, pots, pans, and pottery; peddlers on foot, vending ribbons, laces, and fancy goods. They didn't travel in the winter because the roads were too bad, so housewives had to lay in big stocks in the fall. You saw increasing numbers of pilgrims on their way to shrines. Generally, they traveled in groups, for company and for protection against highwaymen. On his pilgrimage to the shrine at Canterbury, Geoffrey Chaucer joined up with a group of twenty-eight, among them a knight, a squire, a prioress, a monk, a friar, a merchant, a clerk, a haberdasher, a weaver, a carpenter, a shipman, and a miller. Some pilgrims sailed overseas to visit shrines like the renowned one of St. James of Compostella in Spain. Many went to the Holy Land. A guide book was issued in the fifteenth century entitled *Information for Pilgrims unto the Holy Land*. The guide counseled:

> First, if ye shall go in a galley, make your covenant with the patron betimes. And choose you a place in the said galley in the overmost stage, for in the lowest under it is right evil and smouldering hot and stinking . . . Also ye shall buy you a bed beside St. Mark's Church in Venice, where ye shall have a feather bed, a mattress, a pillow, two pair sheets, and a quilt. And ye shall pay but three ducats. And when ye come again bring the same bed again, and ye shall have a ducat and a half for it again, though it be broke and worn. . . . Also when ye shall take your ass at Port Jaffa, be not too long behind your fellows. For an ye come betimes ye may choose the best mule or ass that ye can; for ye shall pay no more for the best than for the worst.

Some efforts were made to improve bridges. Religious orders such as the *Fratres Pontifices* in Italy and the French *Frères Pontifes* made it their good work to build new bridges "for the service of travelers," and they put up stalwart stone bridges, not the shaky wooden structures that had contented European bridge builders for hundreds of years. One of the monks, St. Bénezèt, was beatified for the fine job he did in constructing a bridge at Avignon, the very one in the song "Sur le Pont d'Avignon." Over in England, the monk Peter Colechurch got the public to contribute funds for a stone bridge he wanted to build over the Thames at London. Completed in 1209, London Bridge was 936½ feet long. Originally, it was bare except for a chapel, but people erected so many buildings on it that portions of the masonry crumbled. ("London Bridge is falling down, falling down.")

The most progress came at sea. In the north, the Vikings made their ships fatter, added wooden castles in the bow and stern, and in the twelfth century replaced the traditional right-handed steering oar with a rudder attached directly to the center of the stern. A stern rudder had been used in China in the eighth century, but the Vikings were the first to develop one in the West.

In the Mediterranean, the triangular lateen sail supplanted the square sail on practically all sailing craft around the year 1000. It was a good sail for beating to windward. Then in the fourteenth century, a style of ship was introduced that set both square and lateen sails, had a stern rudder, and the beginning of a raised deck in the stern and a forecastle in the bow. It was a lineal ancestor of the *Santa Maria*.

New instruments and techniques were evolving to help navigators. A primitive compass was invented during the twelfth century. It was still not completely reliable by Columbus' time, but it was helpful. Charts were improving along with a scientific approach to navigation that owed much to an imaginative Portuguese prince who lived from 1394 to 1460. Henry the Navigator, history has designated him.

Prince Henry built his own observatory, formulated a table of declinations of the sun, and made charts. He founded the first school of navigation at Sangres and developed it into a clearing house for geographical and nautical information from all of Europe.

If anyone can be said to have fathered the Age of Discovery, it was Prince Henry. In his day, people derided exploration. Or like the Portuguese Gomes Eannes de Azuram were terrified of its dangers. South of the Canary Islands, Eannes warned, "The currents are so terrible that no ship having once passed . . . will ever be able to return." Prince Henry was not frightened. He sent out expeditions to explore the western coast of Africa and seek a route that would circumnavigate Africa. One of his captains rediscovered the Madeira Islands, others discovered the Senegal and went as far as Sierra Leone. They demonstrated that exploring could be safe and profitable.

Henry died in 1460, but the Portuguese explorations continued. Bartholomew Dias sailed around the Cape of Good Hope in 1486, the first man to do so from the west. Twelve years later, Portuguese Vasco da Gama dropped anchor off Calicut, opening an eastward route to the Indies.

Meanwhile . . .

"And [I] came to the town of Palos . . . where I fitted for sea three ships well suited for such an undertaking . . . and I departed from the said harbor well furnished with much provision and many seamen, on the third day of the month of August of the said year, on a Friday, at a half an hour before sunrise, and took the route for the Canary Islands. . . ." So wrote the Italian-born, Greek-influenced, Portuguese-married, and Spanish-financed mariner named Christopher Columbus.

Columbus had a mission. He believed he was the man specially ordained to convert the Orient to Christianity, and to take possession of its illimitable riches. When the King of Portugal rejected his request for backing, he went to King Ferdinand and Queen Isabella of Spain. They put up the money for a brief sea voyage westward to the East. It was just 2,400 nautical miles from the Canary Islands to Japan, he told them, underestimating the distance by 8,200 miles. He had no idea that another broad continent lay in between.

The three ships in Columbus' little flotilla comprised the *Santa Clara,* his pet, a caravel measuring 70 feet and weighing 60 tons, whose nickname among the sailors was *Niña,* the *Pinta,* a caravel that was a trifle larger, and the flagship *Santa María.* She was a 100-ton vessel with three masts and, probably, a high stern and forecastle; no one knows exactly because she was later wrecked off Hispaniola. The *Santa María* carried four square sails and a lateen sail and the *Pinta* three square sails when they weighed anchor in Palos. The *Niña* carried lateen sails but shifted to square sails after the shakedown run to the Canaries. The crews of all three ships totaled ninety men, or less.

As far as sailing went, the crossing wasn't difficult. All he had to do to reach Japan, Columbus believed, was to turn right at the Canaries and sail west until he got there. So the navigation presented no trouble, nor did the weather.

It was a tense, fear-ridden trip, nonetheless. Most of the men were afraid that Columbus had underestimated the distance to the East, as indeed he had, and they feared that they would die in the middle of the ocean of thirst and starvation. They were panic-stricken when they sailed through the weed-filled Sargasso Sea in the western Atlantic; it was eerie and unfamiliar and it heightened their sense of isolation. They were uneasy at the fact that the winds held fair and northeasterly; to get home to Spain they would have to beat all the way. The threat of mutiny grew serious.

By October 7—sixty-five days out of Spain—Columbus himself began to worry. It looked to him as if they might have sailed past Japan.

He was a canny sailor, though. Flocks of birds were passing overhead, flying west by southwest, and he veered to follow them. Soon the signs of nearby land became many. On October 11th, he saw sandpipers and a green reed near the ship. The crew of the *Pinta* saw a cane and a pole worked with iron in the water, and the men on the *Niña* spotted a small branch covered with berries. The course was west-southwest and they made 104 miles by sunset.

In his monumental *History of the Indies,* the sixteenth-century Spanish priest, Bartolome de Las Casas told what happened then:

> After sunset the Admiral returned to his original west course, and they went along at the rate of twelve miles an hour. . . . At ten in the . . . night, [the Admiral] being on the castle of the poop saw a light, although it was so uncertain that he could not affirm it was land. He called Pedro Gutierrez, a gentleman of the King's bedchamber, and said that there seemed to be a light, and that he should look at it. He did so, and saw it. The Admiral said the same to Rodrigo Sanchez of Segovia, whom the King and Queen had sent with the fleet as inspector, but he could see nothing, because he was not in a place whence anything could be seen. After the Admiral had spoken he saw the light once or twice, and it was like a wax candle rising and falling. . . . The Admiral asked and admonished the men to keep a good lookout on the forecastle, and to watch well for land. . . .

Rodrigo de Triana, a sailor from Seville who was lookout on the *Pinta* was the first to see it. At 2 A.M. on October 12, he spied a white cliff glistening in the moonlight.

"Tierra! Tierra!" he shouted.

It was the Bahamas—San Salvador Island, to be precise.

The great explorer made four voyages in all to what he always thought were the Indies. He never realized that he'd discovered a new world.

The seas filled with explorers and settlers following Columbus' westward way. John Cabot landed in North America in 1497 and claimed it for England. Amerigo Vespucci reached the mainland of South America in 1499–1500 and realized that it was a separate land, not part of Asia, Spain's Vasco Núñez de Balboa discovered the Pacific Ocean in 1513, and shortly thereafter Ferdinand Magellan proved that the world was round. In 1519 Magellan, a Portuguese financed by the Spanish, sailed around the bottom of South America into the Pacific on the first successful voyage around the world. His ships got home in 1522, but Magellan didn't. He was killed in a native brawl in the Philippines.

The colonists came hard on the trail of the explorers, and started building great new empires. By 1493 the Spanish had a colony on Hispaniola, the start of a New World realm that stretched from the Argentine to Florida. By 1506 the Portuguese were settling in India and Brazil. By 1541 the French were trying to colonize Canada. By the early years of the seventeenth century, the Dutch were active from Brazil to New York. The British founded a colony in Virginia in 1585 that had to be abandoned, and another that simply vanished. In 1609 they settled a colony at Jamestown that survived through the leadership of John Smith and the assistance of his Indian sweetheart, Pocahontas. Massachusetts was settled by the British in 1620. Two boatloads of colonists started out on this expedition, but one of the ships, the *Speedwell*, leaked like a sieve and had to return to port. The other vessel, the *Mayflower*, made it to Amer-

The MAYFLOWER. Model by R. C. Anderson, Pilgrim's Hall, Plymouth, Mass.

ica with 102 passengers, half of them Pilgrims fleeing persecution, the other half Anglicans out for fun and adventure.

The size of the inhabited world had been more than doubled in a little over a century.

While pioneers sailed unknown seas and carved hard livings from forests and jungles, pioneers of a different sort were at work in the Old World.

Before the end of the seventeenth century, the basis was being laid in Europe for one of the world's biggest revolutions in transport: widespread canal building. To do it, a solution had to be found to a tricky engineering problem: how to make water run uphill as well as downhill and carry boats safely.

The answer was the canal lock by which a boat could be lifted on steps up a hill and lowered down steps on the other side. On each step up, the boat moved into a chamber with watertight gates and the water level was raised to that of the water ahead. The forward gate was then opened and the boat proceeded. The process was reversed on the downhill side.

A Chinese engineer, Ch'iao Wei-yo, built the first known canal lock in 984 but the concept was brought to fruition in Europe. Among the Europeans contributing their genius was Leonardo da Vinci, who lived in Italy from 1452 to 1519. The modern gate for canal locks was his invention.

Previous gates had been single doors hung from above the stream and worked by raising and lowering. Leonardo's brilliant innovation was the use of a pair of gates which formed a wide V when closed and which could be opened like ordinary doors. To this he added a gate within a gate, a small door placed below the surface of the water which let water in and out at a slower, safer rate than the main gates.

All over Europe people started to build canals with locks. The Swedes constructed one from Eskilstuna and Lake Mallaren as early as 1606. The French built one—the Languedoc Canal—in the reign of Louis XIV that was 150 miles long, from the Mediterranean to the Atlantic at Bordeaux. It took twenty-six years to finish and cost its builder a fortune, including the money intended for his daughters' dowries. His name was Pierre-Paul Riquet, and he explained that he had used his daughters' dowry money because "The canal is my dearest child." It was a remarkable progeny, a milestone, although Riquet died before it was opened in 1681. Twenty-six locks lifted the canal 206 feet in the thirty-two miles from Toulouse to Narouse, its summit; seventy-four more locks lowered it 620 feet to the level of the Mediterranean. It continues in operation to this day.

There was pioneering with bridges. Seventy-five-year-old Antonio Da Ponte, the supreme Italian bridge designer, erected the celebrated Rialto Bridge with its graceful single arch in Venice in 1588. At the end of the century in Paris, Jacques Androuet du Cerceau designed the massive Pont Neuf, the most modern bridge of its era. It is still called the New Bridge for all that twenty-five more bridges have since spanned the Seine in Paris. And in 1610 the Spanish put up an exceptional stone bridge in Lima, Peru, with the help of 100,000 eggs. They mixed the egg whites with the mortar to make it bind better.

One of Japan's most famous spans—the Sacred Bridge at Nikko—went up about this time. A beautiful arch of vermilion lacquer and gilt, it was hung over the rampaging Daiya from torii gates of granite. It was erected for the exclusive use of the Shogun, and it still is barred to the Japanese public.

European roads, it must be said, remained dreadful. Most governments relied on statutory labor for road maintenance. Under this system, people residing along each road had to donate a number of days' work to repairing it, and their stints were not very enthusiastic.

Some slight signs of improvements on the roads were to be noticed, though. The French Government made a concerted effort in the seventeenth century to better roads, and in England a new idea appeared—the turnpike. The first, on the Great North Road, was authorized by Parliament in 1663. The toll for a horse was one penny, for a score of sheep a halfpenny.

The best news was the development of a splendid new conveyance—the coach. It was a big, closed-in, four-wheeled carriage with doors in the sides, which derived its name from the town of Kocs in Hungary where it was invented around 1450. Initially, it wasn't very comfortable. It was merely a box on wheels with no springs, no brakes, and no glass in the windows. Good Queen Bess of England complained bitterly to the French Ambassador, "I suffered greatly from aching pains in consequence of having been knocked about in a coach driven too fast." Nevertheless, it swept Europe. Every monarch wanted several coaches and wanted them to be more resplendent than his neighbor's. They were covered with gold, jewels, and paintings. Early in the seventeenth century, springs made of heavy leather straps were introduced; later steel springs were added.

Edwin Tunis.

Queen Elizabeth's English coach, 1564.

City streets grew crowded with them. "Sixty or seventy years ago," Fynes Moryson wrote in 1619, "coaches were very rare in England, but at this day . . . there be few gentlemen of any account . . . who have not their coaches, so as the streets of London are almost stopped up with them." Noisy vehicles they were. Londoners referred to them as "hellcarts." On one occasion, Samuel Pepys reported, "It is believed the Queen is with child, for that the coaches are ordered to ride very easily through the streets."

Hackneys started up. London had four in 1634. By 1710, it had 800. Paris began an omnibus line with coaches. Although it charged less than a penny to ride about the city, it failed for lack of business.

By the end of the century, stagecoaches were in operation in England transporting passengers between cities. They were not always very pleasant. John Dryden, the poet, writing to his cousin, Mrs. Steward, in 1698, recounted:

> My journey to London was yet more unpleasant than my abode at Tichmarch; for the coach was crowded up with an old woman, fatter than any of my hostesses on the road. Her weight made the horses travel very heavily; but to give them a breathing time, she would often stop us, and plead some necessity of nature, and tell us we were all flesh and blood. But she did this so frequently, that at last we conspired against her; and that she might not be inconvenienced by staying in the coach, turned her out in a very dirty place, where she was to wade up to the ankles before she could reach the next hedge. When I was rid of her I came sick home, and kept my house for three weeks together.

Travelers stayed overnight with friends when they could, or at abbeys and monasteries; only as a last resort would the well-to-do person put up at an inn. One traveler in Germany wrote of "being lodged at Rodenburgh in a stately inn, where the host, hostess, guests, cows, horse, swine lay all in one room. . . ." Innkeepers were often in collusion with the ubiquitous highwaymen.

There were new developments on water. Warships that regularly used oar power were on their way out, and the three-masted sailing ship known as the galleon had come to form the core of European navies. The largest of the galleons, England's gilded *Sovereign of the Seas,* hoisted thirteen sails. Other new types of vessels included the Dutch *fluyt* and *jacht,* the pinnace, the brigantine, the frigate, the polacca, the cutter.

The fact is that Europe had awakened. With its new canals, bridges, turnpikes, coaches, and ships, it was bracing itself for an industrial expansion equal to its geographic one.

IV

Building Up Steam

THE EVIL CONDITION of roads continued unabated into the eighteenth century. One of the most often-told jokes in England concerned the man with a wooden leg who turned down a lift in a coach.

"I'm in a hurry," he said.

Fact outdid fiction in this regard. "Blind Jack" Metcalf, an English road builder, was once offered a coach ride from London to Harrogate. He declined, saying that blind as he was he could still walk the 200 miles faster than a coach could travel them. He proved his point, too, by beating the coach to Harrogate.

The Royal Portuguese Ambassador took three months to go from Rome to Lisbon in 1716. And he and his entourage were traveling in the latest, most elegant coaches to be had.

In the American colonies, coach passengers did as much pushing as riding. Even in the most settled corner of this incubating nation, the New York-Boston-Philadelphia triangle, travel was primitive. There were no bridges over the big rivers and the ferries usually ran in daylight only. Many of them were so small that they were in constant danger of being upset. In the early spring, floating ice added extra hazard. Boats were overturned or stove in, and the passengers had to swim to the nearest ice floe. Sometimes, the traveler who managed to escape drowning froze to death on the cake of ice waiting for rescue.

The trip from Boston to New York took a week or ten days at the least. Mrs. Sarah Knight of Boston, newly a widow at the age of thirty-eight, made the journey on horseback in the fall and winter of 1704 to settle some business in connection with her late husband's estate. She was a remarkable woman, traveling independently over an ill-defined route through wild country that abounded in wolves and bears. She rode with the post or other travelers, or she hired guides to lead her from point to point, but those were her only concessions to caution at a time when strong men feared to make the trip. Mrs. Knight kept a delightful diary which gives a lively picture of what travel was like.

According to the diary, she started out by going to a tavern and looking for a guide for the first leg of the journey. John, the son of the tavernkeeper, "arrose, and gravely demanded what I would give him to go with me? 'Give you,' said I, 'are you John?' 'Yes,' sais he, 'for want of a Better. . . .' 'Well, Mr. John,' sais I, 'make your demands.' 'Why, half a pss. of wight and a dram,' sais John. I agreed, and gave him a Dram [now] in hand to bind the bargain. . . .

"We come to Billinges, where I was to Lodg. My Guide dismounted and very Complasantly help't me down and shewd the door, signing to me with his hand to Go in; wch I Gladly did—But had not gone many steps into the Room, ere I was Interogated by a young Lady I understood afterwards was the Eldest daughter of the family, with these, or words to this purpose, (viz.) Law for mee— 'what in the world brings You here at this time a night?—I never see a woman on the Rode so Dreadfull late, in all the days of my versall life. Who are you? Where are You going? I'me scar'd out of my witts'—with much more of the same Kind. I stood aghast, Prepareing to reply, when in comes my Guide—to him Madam turn'd, Roreing out: 'Lawfull heart, John, is it You?—how de do! Where in the world are you going with this woman? Who is she? . . .' "

There was the afternoon when "the Post told mee we had neer 14 miles to Ride to the next Stage, (where we were to Lodg.) I askt him of the rest of the Rode, foreseeing wee must travail in the night. Hee told mee there was a bad River we were to Ride thro', wch was so very firce a hors could sometimes hardly stem it: But it was but narrow, and should soon be over. I cannot express The concern of mind this relation sett me in: no thoughts but those of the dan'res River could enter my Imagination. . . ."

Night came. "The only Glimmering we now had was from the spangled Skies, Whose Imperfect Reflections rendered every object formidable. Each lifeless Trunk, with its shatter'd Limbs, appear'd an Armed Enymie; and every little stump like a Ravenous devourer. . . ."

And then "I knew by the Going of the Hors wee had entred the water, wch my Guide told mee was the hazzardos River he had told me off; and hee, Riding up close to my Side, Bid me not fear—we should be over Imediatly. I now ralyed all the courage I was mistriss of, Knowing that I must either Venture my fate of drowning, or be left like ye children in the wood. So, as the Post bid me, I gave reins to my Nagg; and sitting . . . Stedy . . ., in a few minutes got safe to the other wise, which hee told mee was the Narragansett country. . . ."

Doughty Mrs. Knight was somewhat tired, bedraggled, and saddlesore by the time she got to New York.

Moving inanimate goods overland was still more grueling work. In 1698 the Burgundians bought a bronze statue of Louis XIV, which they intended to set up at Dijon. It was carried by boat to Auxerre and started on the long trek by road to Dijon. En route it got stuck in the road. Nothing the French could do would move it, so they built a shed around it and for twenty-one years they waited for the road to be improved enough to bear it.

Inland transportation at the opening of the eighteenth century, in short, was generally poor. But the seed had been sown for momentous changes. Problems in industrial production were being attacked by new, scientific methods. Wind, water, and steam were being harnessed to supply power. New techniques and machines were being invented—the spinning jenny in textiles, molds for pottery, casting of plate glass were a few—that allowed one man to do many times the work he could do before. This was the Industrial Revolution which began in earnest in England about the middle of the century. The increased production of raw materials and inexpensively made goods intended for mass markets demanded better, cheaper internal transportation. This came as man moved steadily toward the steam age.

The first change was an old idea that blossomed abruptly into maturity—go by water. Since many of the leading manufacturing and mining centers were not on navigable streams, navigable streams had to be built. A great canal-building era began in the Western world in 1759, its immediate impulse provided by the strange combination of a bored young duke, an unhappy love affair, and a few coal mines.

The bored duke was twenty-three-year-old Francis Egerton, the third Duke of Bridgewater. A slim, well-manicured aristocrat, he had inherited much property, had traveled, was engaged to marry a beautiful belle, and could look forward to a life of ease and pleasure. However, the engagement went sour, and he had to find something to take his mind off his troubles.

On the duke's Worsley estate near Manchester were coal mines. His father had talked about building a waterway for carrying the coal into Manchester and young Francis resolved to follow up on the plan. During his travels in France, he had been deeply impressed by the Languedoc Canal, so now he planned a canal that would descend by a steep flight of locks from the mines to the Irwell River, march up the other side and go on to Manchester. Before proceeding with the project, he consulted a self-educated millwright *cum* jack-of-all-trades named James Brindley who at forty-three was making a name for himself as a consultant in another canal undertaking. According to the English poet, Robert Southey, Brindley was "a man of real genius for this particular employment, who thought of nothing but locks and levels, perforating hills, and floating barges on aqueduct bridges over unmanageable streams. When he had a plan to form, he usually went to bed, and lay there working it out in his head till the design was completed. Being asked before the House of Parliament for what he supposed rivers were created, he answered after a pause—'to feed navigable canals.' "

Brindley studied the duke's projected canal and advised him to avoid going down and up again with all those locks, to build instead a canal that ran on one level from the mine by viaduct across the Irwell River and on a built-up embankment across the Stretford meadows to Manchester. The duke agreed, hired Brindley to do it, and stuck by him even when people began making jokes about the elevated canal that traveled overwater on a viaduct. "Brindley's castle in the air," they called the viaduct. It was 600 feet long by 36 feet wide, and the bottoms of its three arches were 39 feet above the surface of the river in order that sailing barges could go underneath them without lowering their masts.

Despite rigorous opposition, the canal was finished in 1761, and an amazing sight it was to see coal barges traveling serenely four or five stories above other boats.

The project was a total success. It cut the delivered price of the duke's coal exactly in half, from seven to three and a half pence a hundred weight. It helped to make Manchester the most important industrial city in northern England, and touched off a wave of canal building that threaded the map of England with navigable waterways.

Brindley did not stop with his first success. The Duke of Bridgewater put him to work on a canal connecting Manchester with the Mersey River and the port of Liverpool. A third Brindley project, the Grand Trunk Canal, linked up the Mersey with the Trent and Humber Rivers. In all, the untutored Brindley designed some 360 miles of canals and became the most famous canal builder of his time—before he died in 1771 at the age of fifty-five from overwork.

Torrents of money poured into canal building. When the promoters of the Ellesmere Canal set out to raise the necessary funds by public subscription, around 1790, they obtained four times the backing they thought they needed. Unavoidably, this kind of enthusiasm led to wild speculation which ruined some unwise investors, but it was wonderful in terms of the canals it built. In 1750, there were about 1,000 miles of navigable rivers in England. Within a century, the inland waterway mileage jumped to 4,250. Freight rates were overturned. The rate for moving pottery from Staffordshire to Liverpool had been £21.10s. a ton. By canal it fell to thirteen shillings a ton.

Canal building was not limited to England; some singular waterways were laid down on the Continent during the eighteenth century. The Canal du Centre in France tied the English Channel to the Mediterranean. The Eider Canal opened a passage across the foot of Denmark and eliminated a long and dangerous journey around the peninsula.

In America, the last decades of the century saw a growing interest in canals. In 1772, Benjamin Franklin was writing to the Mayor of Philadelphia, "Rivers are ungovernable things, especially in Hilly Countries. Canals are quiet and very manageable." During the last ten years of the century, the Middlesex Canal in Massachusetts, the Little Falls in New York, and the million-dollar, 22-mile Santee in North Carolina were built, and they were merely hints of things to come.

Slowly the roads began to improve, too. At first, people tried to achieve good roads backwards—by improving the vehicles. If the coach were better built and more comfortable, they figured, the passenger would not notice the bad roads as much. Another approach was somewhat more reasonable: construct and regulate vehicles so that they would do less damage to the existing road surfaces. Laws were, therefore, enacted controlling the size of wheels, the weight of wagons, and the number of animals employed to draw them. At most these were stopgap measures. The only workable solution was to build roads that could stand the growing traffic.

France, again the pace-setter, created in 1716 the first modern state-maintained organization of civil engineers, the *Corps des Ponts et Chaussées*, and, in 1747, the world's first engineering school, the *École des Ponts et Chaussées*. The *Corps* supervised bridge and road building throughout the country, and the *École* trained engineers for the future. In the 1770's, a French engineer, Pierre Trésaguet, developed a style of road building that affected road construction throughout the world. Very simply, Trésaguet designed roads with three fairly shallow layers of hard-packed, tightly fitting stones. The roadbed and the surface sloped gently down on either side from the center to ensure proper drainage.

In England, the first of several world-renowned road builders had begun his career. This man had been a soldier and a businessman before he became a road builder. He'd also been an athlete, a splendid horseman, and an itinerant dance fiddler although he had been blind since he was six years old. His given name was John Metcalf, but most people addressed him as "Blind Jack." It was he who hiked from London to Harrogate. That sort of bravado was characteristic.

"Blind Jack" was in his late forties when he started work on his first strip of road around 1765, but he soon made himself and his roads famous. He originated a shrewd technique for keeping road foundations dry. He took off the soft topsoil, dug deep ditches on both sides of the road for drainage, and lifted the roadbed with the soil he'd removed from the ditches. Then he covered the surface of the road with gravel.

For thirty years, "Blind Jack" distinguished himself with the excellent roads and bridges he built. One of his triumphs was the suc-

Stagecoach, circa 1835.

Firestone Archives

cessful construction of a road across a swampy marsh. He kept the stone and gravel road dry and stable with a packed bed of thousands upon thousands of small bundles of heather.

The British road system owes him much.

Traffic got heavier. There were "flying wagons" carrying light goods, mail coaches, private vehicles, horseback riders. Huge stage-wagons, usually borne by four, sometimes by eight, great broad wheels, 9 to 16 inches across, rumbled and creaked from town to town with large freight. Stagecoaches clattered and slithered past them, averaging as high as eleven miles per hour. Each year more of them could be seen. In 1740, one stagecoach a week left London for Birmingham. By 1783, four or five a day covered that route—thirty a week.

These stagecoaches carried incredible loads. Some emptyings of coaches at a journey's end resembled the modern circus stunt in which the tiny car comes in, stops, its doors open, and unbelievable numbers of clowns climb out. A 1770 record notes that "thirty-four persons were in and about the Hertford coach this day when it broke down by one of the braces giving way." Some staid passengers used to ride inside the coach, but many others, for half-fare, clung all over the outside—on top, in back, and up front beside the driver. "He who can properly balance himself rides not incommodiously on the outside," wrote a German visitor to England in 1772, "and in summer time, in fine weather, on account of the prospects it certainly is more pleasant than it is within, excepting that the company is generally low."

Turnpikes were the big thing now. The British government chartered private companies to build and maintain roads in return for which they were authorized to charge tolls. The tolls were paid at revolving gates—hence, the word turnpike. Since it cost the government nothing, Parliament was very partial to the arrangement. By 1829, 3,873 turnpike companies were in operation in Britain with 20,000 miles of highway.

Not that these companies did much about maintaining their highways. Most of them let their roads go to pot. Nor could you blame them. They were systematically cheated by the toll-takers.

In America, most early roads were outgrowths of Indian trails. When a young surveyor named George Washington was sent to plot a road from Virginia to Pennsylvania in 1754, he followed an Indian trail known as Nemacolin's Path. When Daniel Boone laid out the famous Wilderness Road in 1775, he retraced the Warriors' Path through the Cumberland Gap. Road construction was generally slow and backward. By 1776, a continuous set of highways reached from Boston to Savannah, but there was only one hard-graveled road in the country, heading out of Portsmouth, Maine.

The first stagecoach line that catered to the public started service in 1732. It ran from Burlington, New Jersey, across the state to Amboy. You had to go the remainder of the way to New York by boat from Amboy, or to Philadelphia by boat from Burlington. A through stage went from Philadelphia to New York in 1756, but it required three days' time with the coach traveling eighteen hours a day.

Turnpikes were needed to better matters.

The United States got the turnpike craze toward the end of the century and got it badly. The first was built in Virginia in 1785. The Little River Turnpike was its name, and it went west from Alexandria. The first important one was the Lancaster Turnpike which reached sixty-two miles from Philadelphia to Lancaster, Pennsylvania. It cost $415,000 to construct, a fortune for that period. The builders quickly made a fortune out of it, though, and no wonder with the tolls they charged.

The fee for "a four wheeled pleasure craft drawn by two beasts" was generally about fifty cents in those days, plus four cents for each additional beast. A wagon drawn by two beasts cost twenty-five cents, a pleasure sleigh drawn by two horses twenty cents, by one horse twelve and a half cents. It was six cents for each horse and rider.

The turnpikes proved so profitable that hundreds of companies went into the business. In New York State 278 different companies built over 4,000 miles of turnpike before 1821.

While the turnpike craze lasted, it was a boon. It opened much new country to land transport, and cut travel time appreciably.

Railroads weren't so far off now.

In sixteenth-century German mines, wooden rails had served as roads for hand-pushed ore carts. By the start of the seventeenth century, wooden rails led downhill from certain English coal mines; wagons full of coal coasted down to riverside wharves, were emptied into barges, and hauled back up to the mines by horse. By the end of the eighteenth century, all the important collieries in England had horse-drawn railways. Some of these used cast-iron rails.

Everything was in place awaiting the arrival of the engine. The world was building up toward steam.

At sea, sailors and travelers continued at the mercy of the weather. A ship bound from Dublin to Philadelphia in 1741 had to be abandoned in the mid-Atlantic after 144 days at sea, more than twice the normal time for the whole trip. There was just no wind. Lieutenant William Bligh's expedition to the South Seas aboard H.M.S. *Bounty* in 1787 was kept nearly a month by "contrary winds and bad weather" from sailing down the English Channel to the open Atlantic.

Travel by water could be miserably uncomfortable. In his autobiography, Ben Franklin told about a trip he made from New York to Philadelphia in 1723. Starting out by boat from New York to Amboy, New Jersey, he wrote:

> We met with a squall that tore our rotten sail to pieces . . . and drove us upon Long Island . . . at a place where there could be no landing, there being a great surff on the stony beach. . . .
>
> We had no remedy but to wait till the wind should abate; the boatman and I concluded to sleep, if we could; and so crowded into the scuttle, and the spray beating over the head of our boat, leak'd thro' to us. . . . In this manner we lay all night, with very little rest; but the wind abating the next day, we made a shift to reach Amboy before night, having been 30 hours on the water, without victuals, or any drink but a bottle of filthy rum. . . .

On longer trips the diet was a terrible hazard. Usually it was hardtack, salted meat, fish that might not, if you were lucky, be rotten, stagnant water and sometimes filthy rum. Men became weak, caught scurvy, or a fever, and died.

An allied danger was overcrowding. Diseases could sweep the close quarters of a ship at sea. This condition was not eased by owners who frequently signed on larger crews than their ships needed to make up for the men they knew they'd lose in the normal course of events.

If the ship was not wrecked by a storm, or becalmed for weeks on end; if it didn't get lost or sunk due to poor charts, or no charts, and poor navigation; if the food did not run out; if scurvy did not infect half the men with spongy gums, loose teeth and weak limbs; if some fatal illness didn't decimate the crew—there were always pirates.

Mariners had to keep a sharp lookout for a white flag that appeared to have been dipped in blood. It was one of the pirate ensigns. Or they feared plain black flags, or black flags decorated with various combinations of devils, sailors, swords, skeletons, skulls and crossed bones. All of them meant *Run!*

It was a rough life, and sailors were a rough lot. Jonathan Swift's traveler, Gulliver, depicted them pretty accurately. Sailors, he said, were "Fellows of desperate Fortunes, forced to fly from the Place of their Birth, on Account of their Poverty or their Crimes. Some were undone by Law-suits; others spent all they had in Drinking, Whoring and Gaming; others fled for Treason; many for Murder, Theft, Poysoning, Robbery, Perjury, Forgery, Coining False Money; for committing Rapes or Sodomy; for flying from their Colours, or deserting to the enemy; and most of them had broken Prison. None of these durst return to their native Countries for fear of being hanged, or of starving in a Jail; and therefore were under a Necessity of seeking a Livelihood in other Places."

Despite all this, the century's true symbol of surging travel was the crowded harbor, the sail-dotted horizon. Fat, blunt-nosed, heavily-armed East Indiamen plowed all the seas, along with a bewildering variety of frigates and corvettes, luggers and cutters, speedy Baltimore clippers, brigs, brigantines and barkentines. Legitimate traders, most of them, but naturally, there were some privateers, smugglers, slavers, pirates and men-of-war.

One of the era's most colorful ships was the schooner. This was a type rigged with at least two sets of large fore-and-aft sails plus a minimum of one jib. The big fore-and-aft sails were of the old lateen family, with a significant modification: that part of the sail that had once projected forward of the mast was now gone, and the leading edge of the sail was attached to the mast. This was called a gaff rig. The jib was triangular, hung fore-and-aft, and it served like any other sail when the wind was behind the vessel or off its beam —i.e., it tugged forward—but its main function when the ship was beating to windward was a new one: it served to speed the air past the outside of the sail behind it, which made the ship go faster to windward.

The schooner rig was an invention of the Dutch, but New England fishermen named it in 1713 and made it famous.

It happened in this way.

A favorite water's-edge pastime was skipping stones. As the flat stone pattered across the water, it was said to be "scooning." Captain Andrew Robinson sent a trim, double-masted ship down the ways in Gloucester, Massachusetts, and when she hit the water, so the story goes, a fisherman shouted, "See how she scoons!"

"Scooner let her be called," declared Captain Robinson.

The schooner needed only a small crew, seven men including the cook. She was therefore an economical vessel for trading or for

Newcastle-on-Tyne, 1724. Captain James Cook began his career here.

Phineas Pett's three-decker, THE PRINCE, 1670.
Model from Samuel Pepys' collection.

fishing. The New Englanders sailed their schooners to George's Banks off Cape Cod, and north to the Grand Banks, packed their holds with cod, bluefish, mackerel, halibut, and hake and headed home with the lines for lowering sail tied well out of reach in the rigging, and, like as not, the craft heeled over on her side, booming along in a nor'easter. It was said that a schooner was at her best "with her lee rail under water and her cabin dragging."

At the other end of the scale was the full-rigged ship, which came into its own at the end of the century. On this one they really could crowd the canvas; a three-masted ship often hoisted two dozen or more sails.

When it came to building ships, the American Colonials excelled. By 1650 shipbuilding was a thriving industry in Massachusetts and long before 1750 American ships equaled any in the world for quality. At the time of the American Revolution, one out of every three British ships had come out of an American shipyard.

Great Britain led the world, of course, in both naval and merchant shipping. In the mid-eighteenth century, Britain had twice as many warships as did France, six times as many merchant ships, and ten times as many experienced seamen. With each generation, British sea trade increased. Between 1663 and 1669 an average of 93,000 tons of shipping a year cleared British ports. Between 1700 and 1702 this figure was 274,000 tons. Between 1778 and 1789 it was up to 1,722,000 tons.

The boom in trade called for an increase in marine insurance, and at a coffeehouse in London the men of this growing business met to talk and keep abreast of events. Beginning in 1734, a list was kept there, containing the names of the merchant ships currently at sea, where they were, and where bound. A firm grew in this meeting place and when it moved from the coffeehouse in 1774 it took the name of the coffeehouse—Lloyd's—with it.

Among the technical advances that came into common use in this period were the wheel for steering—which replaced various arrangements of tillers and cables—and the sheathing of ship bottoms with copper to protect ships against parasites and rot.

For navigating by the heavens the sextant grew out of the old quadrant. And in 1714, the English Parliament, attempting to spur on an old search, put up a prize of 20,000 pounds to be awarded to the inventor of a method for precisely determining longitude at sea. An Englishman, John Harrison, after developing three chronometers that weren't good enough, devised one that was. It was hung in gimbals so that it would stay level regardless of what the ship was doing. In one test it was accurate to within fifty-four seconds in five months. Harrison earned the prize.

While some men worked on the development of better navigating equipment and techniques, others studied the shape and size of the earth. One fact discovered by eighteenth-century scientists was that the earth was not a perfect sphere, but was flattened at the poles. This kind of study, in combination with careful geographic exploration, made accurate charting possible.

The eighteenth century saw world maps and charts for the first time really begin to conform to actuality. Until this century what little the geographers knew got mixed up on the maps with what men "had always been told" and what they thought should be true and what they wished were true.

There should be a westward route to the Indies, they had thought. That was only reasonable—the world was round, wasn't it? And it would be wonderful, they had figured, if ships didn't have to sail a great southern loop around Africa on their way to India, China and Japan. So the early explorers visualized the New World not as the shores of a new continent but only as a narrow hurdle in their westward voyage, just a "barrier reef," to use Bernard De Voto's phrase. That illusion vanished as known America slowly began to thicken out, but still it seemed certain to the geographers that the land was not very wide and that there was a passage through it somewhere. Much of the early exploration of North America was done because of that mistaken belief. As De Voto pointed out:

> The Pacific was so near that the charters of Massachusetts (1628 and 1691) granted the colony the full extent of the land west to the ocean. Virginia (second charter 1609) extended from sea to sea. Connecticut too ran to the Pacific (1662). . . . So did both Carolinas.

The scientific approach of the eighteenth century insisted that there be no more of these wishful fantasies. Everything had to be carefully observed and well documented. Not everyone responded to this demand, but the maps of the French cartographer J. B. Bourguignon d'Anville symbolized a beginning. For instance, Europeans had been drawing rivers on the map of Africa although they knew very little about the African interior. All right then, d'Anville in his maps left the African interior blank. *They* would start from scratch. Now that they had the tools, the knowledge of the world would be built with facts.

To fill in the gaps and give the mapmakers more to work with came such men as Vitus Bering, James Cook, and the Comte de La Pérouse.

Bering discovered that America and Asia were separate continents. He proved that there was no land bridge connecting Siberia with Alaska. The Danish explorer's findings were instigated by Czar Peter the Great who is supposed to have said, "Now that the country is in no danger, we should strive to win for her glory along the lines of the Arts and Sciences." In 1728 a Russian expedition led by Bering coasted north along the Pacific peninsula known as Kamchatka and into the straits that now bear the name of Bering. It reached East Cape, the farthest northeast point on the Asian land mass before it headed back. A second expedition set out in 1741 and touched in at Alaska.

Then there was Cook, an amazing gentleman who made three voyages of discovery in the Pacific between 1768 and 1779. His ships were reformed coal carriers. (He had apprenticed aboard one and he knew their toughness.) With them he staked out New Zealand and Australia for the crown of England and laid to rest a very old myth that there was a vast southern continent, bigger than all the known lands of the world combined—*Terra Australis Nondum Cognita*. Into the bargain he did a job of charting such that a Frenchman who sailed to New Zealand after him remarked that Cook's charts were "of an exactitude and of a thoroughness of detail which astonished me beyond all powers of expression: I doubt whether our own coasts of France have been delineated with more precision."

An excellent sailor, navigator, and leader, Cook took great risks in shallow waters filled with coral reefs in order to plot coastlines accurately. One time, having unknowingly trapped himself into running between the northeastern coast of Australia and its Great Barrier Reef, his ship and expedition nearly came to an end on a jagged bar of coral. But he skillfully kept his crew from panic long enough to get the ship repaired and out of peril.

Cook was a Yorkshire farmer's son. He stood more than six feet tall and he had a sensitive face marked by prominent brows and a wide-eyed, direct glance.

For his day he was a revolutionary. He required cleanliness aboard his ships, and had them scrubbed down regularly with vinegar. The normal captain couldn't have cared less what his men ate, so long as they were full enough not to make trouble. Cook believed strongly in the well-balanced diet, though, and made sure his crew stuck to one. He displayed patience and humaneness toward his men. He went further. In contrast to the brutality so evident in the white man's approach to "savages," he was kind. At Tahiti, he gave his sentries strict orders not to fire upon Polynesians whom they caught thieving. As he explained, "That thieves are hanged in England I thought no reason why they should be shot in Otaheite; because, with respect to the navies, it would have been an execution by a law *ex post facto*. They had no such law amongst themselves, and it did not appear to me that we had any right to make such a law for them. That they should abstain from theft, or be punished with death, was not one of the conditions under which they claimed the advantage of civil society, as it is among us; and I was not willing to expose them to firearms, loaded with shot."

A great man as well as a great explorer, he.

France had Jean Francois de Galaup, the Comte de La Pérouse. He took an expedition into the Pacific between 1785 and 1788, discovered bleak, foggy La Pérouse Strait north of Japan, and made the first exact record of geographical points in Chinese and Japanese waters.

He never got back to France. He was shipwrecked in the New Hebrides and his entire expedition lost.

Cook never got back to England either. He was killed in Hawaii at the age of fifty-one in a scuffle with some natives he tried to befriend.

To turn to a happier note: a scientific advance of the eighteenth century saved countless lives on shipboard. On the advice of British naval surgeon, James Lind, the Royal Navy made lime juice a compulsory part of its diet in 1798. It wiped out scurvy among British sailors, and soon most of the world's ships were serving citrus juices to their crews. The English people thereby got a nickname: "limeys."

Some interesting bridges were erected in this century. France produced Jean Rodolphe Perronet, the "Father of Modern Bridge Building," who perfected the masonry arch and devised a new pier

The ESSEX, American frigate, 1813.

construction. He designed the beautiful Place de la Concorde Bridge in Paris in the 1780's and the pioneering Pont Saint-Maxence over the Oise that had the flattest arches yet seen. It stood strong for almost a century until German invaders demolished it in 1870.

The British put up two more spans over the Thames in London despite horrified outcries from conservative Londoners who maintained that the old London Bridge was more than enough. "A new bridge," the die-hards feared, "would make the skirts of London too big for the body."

America got its first bridges in this century. One of the earliest was a fine wooden structure over the Connecticut River at Bellows Falls, Vermont. A Colonel Enoch Hale built it and lost it when a mortgage on it was foreclosed. Many of these early American wooden bridges were covered. They were built to look just like a barn with open ends so the horses wouldn't be frightened by the wild white water of spring thaw. Besides, the cover protected the bridge against the weather. Some claimed it lengthened the life of a wooden bridge by forty years.

All over the world, travel was gradually becoming easier now, and more people traveled for pleasure and education. The well-to-do of England made a ritual of going on a Grand Tour of the continent.

"I am told, but it seems incredible," Edward Gibbon wrote in 1785, "that upwards of 40,000 English, masters and servants, are now absent on the continent."

It worked in both directions. A Frenchman noted in 1765 that, "At Dover the inns were entirely full of Frenchmen, and their numbers were so considerable that they could not provide themselves with carriages. . . ."

Apparently the inns were so crowded that they resorted to the "hot bed" system. "The servants of the house came to awake me at 3 o'clock in the morning to make me give up my bed to newcomers," the Frenchman complained. He stood up for his rights, though. "Notwithstanding all the rout they made, I kept my place, and did not leave the bed till 5 o'clock."

Private coaches—particularly royal ones—grew increasingly luxurious. They had gilded decorations with beautiful wooden carvings, linings of lush velvet, built-in lanterns, pistol cases, and chamber pots.

Across the Atlantic the going was somewhat more difficult, the life considerably more rugged. Most of the travelers in America went long distances only when they had to; say, to start new communities. In the closing years of the century, they started to use Conestoga wagons for this, rumbling over the Allegheny Mountains into the Northwest Territory. The larger Conestoga wagons were pulled by six horses and carried up to eight tons. Customarily, the driver rode behind the left wheel horse, the reason that Americans now drive to the right of the road.

It wasn't always difficult riding. As an English officer in America wrote to his brother about a sleigh ride in America, "You can have no idea of the state of the pulse seated with pretty women mid-deep in straw, your body armed with fur and flannels, clear air, bright sunshine, spotless sky, horses galloping, every feeling turned to joy and jollity."

During some half a million years, man had learned to travel over land only as fast and as far as he could go on foot, or as his animals could carry or pull him; over water he went only as fast and as far as the currents, oars, and the unreliable wind could move his boat.

He had made no important change in his means of transport for more than 4,000 years.

By the eighteenth century one such change was on the way: steam power.

A persistent legend exists that James Watt of Scotland conceived the idea of a steam engine while watching steam jet from the spout of a kettle on his mother's stove. This is nothing more than a homely little fairy tale.

In 1690, nearly half a century before Watt was born, a Frenchman named Denis Papin made public a design for a steam engine. An Englishman, Captain Thomas Savery, took out a patent for a steam engine in 1698. In 1706 a Papin-built improvement on Savery's machine pumped water higher than 100 feet in a leaky pipe. In 1712 the English Thomas Newcomen, working independently and ignorant of Savery's invention, developed a better one. By 1769 more than a hundred Newcomen engines were being used to pump water out of coal mines in England as well as on the continent.

Now came Watt, entering the scene as a trained instrument maker in 1763 when he repaired a model of a Newcomen engine and recognized some serious faults in the design. He got into the steam engine business and, in partnership with manufacturer Matthew Boulton, made a number of significant contributions that cleared the way for the development of an engine efficient and light enough to help men get around.

In the race between the cart and the boat to become the first vehicle driven by steam, the boat won.

A wide disagreement exists as to who gets credit for the first steamboat. Once all the partisans have made their claims, it appears that it was the achievement of a thirty-two-year-old French noblemen, Marquis Claude de Jouffroy d'Abbans, who thought up the concept while he was in jail for dueling. He built a 130-foot-long, steam-driven paddle-wheeler, the *Pyroscaphe,* and ran it on the Saône River in 1783. Not for long. After fifteen minutes, the vibration of the machinery began to shake the good *Pyroscaphe* to pieces, and the marquis had hurriedly to beach her.

An American named John Fitch was also building steamboats about this time—three of them. They were weird-looking contraptions with chains of paddles powered by steam. He launched the first in 1787. By his third, he was confident enough of its economy to start a passenger and freight service on the Schuykill and Delaware Rivers, from Philadelphia to Trenton, New Jersey, with stops in between. He was wrong; it wasn't economical. No one was very interested in his service, and Fitch died by his own hand, a ruined, bitter man, in 1798.

Another American, John Rumsey, developed a boat with a singular system: water taken in at the bow and forced out at the stern by a steam pump. Jet propulsion. He demonstrated it on the Potomac in 1787, but drew scant attention and less financial backing.

Still another American arrived in France to try to sell Napoleon not only a steamboat but a submarine. His name was Robert Fulton.

The age of steam was here.

V

The Great Ships Sailing

THE GREAT SAILING SHIPS didn't surrender their sway over the seven seas to the steamers easily. Their last years were their most glorious.

On Monday, January 5, 1818, the Black Ball Line, of New York, inaugurated the world's first regular schedule of ocean voyages—with a sailing ship. The *James Monroe* sailed from New York for Liverpool at ten o'clock that morning, and the same week the *Courier* left Liverpool for New York. Thereafter, the *James Monroe,* the *Courier,* or one of their two sister ships put out from Liverpool on the first of the month or from New York on the fifth, headed across the Atlantic. Full or not, they weighed anchor at the appointed time.

Soon other lines were following suit, and travelers could finally know in advance when their ships would set sail.

These scheduled ships were called packets because governments used them to carry dispatches and mail. On the transatlantic run, most of them were full-rigged three-masters. They did the voyage from New York to Liverpool in twenty-three days, give or take a couple depending upon the weather; the return trip took approximately thirty-eight. Stalwart ships they were. One Black Ball Line packet ship made 322 crossings between Liverpool and New York in the course of twenty-nine years and never lost one passenger, a crewman or a sail. Some 30,000 passengers traveled aboard her, including 1,500 babies born at sea. And 200 couples who were married at sea. Elegant ships they were. The *Dover* of the Boston-Liverpool Packet Line, had eleven staterooms, each 6 feet square, a library, a barroom, and a bathroom with buckets of salt water available for washing.

Early packet passengers paid $186 for a one-way ticket which provided bedding, mattress, food, and $20 worth of wine. By the 1840's, the price of a ticket was down to $75, but the wine came extra.

Competition between the various packet lines and, with the passing of time, between the canvas sailers and the steamers, led to demands for speed, more speed, and yet more speed. Out of this movement came a beautiful piece of marine sculpture, really suitable only for sailing great distances with luxury cargoes, but, nonetheless, the supreme achievement of the men who designed and built sailing ships: the clipper. She derived her name from the Pennsylvania Dutch word *klepper* meaning "a fast horse."

The clipper was a knife with sails. She was long and narrow, her hull wedge-shaped, and she was designed to cut through waves rather than ride over them. On her back-tilted masts a mountain of canvas could be set to catch the winds, a mountain 200 feet high that began with three to six of the triangular jibs at the bow and continued on with an enormous mass of square sails. An unforgettable sight she was. "A huge seabird, with white wings expanded," old Captain Frank Waters wrote.

The first of this magnificent breed is generally considered to have been the *Rainbow*. She was designed by the famed marine architect, John W. Griffiths, and went into the water at New York in January, 1845. Like most clippers, she didn't have much room for cargo, but she could carry it a long way fast. She was built for the China trade and, naturally, the first cargo she brought back from Hong Kong was tea. Hauling tea from China, and opium, was how many of the early clippers made their money. Premium prices were paid in England for the first shipments of each tender new tea crop and the speedy American clippers quickly cornered this lucrative market.

The clippers were developed just in time. In January, 1848, gold was discovered on the west coast of the United States. Six months later, the east coast heard the news, and what a shipping boom that touched off.

Between April 1, 1847 and April 1, 1848, eleven ships arrived in San Francisco Bay from Atlantic ports. By comparison, the year 1849 saw 775 vessels depart the Atlantic Coast for the Golden Gate. "Round Cape Horn in the months of snow," went the sea chantey, "And if we get there no one knows. Then blow ye winds, hi-ho, for Californio, for there's plenty of gold, so I've been told, on the banks of Sacramento."

Plenty of gold there was. From February 28, 1849, to the end of 1852, the Pacific Mail Company carried more than $121,000,000 worth of gold out of San Francisco.

It was a bonanza for the clippers. Men going to the gold fields were in a hurry and willing to pay the high clipper fares for speed. The miners already there were willing to shell out high prices for goods and services. Beef, pork, and flour sold for forty dollars, fifty dollars, sixty dollars a barrel. Liquor went for forty dollars a bottle. Playing cards were snapped up at five dollars a pack. When the clipper *Sea Witch* took on a cargo of flour, nails, and steam engine parts in New York in 1850, it was valued at $84,626. In San Francisco, it brought $275,000.

Speed counted and the clippers had it. The *Flying Cloud* went from anchor up in Boston Harbor to anchor down in San Francisco Bay, 16,000 miles, in eighty-nine days, eight hours. Another clipper, the *James Blaine,* went clear around the world, via Australia, in 132 days. On January 17, 1856, she set the world's record for a sailing ship—twenty-one nautical miles per hour. One day in 1854, the clipper, *Lightning,* reeled off 436 miles. Her mark was not to be excelled by a steamer for many a year.

The clipper sailors were fortunate to have the help of a brilliant, Virginia-born, U.S. Navy officer, Matthew Fontaine Maury, who was crippled in a stagecoach accident and quit the sea for scientific research at the U.S. Naval Observatory. Maury made an historic study of winds, currents, and weather conditions on the Atlantic, Pacific, and Indian Oceans and, beginning in 1851, published an up-to-date guide to the sea lanes which immensely shortened sailing times. From intensive reading of ships' logs, he learned that the best route to Cape Horn from New York was not a more or less straight line south, but a wide arc out into the Atlantic. His findings are credited with lopping forty days off the trip from New York to San Francisco, and *Merchants' Magazine* stated in 1854 that the "Pathfinder of the Seas," as Maury was named, was saving shipowners over $2,250,000 a year in time on voyages to Rio de Janiero, California, and Australia. Largely because of his work, a big international conference on oceanography was held in Brussels in 1853. By 1856 sea captains of many countries were supplying him with observations in return for the latest charts and nautical information. The modern system of global weather forecasting is rooted in Maury's labors.

To satisfy their money-hungry owners who'd spent $75,000 and more for a ship and wanted it back fast, the captains drove their vessels hard. No matter how high the wind, they kept on, squeezing out the last bit of mileage from their sails. Often a gale tore away a topmast that was carrying too much canvas or split a mainmast or worse. That didn't stop them. Unless the damage was catastrophic, the captains raced on. The snarls of splintered wood, broken lines, and shredded sails would be cleared off, and the clippers would plunge ahead while the crews rushed to make hasty, jury-rigged replacements.

The crews were a motley lot. Wages were down to $8 a month and it was difficult to get good men to sail for that. Frequently, the crews were provided by shoreside crimps who drugged sailors, or got them drunk, and delivered them in a comatose state on sailing day. When the men awakened, they found to their misery that they were aboard another one of those "damned blood boats." During the early stages of a voyage, almost every man was dangerous, unwilling, unskilled, or all three. Belaying pins were used by the clippers' captains and the mates in an effort to shape a crew out of the mob; pistols, brass knuckles, and whips, also.

Yet most of these clipper crews turned out well. The inherent danger of the voyages was on the side of the captains. When the crew members realized that no one else would take sail in a squall if they didn't, they became much quicker to obey orders. Many of them were Liverpool Irishmen who had an international reputation as troublemakers. They "were tough, roustabout sailormen and difficult to handle, so that it was sometimes a toss-up whether they or the captain and officers would have charge of the ship," Captain Arthur H. Clark wrote. Still, he said, "to see these fellows laying out on an eighty foot main-yard in a whistling gale off Cape Horn, fisting hold of a big No. 1 Colt's cotton canvas mainsail, heavy stiff with sleet and snow, bellying, slatting, and thundering in the gear, and then to hear the wild, cheery shouts of these rugged, brawny sailormen, amid the fury of the storm, as inch by inch they fought on till the last double gasket was fast, made it easy to forget their sins in admiration of their splendid courage."

As the California rush began to subside, gold was discovered in Australia, and clipper speed was wanted there. By the end of 1853 about 270 clippers had been built. The demand for them was drawing to a close, though. They went on sailing, carrying tea, cotton, and wool, serving on the packet lines, bearing English and Scottish settlers to Australia, helping to transplant hordes of German and Irish immigrants to the United States. But their golden age was over, done, by 1860. Steam won out.

Some authorities have called the clipper an overrated freak. A truer judgment is that the times demanded ships with steamer speed and the steamers were not yet ready to answer the need, so the clippers filled in epically, if briefly.

Such brave ships they were. The 1,619-ton clipper *David Crockett,* which was built in 1853 at a cost of $93,000, made fifty-four trips around the dangerous, storm-swept Horn and sailed the waters of the world without any interruption for thirty-seven years. She earned her owners over a half-million dollars in profits. Alas, she was converted into a coal barge in 1890 and foundered on Romer Shoals, New York, in 1905.

There were other superb sagas of sailing ships. Staunch whalers coursed the Atlantic and the Pacific, and pushed deep into the ice-choked waters of the Arctic Ocean in quest of the mighty bowhead whales. American seamen were preeminent here as well. In the peak year 1846 the whaling fleet of all Europe numbered 230 ships while the United States alone had 735. These American whalers did handsomely. One year, they brought in 10,074,866 gallons of whale oil worth fifty-nine and five eighths cents a gallon, and 3,445,200 pounds of whalebone worth thirty-nine and one fifth cents a pound for use in women's corsets. The streets of all the principal American cities were lit by the whale oil.

Explorers were still going under canvas. The Russian admiral Fabian Gottlieb von Bellingshausen led an expedition of two sailing ships into the South Pole regions in 1820–1821 and found Peter I Island, the first land sighted inside the Antarctic Circle. Up north, the doughty Britisher Sir John Ross discovered the North Magnetic Pole in 1831 and got his ship frozen in the polar ice four winters in a row.

The most renowned of all sailing races was started in this period. In 1851 a syndicate of Americans sent the schooner-yacht *America* to England to compete against British sailing vessels. After vainly trying for weeks to get someone to race with, the head of the syndicate, John C. Stevens, threatened to take his boat and go home. The Royal Yacht Squadron then decided to give the Americans a chance.

In making arrangements for the race, the British committed a silly blunder. They issued two different sets of racecourse instructions. This bailed out the *America* when she really needed it.

Off to a poor start, the *America* had almost caught up with the four leading English yachts by the time they'd approached the first mark, a lightship. But the Britishers were all in a pack and Stevens would have had difficulty breaking the *America* through to get the lead. Here the two sets of instructions came in handy. Obeying one set of instructions, the quartet of English yachts went outside the lightship before coming about and heading for the next mark. Conforming to the other set, Stevens took the *America* inside, thus neatly grabbing the lead, a lead he never relinquished. The closest English boat was a mile back when the *America* crossed the finish line.

Afterwards, Stevens ordered the *America*'s ensign dropped and all hands to attention as they passed the royal yacht where Queen Victoria was sitting. The London *Times* commented that this was "a mark of respect to the Queen not the less becoming because it was bestowed by Republicans."

At the beginning of the nineteenth century, water travel was far faster, cheaper, and more practical than land transport. There

The EAGLE, U. S. Coast Guard training ship.

wasn't a railway in America and most roads were dreadful. Artificial waterways were sorely needed to link the Atlantic coast with the interior of the fast-sprouting young nation. They were quick in coming. Too quick, in some cases.

As early as 1724 one man had seen a good route for a canal: from the Hudson River at Albany to Lake Erie. His name was Cadwallader Colden and he was Surveyor of the Province of New York. But he was premature. Another visionary, Christopher Colles, won the approval of the New York Legislature in the mid-1780's for building—on his own—a canal between the Hudson River and Lake Ontario. But he couldn't raise the money.

A tough, shrewd politico named DeWitt Clinton put it across. Born in the village of Little Britain, New York, in 1769, Clinton qualified as a lawyer, served as private secretary to the Governor of New York, was elected to the State Assembly, the State Senate, the United States Senate, and the mayoralty of the city of New York, all before he passed his thirty-fifth birthday. After an unsuccessful bid for the Presidency in 1812, he threw himself into a bang-up campaign so effectively that the voters elected him Governor, and the Legislature okayed the building of the canal.

It was the biggest American canal to date—364 miles long, 40 feet wide, and 4 feet deep. Work began on July 4, 1817 and for years nobody knew where the canal was going to terminate: at Buffalo or at the nearby city of Black Rock. Governor Clinton ultimately settled on Buffalo.

The canal was completed in October, 1825. On October 25 three boats left Buffalo for New York, bearing Clinton, assorted other celebrities, some eagles, wolves, fawns, raccoons, and a pacing, unhappy black bear.

All along the route were bands, cheering crowds, fireworks, saluting cannon, feasts, speeches, and unbounded enthusiasm. At Sandy Hook in New York Bay, Clinton presided over a wedding of the waters and emptied two brassbound kegs of Lake Erie water overboard, together with water from the Rhine, the Seine, the Nile, the Indus, and the Ganges.

The canal was the making of New York City as a seaport. Previously, east-west freight rates had been $32 per ton per 100 miles by wagon. By canal they fell to $1 a ton per 100 miles.

Travelers could ride the Erie Canal in packet boats or line boats. The packets took people from Albany to Buffalo in five days for $5.50 each, plus $2 for food. Fare on the freight-carrying line boats was $3.64, but they went slower and passengers had to supply their own beds and meals.

The packet boats zipped along the canal at four miles an hour. Fanny Kemble, the famed British actress, rode a packet in the 30's. "I like travelling by the canal boats very much," she wrote. "Ours was not crowded, and the country through which we passed being delightful, the placid moderate gliding through it . . . seemed to me infinitely preferable to the noise of wheels, the rumble of a coach, and the jerking of bad roads. . . . The only nuisances are the bridges over the canal, which are so very low, that one is obliged to pros-

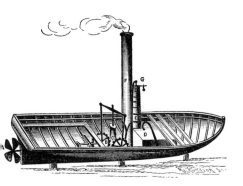

SOME EARLY STEAMERS:

1. Stevens' Screw Steamer, 1804

2. The CLERMONT, 1807

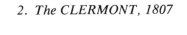

3. The ATLANTIC, 1851

4. A Mississippi steamboat

From *Growth of the Steam Engine*
by Robert H. Thurston, N. Y. 1878.

trate oneself on the deck of the boat to avoid being scraped off it. . . ."

Miss Kemble didn't like one other thing—the sleeping arrangements for women. "We sat in the men's cabin," she said, "until they began making preparations for bed, and then withdrew into a room about twelve feet square, where a whole tribe of women were getting into their beds. Some half undressed, some brushing, some curling, some washing, some already asleep in their narrow cribs, but all within a quarter of an inch of each other; it made one shudder. . . ."

The Erie was a whopping success. By 1836 more than 3,000 boats were moving goods and people over its length, and Albany was crowded with immigrants awaiting passage to the west. Up to 1882 when toll charges were eliminated, the Erie Canal had cost $78,862,153 to build and maintain, but it had taken in $121,-461,871. All told, it stayed in operation for almost a century until the wider, deeper New York State Barge Canal was dug practically parallel to it. That was completed in 1918.

The Erie's success set the canal diggers off in all directions. By 1830 there were 1,277 miles of canals in the United States; by 1840, 3,326, and still the canal digging went on. Before the great canal era in the United States ended, 4,500 miles of canals had been dug at a cost of over $210,000,000. It got to be a worse mania than in England. Several states strained their credit virtually to the point of bankruptcy. Indiana spent so much money on canals that it couldn't meet its payrolls or the interest on its bonds.

Much good was done by the canals in opening up the interior of the nation. The 452-mile-long Wabash and Erie Canal, the longest in the country, helped vastly to settle northern Indiana. In the one year of 1851, 3,083 people arrived in Fort Wayne by this canal. In 1852, 291,489 pounds of passengers' baggage and household belongings came by canal boat to Lafayette, Indiana. The Ohio and Erie Canal which let passengers and freight go by boat all the way from Cleveland to Portsmouth in the south of Ohio, and on to the Mississippi River, did much for Buckeye prosperity. The first section, from Portsmouth to Akron, opened on July 4, 1827, and Governor Allen Trimble of Ohio reported to the legislature that the first boat "was cheered in her passage by thousands of our delighted citizens."

The scrawny little town of Chicago, Illinois, had fewer than 4,000 inhabitants in 1834 when Governor Joseph Duncan and a young Whig Assemblyman named Abraham Lincoln started working for a canal to connect the Illinois River with Lake Michigan. A canal was much to be preferred to a railroad, the Governor ardently argued, since railroads "are kept in repair at very heavy expense and will last but about fifteen years." By 1848 when the Illinois and Michigan Canal was opened, Chicago's population was up to 20,000. It can be said that the canal made the Windy City rich. Chicago's exports came to $1,000.64 in 1836. In 1848 they soared to $10,700,000.

But most of the canals were not useful. Twenty-six years of labor and $14,000,000 went into the Chesapeake and Ohio Canal before it was completed in 1848, and it never did reach its goal, the Ohio River. The canal, a brainchild of President George Washington, only got as far as Cumberland, Maryland, 184 miles from the District of Columbia, and it was a total financial failure.

An even crazier project was the 394-mile-long Pennsylvania Portage and Canal System which was supposed to rival the Erie Canal by linking Philadelphia with the Ohio River at Pittsburgh. The difficulty was that the Allegheny Mountains stood squarely in the way.

One section of the canal began at Columbia, on the Susquehanna River west of Philadelphia, and marched up 108 locks over a distance of 172 miles to Hollidaysburg where the Alleghenies blocked its path. On the other side of the mountain, at Johnstown, a series of sixty-six locks carried the canal down to Pittsburgh 104 miles away. In effect, these were two canals hyphenated by the mountains. At first, when the Pittsburgh-bound passenger got to Hollidaysburg, he changed to a stagecoach that conveyed him over the top to Johnstown. Later, the stagecoaches were replaced by railroad carriages that were hauled up and let down by stationary steam engines. Still later, some canal boats were built to be broken into sections for placement on flatcars, and the traveler from Philadelphia to Pittsburgh could cover the entire distance in a canal boat, although 118 miles of the trip were overland on railroad cars drawn by horses or steam engines.

Explicably, the Pennsylvania Canal gave up the ghost when the railroads came along.

The fact is that few canals could stand up to railroad competition. A freight shipment from Cincinnati to New York by canal took eighteen days in 1852, by rail six days. Furthermore the railroads were much more flexible: feeder lines could be laid right to the doors of factories. As the railroad boom grew, the canal fever fizzled out. Between 1840 and 1860, 28,000 miles of railroad were built in the United States, and not one major canal. By 1850 more canals were being abandoned than were being built. A U.S. Census report for 1880 sadly records that of the 4,468 miles of canals built in the United States, 1,953 miles had been abandoned and most of the remaining 2,515 were not paying expenses. Every canal in New England had been abandoned for commercial purposes, the report stated.

The decline and fall of American canals was a repetition of what had happened in Great Britain. Most canals there were given up and filled in. A fine canal from Manchester to the sea was opened in 1894, but less than 2,800 of the 12,000 miles of canals that once wound through England, Scotland and Wales were left.

Some excellent canals were built in countries like France, Hungary, and Russia. In northern India, a magnificent 500-mile-long canal was constructed on the upper Ganges, and in Egypt a thousand-year-old dream came true when a new Suez Canal was built.

The ancient water route from the Mediterranean to the Red Sea had been closed since A.D. 767 when the Caliph al-Nansur in Baghdad ordered it filled in to prevent an attack on him by his Egyptian subjects. Now, in the face of stiff British opposition, a fast-talking French promoter, Ferdinand de Lesseps, persuaded Sa'id Pasha, the 300-pound Egyptian Khedive, to grant him a concession to dig a canal from the Mediterranean at Port Said to the Red Sea at Suez about a hundred miles away.

After ten years' toil by whip-lashed Egyptian slaves working in 120-degree heat, the canal was opened on November 17, 1869. The voyage between Europe and India had been shortened by

3,700 miles, and the French Government had a stranglehold on the British line of communications to India.

In the end, the British got control of the canal anyway. Upon Sa'id's death, his son, Ismael, squandered his colossal fortune on incredible extravagances, went bankrupt, and had to sell his controlling interest in the canal. The masterly Benjamin Disraeli, Britain's Prime Minister, heard of Ismael's plight and agreed to buy his shares in the canal for a pittance—four million pounds sterling. Since the British Government didn't have the money, Disraeli borrowed it from the Rothschilds.

"It is just settled," he jubilantly wrote his dear friend, Queen Victoria. "You have it, Madame: the French Government has been outgeneralled."

Afterwards, de Lesseps became involved in a project to cut a canal across the narrow waist of the New World, at Panama. In 1889, after eight years, 50,000 lives and more than one billion francs had been expended, de Lesseps called it quits. Other Frenchmen continued to work on the project until 1904, but to no avail.

Someone else had to dig the Panama Canal.

Clinton had his "ditch," or when a critic was feeling particularly vindictive, his "gutter." Robert Fulton had his "folly." Both turned out to be triumphs.

Artist, engineer, inventor, Fulton was one of those da Vinci-like men who could do practically anything well. Born in a little Pennsylvania town in 1765, he trained as a gunsmith and worked as a draftsman in his teens. In 1786 he went abroad for twenty years during which he painted, invented a power shovel, and designed steamboats, torpedos, mines, and submarines. He hoped to make all navies equal through the use of his submarines so that war would be impossible. Napoleon snubbed his submarine the *Nautilus* when it failed its tests; the British government rejected it when it passed them. Consequently, Fulton returned to America and made a fortune. He had the financial backing of one of the United States' most illustrious citizens, Robert R. Livingston, member of the Continental Congress, negotiator of the Louisiana Purchase, and Minister to France. Livingston employed his political influence to get

Fulton and himself a monopoly from New York State on all steam-boat business on the Hudson River.

The forty-year-old Fulton built a long, narrow paddle-wheeler with a tall funnel amidships and two masts to carry sails in case of emergency, and he put an English-made Boulton & Watt steam engine in it. The name of the boat was *not* the *Clermont* then. It was called the *North River Steamboat*. Only later did it get to be called the *Clermont* after Livingston's country estate.

On August 17, 1807, a fire was set under the boiler of "Fulton's Folly" and, as Fulton related, "The moment arrived in which the word was to be given for the boat to move. My friends were in groups on the deck. There was anxiety mixed with fear among them. . . . I read in their looks nothing but disaster. . . .

"The signal was given, and the boat moved a short distance and then stopped. . . . I could distinctly hear repeated, 'I told you it was so.' . . . . I elevated myself upon a platform and addressed the assembly. I stated that I knew not what was the matter, but if they would be quiet and indulge me for half an hour, I would either go

Robert Fulton.

on or abandon the voyage. . . . I went below, and examined the machinery, and discovered that the cause was a slight maladjustment of some of the work. In a short time . . . the boat was again put in motion. She continued to move. All were . . . incredulous."

Upstream the steamboat chugged at five miles an hour. One farmer caught sight of her and turned tail for his house. "The devil is coming up the river in a sawmill!" he shouted. The steamer made the 150-mile trip to Albany in thirty-two hours' traveling time, the return trip in thirty hours, and on September 4, Fulton inaugurated commercial service from New York to Albany, carrying passengers for $7 apiece.

At the end of the year he declared a profit for the company. The steamboat was a success in America. In Europe it soon succeeded, also. The first one to run commercially there was the *Comet,* on the River Clyde in 1812.

Fulton produced twenty-one more paddle-wheelers before the end of 1815. One of them was history's first steam-driven battleship, the *Demologos,* a bizarre design which carried the paddlewheel between the twin hulls and had sides 13 feet thick. Built for the War of 1812, the *Demologos* guarded New York Harbor and never had to fire a shot at an enemy.

The most lasting image of the paddle-wheeler in American minds is that of the triple-decked, gingerbready "floating palaces" that steamed the midwestern rivers. Fulton also launched that legend. In 1811 he sent a group of men to Pittsburgh to build a boat and steam her down the Ohio and Mississippi to New Orleans. The leader of this expedition was a Nicholas J. Roosevelt, whose pregnant wife insisted on coming along and had her baby en route. That and shooting the wicked falls west of Louisville would have been excitement enough for one trip, but no sooner had they cleared the falls than the land was shaken by a violent earthquake. For days they felt the effects. One evening they moored their steamer the *New Orleans* to an island, and by morning the island had disappeared. The quake changed the course of big sections of the Mississippi River so that the pilot's knowledge of the river was suddenly outdated.

Nothing else occurred during the trip except for a fire breaking out in the cabin.

With that voyage a romantic chapter in America's history commenced. Hundreds of paddle-wheelers got to plying the inland water routes.

On these great paddle-wheelers, the pilot was king; the captain was his inferior. Perched in the wheelhouse high above the water, the pilot had to be able to read the surface of the river and tell its depth, to know when a ripple meant current, or wind, or sandbar, or a pile of submerged driftwood that could tear a hole in the bottom of a boat and sink it in a minute. He had to know the riverbank by heart, backward and forward, in daylight and on moonless nights. He needed a memory thousands of miles long, and he had to be ready to change it as the river varied its course.

"Take this place where we are now," Mr. Bixby, one of the river pilots, told his apprentice, young Sam Clemens (who grew up to be Mark Twain). " 'As long as that hill over yonder is only one hill, I can boom right along the way I'm going; but the moment it splits at the top and forms a V, I know I've got to scratch to starboard in a hurry, or I'll bang this boat's brains out against a rock; and then the moment one of the prongs of the V sweeps behind the other, I've got to waltz to larboard again, or I'll have a misunderstanding with a snag that would snatch the keelson out of this steamboat as neatly as if it were a sliver in your hand.' "

There were other dangers. A guidebook of the period cautioned, "It has been truly stated that more accidents by explosion, burning or sinking of steamboats occur annually in the United States, and more lives are lost, than in crossing the Atlantic."

Nor were the cuisine, the table manners and the conversation always very elegant. Charles Dickens bore witness to that. In his *American Notes,* he reported on a trip he and his wife took on the steamboat, *Messenger,* down the Ohio from Pittsburgh to Cincinnati in the early 1840's:

> There are three meals a day, breakfast at seven, dinner at half past twelve, supper about six. At each, there are a great many small dishes and plates upon the table, with very little in them; so that although there is every appearance of a mighty 'spread,' there is seldom really more than a joint: except for those who

fancy slices of beet-root, shreds of dried beef, complicated en-
tanglements of yellow pickle; maize; Indian corn, apple-sauce
and pumpkin.

Some people fancy all these little dainties together (and sweet
preserves beside), by way of relish to their roast pig. They are
generally those dyspeptic ladies and gentlemen who eat unheard-
of quantities of hot corn bread (almost as good for the digestion
as a kneaded pin-cushion), for breakfast, and for supper. Those
who do not observe this custom, and who help themselves several
times instead, usually suck their knives and forks meditatively,
until they have decided what to take next; then pull them out of
their mouths: put them in the dish; help themselves; and fall to
work again. . . . Nobody says anything, at any meal, to anybody. . . .

It wasn't many years before the steamboat went to sea.

John Stevens wanted to run a ferry service from Hoboken, New
Jersey, to New York City with his paddle-wheeler *Phoenix*. Since
he couldn't get around Fulton's monopoly, he sailed the *Phoenix*
down the Atlantic coast to Philadelphia, a thirteen-day voyage for
her in 1809, and went into the ferry business between Philadelphia
and Trenton. Soon steamers were sailing regularly up and down the
coast.

By mid-1819 the first steamship, an American one, had crossed
the Atlantic. She was the 320-ton *Savannah* under Captain Moses
Rogers, and she was a three-masted sailing ship with two paddlewheels that could be folded and lifted on deck in rough weather. It
was a twenty-seven-and-one-half-day trip during which the *Savannah* ran only seventy hours under steam. That was as much fuel
as she could carry. Her engine was working, however, when she
arrived off the coast of Ireland on June 17. She was reported to the
customs as a ship on fire.

Not one passenger dared sail the *Savannah* on her historic voyage, and she couldn't get an ounce of cargo.

Nineteen years later the 703-ton British paddle-wheeler, *Sirius*
crossed the Atlantic entirely under steam. She had to burn her mast
and furniture to do it, but she got to New York in eighteen days, ten
hours, at a mean speed of 6.7 knots, and she was followed the next

day by the 1,320-ton *Great Western* which made it in fifteen days, five hours, at a mean speed of 8.8 knots. (Three years before, the noted British science writer, Dr. Dionysius Lardner, had told the English Association for Advancement of Science that there was as much chance of crossing the Atlantic by steam as there was of going to the moon!)

In no time now, steamships were crossing both the Atlantic and the Pacific on firm schedules. The first was the *Brittania*, which departed from Liverpool on July 4, 1840, and reached Boston, after a stop at Halifax, in fourteen days, eight hours. Coming back, she did better, a little over ten days.

These small steamers were not exactly stable in a storm. Dickens rode the *Brittania* in winter weather going to America in 1842, and he had a rough time of it. His report is a feeling one:

> I am awakened out of my sleep by a dismal shriek from my wife, who demands to know whether there is any danger, I rouse myself, and look out of bed. The water-jug is plunging and leaping like a lively dolphin; all the smaller articles are afloat, except my shoes, which are stranded on a carpet-bag, high and dry, like a couple of coal-barges. Suddenly, I see them spring into the air, and behold the looking-glass, which is nailed to the wall, sticking fast upon the ceiling. At the same time the door entirely disappears, and a new one is opened in the floor. Then I begin to comprehend that the state-room is standing on its head.
>
> Before it is possible to make any arrangements at all compatible with this novel state of things, the ship rights. Before one can say, 'Thank Heaven!', she wrongs again.

Painfully, Mr. Dickens continues:

> . . . What the agitation of a steam-vessel is, on a bad winter's night in the wild Atlantic, it is impossible for the most vivid imagination to conceive. To say that she is flung down on her side in the waves, with her masts dipping into them, and that, springing up again, she rolls over on the other side, until a heavy sea strikes her with the noise of a hundred great guns, and hurls her back—and that she stops, and staggers, and shivers, as though stunned, and then, with a violent throbbing at her heart, darts onward like a monster goaded into madness, to be beaten down,

and battered, and crushed, and leaped on by the angry sea—that thunder, lightning, hail, and rain, and wind are all in fierce contention for the mastery—that every plank has its own groan, every nail its shriek, and every drop of water in the great ocean its howling voice—is nothing.

The *Brittania* was the first ship built for a daring Canadian named Samuel Cunard. With the help of a British government mail subsidy he developed her into the illustrious Cunard Line.

There were more technical advances at sea. Screw propulsion, an outgrowth of an idea patented by Samuel Miller in England in 1773, came into use and, in the long run, made the paddlewheel as obsolete as the sail. Some accounts say that the Royal Navy staged a tug-of-war between a paddle-wheeler and a propeller-driven ship to see which was stronger. The screw ship dragged the poor paddlewheeler every which way. The 237-ton *Archimedes* was the first steamer to be powered by a propeller. It was in 1838.

Iron began to replace wood in shipbuiding. In 1821 the British riverboat *Aaron Manby* was built of steel, the first steamer to be constructed of this material. She crossed to France and sailed merrily along the Seine for years.

Ships got faster. By 1860 their speed was up to thirteen knots. And they grew bigger, incredibly so. In 1858 a steamship was built of iron in England that was 692 feet long, displaced 32,000 tons, had five funnels, six masts, four boilers, two 56-foot paddlewheels, and a 24-foot propeller. She was christened the *Great Eastern,* and she could have carried 4,000 passengers if they'd have purchased tickets.

An unhappy ship she was. Badly mismanaged, she bankrupted several companies and ended up laying transatlantic cable. In 1888 she was sold for scrap. But she did point the way. The great ocean liners of today are her legacy.

Sea stride came after sea stride. In the 1870's shipbuilders started to use steel widely. High-pressure boilers increased fuel economy, and a wonderfully powerful steam turbine was developed by Sir Charles Parsons in 1894. He built a fabulous little ship, the *Turbinia,* which achieved the then incredible speed of 34.5 knots.

To attract attention to his invention, Sir Charles crashed a naval

review held in honor of Queen Victoria. The *Turbinia* zipped in
and out among the arrayed ships of the Royal Navy and ran away
from everything that attempted to catch her.

Acceptance of the turbine engine was assured.

What a century it had been on water! From the Erie Canal to the
Suez. From canvas to paddlewheel to propeller. From thirty-eight
days to less than six for the England-to-America passage. It was a
period when 17,500,000 immigrants moved by sea from Europe to
the new, free world. It was a period when Commodore Matthew C.
Perry sailed to Japan, impressed her with America's naval might,
and, in 1854, terminated over 200 years of Japanese isolation. It
was a period when the American merchant marine lost its primacy
for generations to come because of its reluctance to switch from
sails to steam, because American industry couldn't manufacture big
enough steam engines, because the United States Congress wouldn't
grant subsidies as large as those granted by the British Parliament.

This was the century when the navies of the world grew ever
more powerful; when the French built the first armored battleship,
the *Gloire,* in 1859; when two armored battleships, the *Monitor*
and the *Virginia,* fought each other to a pointless draw in the
American Civil War, in 1862; when capital ships got their first
mammoth 15-inch guns. It was the century when the Earl of St.
Vincent, First Sea Lord of the British Admiralty, insisted that
Prime Minister William Pitt spurn Fulton's submarine. "Don't look
at it, and don't touch it," he said. "If we take it up, other nations
will; and it will be the greatest blow at our supremacy on the sea
that can be imagined." It was the century when the Confederate
submarine *Hundley* sunk the Union corvette *Housatonic* in the first
effective submarine assault on a surface vessel; the century when
the French Navy built the first successful electric submarines,
twenty-nine of them; when a British minister, the Reverend G. W.
Garett, constructed a steam-propelled submarine named *Resurgam*
(I Shall Rise) which the Swedish engineer Thorsten Nordenfeldt
adapted and sold to the Greek Navy; when the U.S. Navy continued for decades to ignore submarines. "The navy doesn't like
submarines because there's no deck to strut on," the inventor John

Holland aptly commented. It was not till 1900 that the U.S. Navy caught up with the rest of the naval world and bought its first submarine, *Holland Number 9*.

And all that isn't the half of the nineteenth century. The land side of it is yet to come.

VI

Iron Horse

SOME MAGNIFICENT THINGS happened to transportation on land in the nineteenth century. The road builders learned what to do about the weather, trains of covered wagons moved thousands of pioneers across the vast North American continent, the Iron Horse was born and grew to maturity, mass urban transit became a reality, and little Nelly Bly took a trip.

Travel by road was still a miserable ordeal when the century started. There was more rut than road. One newly appointed French *préfet* arrived at his post so caked with mud that the gendarmes didn't recognize him. Instead of saluting him, they chased him away as a vagabond. Most main roads in France were lined with wrecked carriages, and we have it on the authority of Queen Hortense Bonaparte of Holland that coach riding anywhere in Europe was as torturous as the rack. "And so we travelled on, growing visibly thinner with every mile," she pitifully noted in a letter.

Three men, two Scots and a Frenchman, with a helping hand from the Emperor Napoleon himself, changed the road scene for the better in the early decades of the century. The first was the versatile Thomas Telford, an engineer born in Scotland in 1757 who could do well practically anything in the construction line. He built more than thirty harbors, plus roads, canals, and bridges, from Wales to Poland, along with a network of internal waterways that transversed most of Sweden. Somewhere along the way, he found time to invent the Telford pavement, a road made of two layers of stone covered by a blanket of gravel. It was expensive to lay and maintain, but it was the first real improvement in road building of the past fourteen centuries.

The second man was the most famous road builder of all history, John Loudon McAdam, who through some etymological legerdemain has come to be known as Macadam. The former spelling is the correct one.

A Scotsman, too, and an engineer, a year older than Telford, McAdam sailed to New York in 1770, stayed there through the Revolutionary War, and made himself a pretty penny as agent for the sale of war prizes. After the war, he secured a nice governmental post in Scotland as a naval purchasing agent and set to perfecting some ideas he had on building weatherproof roads. In 1815 he got himself appointed Surveyor General of the Bristol Roads, a post which afforded him the opportunity to try out his ideas in practice. They proved beautifully successful.

McAdam believed that laying down a special strong foundation for a road was waste motion and money. "The native soil," he said, ". . . really supports the weight of traffic. While it is preserved in a dry state," he maintained, "it will carry any weight. . . ." He therefore concentrated on keeping the native soil dry.

To commence, McAdam raised the road above the level of the ground to ensure that the roadbed of native soil was not weakened by rain water flowing in from either side. Then he spread a thick layer of small, sharp stones on the roadbed. The rest he left to traffic. Moving over the road, the traffic packed down the stones until they cohered into a smooth, solid surface, 10 inches deep, that was completely waterproof.

One of the happiest things about this kind of surface was that any part that became rutted or worn away could be simply repaired by pouring in new stones. Passing traffic tamped the stones into place.

Macadamizing was the name the system got, and it revolutionized road travel. On these new, hard roads, vehicles could move infinitely faster. Previously, it had taken two full days for a coach to go from Oxford to London, with a night's sleep at an inn en route. Now, a coach could do it in six hours.

The third great road builder was the daring French engineer Nicolas Cèard. Cèard built the first road over the Alps that had been constructed for 1,500 years. He went up 6,590 feet and over the Simplon Pass into Italy, blasting his way through dense rock with gunpowder set off in hand-drilled holes. When it was completed in 1805 the road was wide enough for two carriages to pass, and it showed that towering mountains could be surmounted. It was as great an achievement as anything the Romans had done. Greater, perhaps. This Simplon road was the first of many superb roads that Napoleon sponsored. Between 1804 and 1812 he spent twice as much money on roads as he did on military fortifications.

Other advances in roadbuilding appeared. Concrete, once utilized by the Roman engineers and long-forgotten, was reintroduced in England during the late 1820's. Asphalt began to be used on French roads in 1835. Wooden paving blocks were first laid in St. Petersburg, Russia in 1820, in New York in 1835, in London in 1838.

Over the highways the best of the stagecoaches raced at speeds of ten miles an hour and up. They charged into the yards of coaching inns, took on passengers and packages, and in less than a minute were off again with a blast of the coach horn. Who can forget the English writer Thomas Hughes' description of young Tom Brown's departure for Rugby in the 1830's? Tom rode on the coach *Tally-ho,* "a tip-top goer, ten miles an hour including stoppages, and so punctual, that all the road set their clocks by her." The coach left Islingston at three in the morning. Tom had just finished his pre-dawn breakfast at the Peacock Inn when:

> the horn sounds, Boots looks in and says, "Tally-ho, sir;" and they hear the ring and the rattle of the four fast trotters and the town-made drag, as it dashes up to the Peacock.
>
> "Anything for us, Bob?" says the burly guard dropping down from behind, and slapping himself across the chest.
>
> "Young gent'm'n, Rugby; three parcels, Leicester; hamper o'game, Rugby," answers Ostler.
>
> "Tell young gent to look alive," says Guard opening the hind-boot and shooting in the parcels after examining them by the lamps. "Here, shove the portmanteau up a-top—I'll fasten him presently. Now, then, sir, jump up behind."

"Good-bye, father—my love at home." A last shake of the hand. Up goes Tom, the guard catching his hat-box and holding on with one hand, while with the other he claps the horn to his mouth. Toot, toot, toot! The ostlers let go their heads, the four bays plunge at the collar, and away goes the *Tally-ho* into the darkness, forty-five seconds from the time they pulled up.

Three thousand coaches were rattling over the fast-improving roads of England by 1836. In one twelve-hour period in 1850 more than 13,000 vehicles crossed London Bridge, including two- and four-horse cabs, hansoms, wagons, coaches, and private carriages.

The United States was not doing nearly as well. Its roads were dreadful. The turnpike boom was over by 1825, and few of the pikes were commercially successful. The famous National Pike, the first important road to be built with Federal funds, started out from Cumberland, Maryland, in 1811 and got as far as Columbus, Ohio, in 1833, but, for the most part, the road network of the new nation consisted mainly of tracks and mud paths. The best traveling was in the winter when the ground was covered with snow and sleighs could glide along.

For all that, stagecoach lines proliferated and the competition between them was cut-throat. The fare for the forty-mile trip between Boston and Providence was usually three dollars each way, but it was standard procedure for the older lines to slash prices whenever a new stage line began operating.

One time, a smart entrepreneur got the jump on the established lines and commenced operations with a fare of $2.50. A fierce rate war ensued that ended in all the lines offering the ride plus dinner and a bottle of wine free.

Transportation wasn't always so cheap. During the War of 1812, freight shipments to the south had to go by land in Conestoga wagons because the sea lanes were cut off. The freight rate from Boston to Charleston was forty cents a pound—eight hundred dollars a ton.

Those days, Americans resembled a man and wife who had spent all the money they had in the bank to buy a huge, unfurnished farmhouse. They were clattering around in the space of a continent, with a sofa and a pianoforte in the front parlor, as it were, but not much else in the house, little money to spend, and lots of conflicting ideas on how to expend it. They hadn't even explored all the rooms yet. Predictably, "going places" grew to be something of a national religion in the United States.

The big surge was toward the wide open West, and the trappers, the traders, and the missionaries led the parade. A Missouri trader, William Becknell, blazed the Santa Fe Trail to the southwest in 1821; a fur trader, James Bridger, discovered the Great Salt Lake in 1822; the Reverend Jason Lee founded the first mission in the Oregon country in 1834; and in 1836 Dr. Marcus Whitman, a religious young physician, brought the first two white women to Oregon. In 1841, the Bidwell-Bartleson party made it safely to California, opening the California Trail through Nevada. A year later, "Oregon Fever" swept the midwest and the "Great Migration" to the Oregon country began. The historic Oregon Trail entered geography; it ran west and northwest across Nebraska beside the Platte River, over the Rockies at South Pass, north to the Snake River, to the Columbia River, and into fair Oregon.

People migrated by the tens of thousands, to Oregon, to California, and to points along the road, seeking homes, farmlands, gold, religious freedom. The first wagon train to reach the Pacific got there in 1841. In 1843 the first big train set out, 120 wagons carrying 200 families. In the next two years, some 4,500 more settlers headed for the west coast. Then, in 1846, 17,000 Mormons were forced by violence to leave the town of Nauvoo, Illinois, and began a fantastic trip toward an unknown promised land. They found it, those that lived, in the valley of the Great Salt Lake, in July, 1847. And that exodus was nothing compared to the flood let loose by the cry of "Gold!" uttered at Sutter's Mills in 1848. Between January 1 and July 8, 1850, 9,720 wagons with 42,300 emigrants trundled westward through Fort Laramie, in Wyoming.

Most of the pioneers traveled by prairie schooner, and a spunkier vehicle there never was. A covered wagon with a white canvas top, it was smaller and lighter than the Conestoga wagon. It needed only four horses, sometimes merely two, even on the worst prairie trails. (Often oxen were employed in place of the horses.) Both ends were closed save for small oval openings that allowed air and light into the interior where the women and children rode and slept.

Nothing daunted these prairie schooners, not the endless plains, the racing rivers, the brutal mountains, the warring Indians. On they rolled, bearing the settlers, their families, their food, and all their possessions to their new world.

The prairie schooners wound across the plains two or four abreast while the guide rode ahead with a group of men to check the route and, if necessary, make it passable. Off in the distance another group of men went hunting for game. The train stretched along the trail for miles, raising columns of dust in the lonely landscape. The livestock—milk-cows, horses, oxen, and mules— brought up the rear. Each night the train performed a maneuver that was martial in purpose and appearance. Like a well-trained drill team, the wagons turned out of the line of march to form a big circle or square and were locked together to act as both a fort and a corral into which the animals were herded.

The farther the wagon trains went, the smaller they grew. Men and horses died, families turned back, wagons were abandoned.

"It's not high mountains ner great rivers ner hostile Injuns that'll give us most grief," warned a scout for a California-bound wagon train. "It's the long grind o' doin' every day's work regler an' not let-up fer nobody ner nothin'. Figger it fur yourself; 2100 miles—four months to do it in between April rains and September snows—123 days. . . . And every day rain, hail, cholera, breakdowns, lame mules, sick cows, washouts, prairie fires, flooded coulees, lost horses, dust storms, alkali water. Seventeen miles every day—or you land in the snow and eat each other like the Donner party done in '46."

The Donner party was a band of eighty-seven emigrants who were trapped by winter crossing the Sierra Nevada, suffered agonies, and ended by eating human flesh.

Regardless of hardships, most of the pioneers made it. Over 1,500,000 people completed "the long overland march" to California and intermediate points between 1849 and 1868.

Civilization came after them fast. Stagecoach service commenced between Independence, Missouri, and Salt Lake City in 1850.

Shortly after, another line connected Salt Lake City and Sacramento, California, to take passengers the remainder of the way. In 1857 Congress authorized a mail coach service, and the Overland Mail began doing business between St. Louis and San Francisco. On April 3, 1860, the romantic Pony Express started to carry mail between St. Joseph, Missouri, and Sacramento. The eighty relay riders rode the 1,960 wilderness miles in ten days. Initially, they charged five dollars an ounce, but they reduced the cost to one dollar an ounce. Each rider had to be over twenty years of age, weigh no more than 125 pounds, read the Bible, and vow always to act like a gentleman. The service lasted nineteen months; the completion of the transcontinental telegraph killed it.

For a time, it was hoped that camels could deliver the mail across America. At the instigation of Secretary of War Jefferson Davis, Congress appropriated $30,000 in 1854 for the purchase of some "desert ships." About seventy-five dromedaries and Bactrians were bought in Egypt and Arabia, dispatched to the United States on the Navy ship *Supply,* and unloaded at Indianola, Texas, on February 10, 1857. They were assigned to the U.S. Army under the command of Lieutenant Edward F. Beale, and proved a total flop. The camels, with their usual hauteur, hated the tough-talking Army mule drivers, and the Army men loathed them in return, so much so that both came close to mutiny. Ultimately, all seventy-five camels were either killed and eaten or turned loose on the American desert.

To speed east-west communications, the National Highway continued to creep westward. It reached Vandalia, Illinois, in 1852. There its broken-rock-and-gravel path ended.

By 1852 it was obvious that there was a better way to cross the country than in a racing, rattling, breakneck stagecoach. What's more, it would soon be possible.

Clear the track! Here comes the railroad.

The ancestry of the railroad is a bit like a church supper. Everybody had a hand in it. Centuries before Christ, the Hittites, it will be remembered, constructed their roads with grooves for wagon wheels to roll in. Sixteenth-century German miners utilized wooden

PROGRESS ON WHEELS:

1. Oliver Evans'
ORUKTOR AMPHILBOLIS,
1804

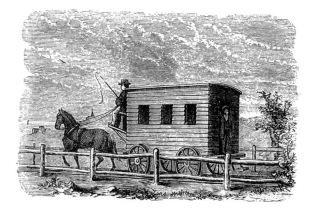

2. The first railroad car,
1825

3. The ROCKET, 1829

From *Growth of the Steam Engine*
by Robert H. Thurston, N. Y. 1878.

rails for the ore carts they laboriously pushed. Some English mines of the period had wooden rails, so that coal wagons could coast down to river landings. Horse-drawn railways came into use in English mines in the eighteenth century, and some had cast-iron rails.

Probably the grand-paternity of the railroad should be ascribed to an ingenious Frenchman by the name of Nicholas Joseph Cugnot. In 1769 M. Cugnot built a bizarre three-wheeled steam carriage to haul cannon, and drove it through the streets of Paris at a speed of two and a quarter miles per hour. It looked rather like a wheelbarrow with a heavy kettle on its prow.

Cugnot's contraption was very difficult to steer and it could only travel fifteen minutes before it ran out of steam. Nonetheless, the French government showed interest, and Cugnot worked on it until it could pull a four-and-one-half-ton load. He never did succeed in improving its maneuverability. One day in 1770 he ran into a stone wall and landed in jail. That terminated his experiments.

The direct paternity of the railroad must be credited to a smart Englishman by the name of Richard Trevithick. Born in 1771, Trevithick followed in his father's footsteps and in 1797 became a top mining engineer. After he'd invented a pump and a high-pressure steam engine, he turned his mind to transportation and built a steam-propelled coach with 10-foot wheels that could go eight miles an hour. On Christmas Eve, 1801, he and seven friends took it for a test run up a steep hill in the little Cornish town of Camborne. The carriage, reported one of the friends, "went off like a little bird."

Trevithick got steam railroads rolling by telling the owner of a Welsh coal mine that a steam carriage could be built to pull a load weighing ten tons along the colliers' railway. The mine owner didn't believe him. The idea was so laughable that he bet Trevithick 500 pounds it couldn't be done. Trevithick won the bet. In February, 1804, the world's first working locomotive chugged along nine miles of flimsy track at Pen-y-darren, Wales, at a speed of four to five miles an hour, hauling five cars and a total weight of twenty-five tons.

The one trouble was that the heavy locomotive damaged the rails, and the mine owner was unwilling to go to the expense of erecting a sturdier track. He decided to stick with flesh-and-blood horses.

Yet it was a start.

Very few men alive could foresee what it was a start for. An American visionary, Oliver Evans, did. He predicted the coming of a great railway network in which passenger trains would run at a rate of 300 miles a day. Furthermore, he prophesied that these trains would be equipped with sleeping and dining cars. Most of Evans' countrymen thought him mad.

Trevithick didn't do well either. He died in sad poverty.

The man who proved railroads were practicable was a husky English miner, born in 1781. He was eighteen years old before he learned how to read and write. His name was George Stephenson, and he was a natural-born engineer. He built a locomotive engine in 1814 that drew eight ore-laden wagons at a speed of four miles an hour. In 1825 he built the first steam railroad in England, from Stockton to Darlington. Initially, it hauled only freight. Until 1835 the passengers on the line rode behind horses.

The Stockton and Darlington Railway was comparatively successful, but no one paid much attention to it. Stephenson, therefore, resolved to try something bigger. He learned that a horse-drawn railway was to be constructed between Liverpool and Manchester, and he proposed to build a steam railway in its place. The opposition was strident. Canal owners screamed that it would wreck their business. Farmers protested that the cinders would damage crops. Despite this, Parliament franchised the road, and Stephenson designed a husky new locomotive, the *Rocket,* which could draw three times its own weight at twelve and a half miles an hour.

On September 15, 1830, the Liverpool and Manchester Railway, the first railroad in the world to haul both passengers and freight exclusively by steam power, opened with loud festivities and the first recorded railroad fatality. The celebration included the presence of the Duke of Wellington, riding in a private car. The fatality involved a friend of the Iron Duke, a Mr. Huskinson or Huskisson, who was run over by the *Rocket.*

The railway turned out to be a triumph for Stephenson. In its first year the *Rocket* hauled more than 70,000 persons and 4,000 tons of freight and Stephenson was en route to fame and riches.

THE LOCOMOTIVE EVOLVES

1. The STOURBRIDGE LION purchased in England and first operated at Honesdale, Pennsylvania, on August 8, 1829

2. The DE WITT CLINTON, built by the West Point Foundry in 1831

3. Passenger Flyers on the south shore of Lake Erie about 1875

4. The Northern Pacific first NORTH COAST LIMITED, from a photograph made in April, 1900

1. Delaware & Hudson Railroad Corporation 2. New York Central System 3. Standard Oil Co. (N.J.) 4. Northern Pacific Railway

Opposition to railroads continued, to be sure, and it was vehement. Many people held with the outlook of the *Quarterly Review:* "What can be more palpably absurd and ridiculous than the prospect held out of locomotives traveling twice as fast as stage coaches. We should as soon expect the people of Woolwich to suffer themselves to be fired off upon one of Congreve's . . . rockets as trust themselves to the mercy of such a machine going at such a rate."

A panel of London scientists formally decreed that trains could never go any faster than thirty miles an hour.

Otherwise, it admonished, "The passengers would suffocate."

Abroad, it was as bad. The medical faculty at Munich warned that all railroad passengers were sure to contract a new type of mental illness termed delerium furiosum.

The tide of the Industrial Revolution was rising fast, though, washing away the traditions of centuries. Machines, especially those big, smoking monsters, the steam engines, were everywhere bringing change.

The fear of the railroad was overbalanced by the demands of the age, and by a kind of forward momentum that shoved the objectors to one side and let the railroads grow and prosper.

Grow they did. England had 1,600 miles of railway in 1841, 6,890 miles by 1851. Queen Victoria took her first train ride in 1842, and declared herself "quite charmed with it." On the Continent, the first important road was born in 1835 when Kaiser Ferdinand II of Austria awarded a concession to Saloman von Rothschild to build a line 60 miles long between Vienna and Bochnia. The first railroad line in Germany was opened the same year. The Paris and St. Germain Railway, eleven miles in length, was started in 1837 to ecstatic Gallic shouts of *"Triomphe merveilleuse!"* and *"Émotion sans égal!"* and *"Cheval magnifique!"* By 1842 France was embarked on the construction of a carefully thought out 2,750-mile-long network of railroads with Paris at the hub. In 1851, a railroad was abuilding in Africa, and Russia was starting its first railway, from St. Petersburg to Moscow.

By 1871 there were 15,537 miles of track open for traffic in the United Kingdom. They had gross receipts of £45,100,000. In continental Europe, scores of thousands more miles of railroads were in operation. The Rothschilds paid 100,000,000 lire just for the Lombard-Venice railroad line. That was almost $50,000,000.

In America, the first railroad, the Baltimore and Ohio, was opened to traffic in the spring of 1830—horse-drawn traffic, that is, on a thirteen-mile stretch from Baltimore to Ellicott's Mills. It was 1832 before the B & O started steam service with Peter Cooper's overpublicized locomotive *Tom Thumb.* The distinction of being the first "steam-only" railroad to operate scheduled passenger service in the United States goes to the Charleston and Hamburg Railway. It inaugurated a six-mile length of track in South Carolina on December 25, 1830. An American-manufactured locomotive, *Best Friend of Charleston,* pulled a gaily beflagged three-car train that had a squad of artillerymen in the last car firing salutes with a small cannon. A band "enlivened the scene," the Charleston, S.C. *Courier* reported, "and great hilarity and good humor prevailed throughout the day."

When the full 136-mile line was finished in 1836, the Charleston and Hamburg had something else to fete: it was the longest railroad under one management in the world. The Charleston and Hamburg could also boast that it originated railroading's first headlight, a bonfire on a flatcar pushed ahead of the locomotive. (The first whistle was installed on the locomotive *Hicksville* which went into service at Jamaica, Long Island, in 1836. Reports were that it made "a shrill, wild unearthly sound something like drawing a saw flat across a bar of iron.")

With the years trains and their tracks lost some of the pioneering look. The curved stagecoachlike bodies of the cars gave way to oblong boxes with windows. The locomotives began to take on a standard shape—a barrel body with a smokestack at the front and a place for the engineer at the back. Wooden rails with iron strap topping were replaced by all iron T rails. The iron strap had been the cause of many accidents due to its tendency to shake loose and roll up, puncturing holes in cars.

What was railroad travel like in America in the 1840's?

Uncomfortable was one word for it. This being democratic America, no such things as first and second classes existed; everybody suffered equally. The usual railway car held as many as fifty passengers, two to each hard wooden seat, and, generally, there was a coal stove sizzling in the middle that kept the temperature excruciatingly high and the atmosphere miserably close. The trains jolted, shook, and rattled along, scattering sparks and smoke everywhere, including the interior of the cars.

Improvements were coming, though. Back in 1837 the world's first sleeping car, a crudely rebuilt day coach, had gone into service between Harrisburg and Chambersburg, Pennsylvania. Now, a small-town New York State cabinetmaker arrived with some notions that were to make him a multimillionaire and pamper American travelers beyond their best expectations. He was George Mortimer Pullman and he designed a plush sleeping car with cherrywood seats, disappearing beds, curtains to ensure privacy, and two washrooms. The first of these Pullman Palace Cars ran from Bloomington, Illinois, to Chicago on the night of September 1, 1858.

Conductor J. L. Barnes had a worrisome night of it. "I had to compel the passengers to take their boots off before they got into the berths," he recounted. "They wanted to keep them on—seemed afraid to take them off."

A year after, Pullman brought out something more opulent, a "hotel car" with both eating and sleeping facilities. On its première trip from Chicago to New York, the menu suggested steak for sixty cents, Welsh rarebit for fifty cents, and sugar-cured ham for forty cents. In 1868 Pullman went himself one better and introduced a completely separate dining car.

It was in the United States with its swelling population and commerce, its apparently limitless land and natural resources, and its transcontinental aspirations that railroads exhibited their most spectacular expansion. At the end of 1830 the United States had a meager twenty-three miles of railroad track in operation. By 1840 it had 2,808 miles of track in operation; by 1850, 9,021. By 1860 the total was up to 30,626 miles of track in operation, and within a decade the figure had nearly doubled, to 52,922. Most impressive, inside this decade, the east and the west coasts of the wide, wild North American continent were linked by rail.

A public-spirited New Yorker, Asa Whitney, sparked the campaign for a transcontinental railroad in 1844. His plan was for

Congress to deed him a sixty-mile-wide pathway from Lake Michigan west through the Oregon area to the Pacific. Most of the land would be sold cheaply to settlers and the proceeds used to build the line. The railroad itself would become the property of the United States government when it was completed, and the income from operating it would go into the Treasury for public education. Whitney was to get nothing from it personally.

Several Congressional committees reported favorably on Whitney's proposals, but that was all.

The discovery of gold in California lent new impetus to the drive for a crosscountry rail line. But there were obstacles to overcome, such as sectional jealousies. The South, with secession fast becoming a vivid possibility, did not want any railroad if it passed through the free states. By no coincidence, the Mississippi-bred Secretary of War Jefferson Davis chose an all-Southern route for the railroad after an "impartial" survey.

Even after Congress—in the midst of the Civil War—settled on the route and authorized the railroad in 1862, problems persisted. What gauge was it to be? "Standard" gauge, the one adopted in England, was 4 feet, 8½ inches, and many American rail lines had accepted it. But numerous roads had a 5-foot gauge, while other lines used a 4-foot, 10-inch gauge; a 4-foot, 9½-inch gauge; a 5-foot, 6-inch gauge; a 6-foot gauge. Since any gauge picked for the transcontinental railroad would automatically set the standard for the country, some railroads would have to spend a lot of money on gauge changing.

Congress judiciously left the selection of the track width to President Abraham Lincoln. He is said to have replied that he would be glad to decide if someone would only tell him what was the right gauge. Everybody did, naturally. Lincoln listened and nodded. He mulled over it. Then he took a deep breath and said, "Five feet will be the gauge."

"Wrong!" said Congress, and took back the power of choosing. The solons agreed on a standard width of 4 feet, 8½ inches.

For five years the work went on, faster and faster. The Central Pacific Railroad laid eastbound track, the Union Pacific Railroad worked westward, and each perfected assembly line methods. Work trains pushed right up to the railhead with ties, rails, spikes. Teams of men, Chinese coolies and Irish immigrants, ran the ties out along the roadbed, dropping the ties into place, one after another. Behind them came other men with the rails, which they clanged down on the ties, lined up, and spiked. A mile a day or better was the pace.

The Union Pacific laid its thousandth mile in January, 1869, with only eighty-six more to go. In April the Central Pacific track-layers nearing the end of their 689-mile stint, laid ten miles of track in a single day.

May 10, 1869. Outside telegraph offices in Sacramento, St. Louis, New Orleans, Chicago, Boston, New York, and dozens of other cities, crowds began to gather during the morning. The rails were to meet at Promontory Point, Utah, that afternoon, and the last spike, a golden one, was to be driven in. In the telegraph offices, special bell ringers stood poised.

At about half past noon the telegrapher at Promontory Point alerted the waiting operators. "TO EVERYBODY," he tapped out. "KEEP QUIET. WHEN THE LAST SPIKE IS DRIVEN AT PROMONTORY POINT WE WILL SAY 'DONE.' DON'T BREAK THE CIRCUIT, BUT WATCH FOR THE SIGNALS OF THE BLOWS OF THE HAMMER."

Silence. Then, "ALMOST READY. HATS OFF. PRAYER IS BEING OFFERED."

Silence again. Then, "WE HAVE GOT DONE PRAYING. THE SPIKE IS ABOUT TO BE PRESENTED."

Pause. "ALL READY NOW."

Then flashed the word, "DONE." The nation had been spanned from sea to sea. Clang! went bells all over America, to be greeted by tremendous shouts from the waiting throngs. Saluting cannons barked. There were singing and dancing in the streets, banquets, speeches.

The difficult trip between the Atlantic and Pacific coasts had once taken five or six months by river, wagon, and beast of burden. The best of the clippers had carried settlers and prospectors around the Horn in three months. Now the journey from New York to San Francisco could be made in five or six days.

There was other railroad news. Coal replaced wood and coke as fuel. Iron rails gave way to steel. In 1869 a twenty-three-year-old Civil War veteran, George Westinghouse, patented his revolutionary compressed-air brake that made high-speed rail travel safe, and in 1893 the American Locomotive 999 set a world's record of 100 miles an hour. Luxuries were installed in passenger trains that would have made an old-timer blink: electric lights, chandeliers, downy carpets, velvet drapes, libraries. Sometimes, a sonorous pipe organ was built into the "palace cars."

The quality of the food and service kept pace. After a trip on the Chicago and Northwestern line, Charles Nordoff reported in *Harper's Monthly* in 1872:

> You sit at little tables which comfortably accommodate four persons, you order your breakfast, dinner or supper from a bill of fare which contains quite a surprising number of dishes, and you eat from snow-white linen and neat dishes, admirably cooked food and pay a moderate price. It is now the custom to charge a dollar per meal on these cars; and as the cooking is admirable, the service excellent and the food various and abundant, this is not too much. You may have your choice in the wilderness eating at the rate of twenty-two miles an hour off buffalo, elk, antelope, beefsteak, mutton chops and grouse. Breakfast wines are claret and sautern; Champagne wines, Heidsick and Krug.

This was the era that germinated colossal railroad empires, and emperors. Commodore Cornelius Vanderbilt won control of several railroads and pyramided them into the gigantic New York Central lines. James J. Hill, who'd lost one eye in an arrow accident, helped build the Canadian Pacific Railroad and went on to create the mammoth Great Northern Railroad which extended from Lake Superior to Puget Sound. Edward H. Harriman grabbed off three great railroads, the Illinois Central, the Southern Pacific, and the Central Pacific. The struggles for supremacy between these titans and others of their stature were rugged. So it was in Europe, too, where the Rothschild clan did financial battle with many contenders for control of key railroads, and generally won.

Irresistibly, the railroads rolled on, in America and practically everywhere else. In 1850 the world's total railroad trackage amounted to 20,000 miles. By 1900 it was more than 400,000. The United States had far and away the most, 193,346 miles, but other nations had built widely. The United Kingdom had laid down almost 22,000 miles of line before 1900, and France almost 24,000 miles. Germany had constructed a magnificent network of strategically placed railroads, carefully supervised by the General Staff of the German Army to ensure fast mobilization for war. Czarist Russia began its renowned Trans-Siberian Railway in 1891 to tie the Urals to the Pacific; by 1898, 3,300 miles of the planned 4,771-mile route had been tracked. The intrigue-full Baghdad Railway, that was to connect Constantinople and Iraq and endanger Britain's vital communications with India, was under construction. In China, Japan, Australia, railroads were booming. In South America and Africa, too. One South American line, the Transandine Railroad from Valparaiso, Chile, to Mendoza, Argentina, climbed 10,486 feet to get over the Andes.

Everywhere, the railroads brought people, trade, and higher living standards. In 1816 it cost thirty cents to move a ton of freight a mile by wagon in America. In 1900 the same ton of freight could be moved by rail for less than three-quarters of a cent a mile. In 1850 the United States had a population of 23,191,000 and national wealth of $7,066,562,000. In 1900 its population was 75,995,000 and its national wealth amounted to $88,000,000,000. The railroads contributed heavily to that brawny growth.

Through the century, the bridge builders were as busy as were the railroad engineers. Between 1830 and 1860 more than 25,000 bridges were erected in England alone. In 1818, the multigifted Thomas Telford designed a suspension bridge cut of iron to span the Menai Straits in Wales that was one of the wonders of its day. It was still doing sturdy service 148 years after. In 1823 George Stephenson, the resourceful inventor of the *Rocket,* built the world's first railroad bridge, and five years later Ignaz Edler von Mitis used steel for the first time in a bridge—over the Danube Canal at Vienna. Robert Stephenson, George's son, put up a series of extraordinary bridges, too. His High Level Bridge, which spanned the Tyne in 1849, was 4,000 feet long.

Bridge building—and bridge riding—were risky affairs for a while. From 1870 to 1890 an average of twenty-five iron railroad bridges collapsed each year. The wrought-iron bridge at Ashtabula, Ohio, toppled one blizzardy December night in 1877 as a train thundered over it. Ninety people were killed, and the chief engineer

POWER ON
WHEELS:

1. Chicago &
North Western
commuter streliner coach

2. Hudson type
steam locomo

3. Westinghous
Transit Expre
way—completely automated system

of the line committed suicide from shame. The new Firth of Tay bridge in Scotland, on the freezing night of December 29, 1879, went down, and a hundred people fell to their deaths in the icy waters below.

New design techniques and the increasing employment of steel in construction made the bridges safer. Captain James B. Eads, the first engineer to be elected to the Hall of Fame, built a steel-arch bridge over the treacherous Mississippi at St. Louis in 1874 that set bridge-building standards for generations. It made St. Louis a capital city of the Midwest. John A. Roebling, a German refugee who migrated to the United States, threw an 821-foot railway bridge over the gorge below Niagara Falls in 1855 that no one thought possible. He designed the marvelous Brooklyn Bridge in New York with its record-shattering 1,595 foot suspension span, although he never saw it finished. He died of an accident and his son, Colonel Washington A. Roebling, completed it in May, 1883.

Prodigious tunnels were dug. The most awe-inspiring was the St. Gotthard Tunnel, nine miles long, through the Swiss Alps from Switzerland to Italy. Three hundred and ten workers were killed in accidents or suffocated to death, 877 were injured, and $57,500,-000 spent before it was opened in 1881. The Mount Cenis Tunnel, through the French Alps, was another engineering exploit. Eight miles long, it was under construction for fourteen years, from 1857 to 1871. The Peruvians finished another mighty tunnel through the Andes in 1892. It was only 3,596 feet long, but it was 15,781 feet above sea level. It took tough men to work that high.

While travel between such widely separated points as New York and San Francisco was undergoing rapid acceleration, improvements were coming on shorter trips, like those from Battery Park to Thirtieth Street, or between Montmartre and Montparnasse. And necessarily so since the business of getting to work on time, going shopping, or visiting Aunt Jane across town was of far more pressing import to most people than the matter of a journey across the continent. Besides, metropolitan traffic congestion was already a bitter problem.

Horse-drawn omnibuses had been tried without success in Paris in 1662. In 1819 they were reintroduced there. This time they caught hold and spread to other major cities of the world. The horse-omnibuses were put on tracks, first in Boston and New York in 1852, thus getting to be tramcars. City tram railways were soon steam-powered, and some were raised above streets to become "els." The first in America started operations in New York City in 1867. One steam-powered elevated railway, in East Cambridge, Massachusetts, was not only streamlined in 1886 with cars shaped like sections of a pipe, but remarkably foreshadowed the monorails of the mid-twentieth century. Its wheels were canted inward toward a very narrow set of rails until they almost formed a V; the wheels bracketed another rail which was raised nearly as high as the bottom of the cars and served to guide the train.

The first cable cars appeared in San Francisco in 1873.

Electricity made its entry into urban transportation via the Berlin Industrial Exhibition of 1879. A tiny electric engine, about the size of a modern golf cart, sedately drew a long open car around the Exposition, carrying bowlered, bearded gentlemen and full-skirted, bonneted ladies. Experimental electric-powered tram lines sprang up in Hungary, Germany, Ireland, England, and the United States during the next five years, and before the beginning of the Gay Nineties several regular lines were in service. Trolley cars that drew their current from overhead wires were introduced in New York City in 1889. They were quickly very popular.

Running trains under the streets, out of sight and out of the way, was another approach. It was not so easy to implement, however. London built the first metropolitan railroad underground during the 1860's, and a miserable mess it was. The smoky locomotive made underground travel unbearable.

Budapest built the first successful electric subway line, in a steel-beamed tunnel. It opened in 1893, and was followed by similar ones in Glasgow, Paris, and Berlin. In America, Boston was the first city to have an electric underground railway. It opened a streetcar line in a tunnel on September 1, 1897. The effect of the opening was, so *Harper's Weekly* reported, "like that when a barrier is removed from the channel of a clogged up river." More than 100,000 Bostonians crowded into the cars that day, and "the tremendous pressure upon the surface thoroughfares was at once relieved."

A Frenchman, Jules Verne, published a book in 1873 titled *Le Tour du Monde en Quatre-Vingt Jours,* or *Around the World in Eighty Days.* No one had circled the globe in eighty days, but Verne believed it could be done.

In 1889 a pretty, little sob sister for the New York *World,* Elizabeth Cochrane, who signed her articles "Nellie Bly," set out on an assignment to prove that M. Verne was right, in fact a shred slow. She sailed from Hoboken, New Jersey, to London, and across the Channel to France. After a brief visit with M. and Mme. Verne, Nellie sped by train to the heel of Italy, by ship across the Mediterranean and through the Suez Canal to Penang, Singapore, Hong Kong, Yokohama, and over to San Francisco. There she and a pet monkey she'd purchased in Singapore boarded a special Santa Fe train which had been given a green light to Chicago; everything else had to get off the track. The special roared into Chicago in sixty-nine hours, and Nellie had ample time to catch a train for the east coast that put her in Jersey City, New Jersey, seventy-two days, six hours, and eleven minutes after she set sail from Hoboken, 21,740 miles before.

"Hurrah! Hurrah" cabled Jules Verne.

"What took you so long?" asked her editor.

Nellie's wonderful record didn't stand long. Just four months later, George Francis Train chopped it down to sixty-seven days, thirteen hours, three minutes, and three seconds.

"We surely live in a very fast age," sang Mormons grading the Pacific railway in Utah in 1868.

Those Latter-day Saints did not realize how fast-changing an age they lived in. The leap from ox-team to iron horse was a stupendous one, but across the Atlantic a few perceptive tinkerers were wrestling and grappling over something even more startling: horseless carriages.

VII

Comes the Horseless Age

HORSES RULED the open road as the nineteenth century drew toward a close, but their days were numbered. A variety of weird new conveyances, some powered by coal and wood, some by electricity, some by gasoline, and some propelled by human feet were getting set to chase Dobbin off the highway.

The steam carriage was Dobbin's first mechanical rival on the open road. The Englishman Walter Hancock built nine steam carriages from 1829 to 1836 that performed splendidly. One of them named *Infant* became the first commercial steam carriage. It carried paying passengers between London and Stratford in 1831. Another Englishman, Goldsworthy Gurney, built several steam coaches for road travel in the late 1820's that had the English War Office all a'tingle. The Duke of Wellington, then Commander-in-Chief of the British Army, termed them, "of great national importance." They were an amazing-looking lot. Because Gurney was afraid that wheels might not keep his vehicles moving, he added a pair of curved iron appendages beneath the coach bodies. These were supposed to work like horses' legs and push the carriages up hills when the wheels wouldn't. Other English inventors also got into the act, and by the mid-1830's more than twelve steamers had regular "bus" routes in and around London. Some could travel as fast as thirty miles per hour. Over in France, Anesiphone Pequer, a Parisian watchmaker, was experimenting with steam carriages, and a covey of Americans were occupying themselves in the same fashion. Oliver Evans, the railroad visionary, patented the first American "steam wagon" in 1789, and in the 1820's Thomas Blanchard, T. W. Walker, and William T. Jones each built a steam coach.

Many people didn't take kindly to sharing the roads with these puffing, huffing monsters. In England, the farmers thought that Gurney's machine was a threat to their way of life. A mob of them stoned his coach, one day, and beat him unconscious. The turnpike officials were as ugly. Afraid that the heavy steam vehicles might chew their roads to pieces and scare off other traffic, they slapped outrageous tolls on them. It cost a horse-driven coach four shillings to go by turnpike from Liverpool to Prescot, but a steam carriage had to pay two pounds, eight shillings, twelve times as much.

Such onslaughts had their effect and the steam carriage seemed moribund in England by the end of the 1830's.

A few devotees kept it alive and there was a real flurry of interest again in the 1850's and 60's. In 1858 Thomas Rickett of Buckingham started building steam carriages for private use. His customers were men of sporting blood who acted like modern-day sports car fans. One of them, the Earl of Caithness, drove a Rickett steam carriage from Inverness north to the craggy northern coast of Scotland in October, 1860, and he couldn't stop bragging about it. He took along his wife and a friend who rode beside him on the open front seat. A stoker stood at the back, feeding the fire, while the Earl steered with a tiller. During the trip, they drove over a stretch of very hilly country, known as the Ords of Caithness, and the Earl claimed that "such a feat . . . has never before been attempted by steam; as I believe we rose about 1,000 feet in five miles."

"On the level," he crowed, "I got nineteen m.p.h. . . . I passed the mail coach, Lord Lovat's carriages, etc. . . ."

The Earl's good wife was as proud as he. "I am sure," she told a crowd of Scots, "that as long as Caithness can boast of a steam-carriage propelled on its common roads, it has no cause to be ashamed, and may claim to itself what the Americans would style the character of a go-ahead country."

The English steam carriage industry grew to the point where it was exporting its products. Then the opposition struck again. In 1865 Parliament passed the Red Flag Act that limited all steam carriages to a speed of four miles an hour in the country, two miles an hour in town. A minimum of three men was required by the law to crew a steamer while it was underway, and one man had to walk sixty yards in front of the machine, carrying a red flag in the daytime, or, at night, a red lantern.

With that ended the commercial success of English steam coaches.

American steam coach men had it almost as tough. Richard Dudgeon built himself a steam coach, *The Red Devil Steamer,* in 1858 and drove it from his home on East Broadway in New York City to Columbia Street. It frightened the horses so badly that the municipal fathers restricted him to running his carriage on one city street.

The American public remained profoundly disinterested in Dudgeon's steamers. "After seventeen years of effort and convictions of its utility," he wrote in 1870, "I have learned that it is not fashionable, or that people are not ready for it. . . ."

Later, it was to be different.

Another exciting, new development along these lines was the bicycle. It had an incredible impact on road transportation.

An ancestor of the bicycle, the hobby horse, had long been an eccentric, rather dangerous toy. Early hobby horses had two wheels, one ahead of the other like the wheels of a bicycle, but neither of these wheels could be turned from the straight line. The rider sat on the vehicle's back and pushed with his feet, somewhat like a child on a scooter. Now, someone was to make this toy practical.

In 1816 Baron Kurt von Drais, Chief Forester to the Grand Duke of Baden, made the hobby horse steerable so that he could cover his woodlands more readily. He built a machine with two wooden wheels, a padded saddle in the middle of its backbone and just in front of the saddle a kind of T-bar whose horizontal piece was also padded. Beyond that was a set of handlebars. The rider sat on the saddle, leaned forward until his chest rested on the padded T-crossbar, grabbed the handlebars and propelled himself by pushing his feet alternately against the ground. He could go comparatively

SPECIAL CHALLENGE

Ordinary bicycle,
circa 1878.

Wire-driven bicycle,
circa 1900,
Stuttgart.

1954 B.S.A.,
cyclemotor bicycle.

fast. The Baron went from Marlsruhe to Schwetzingen in sixty minutes, one-fourth the time it took on foot.

The Draisine was the first name given this vehicle. Improved versions of it were called the Parisian Curricle, the Pedestrian Curricle, and the Dandy Horse, and they sold like wildfire in England and America around 1819. The countryside swarmed with red-faced, perspiring men and women who labored along the roads until they got up enough speed to lift their feet and coast. When they came to a downgrade, they trusted to luck and quick reflexes, for the curricles had no brakes. To get up a hill, people pushed or carried them. The wear and tear on shoes was something tremendous. Enterprising English bootmakers began to advertise iron-soled shoes for curricle owners.

A Scottish blacksmith, Kirkpatrick Macmillan, added pedals and raised the rider's feet off the ground. A curricle he built in 1831 was propelled by cranks on the rear wheel that were connected by rods to pedals attached to the front wheel. This machine did not depend on spills and obstacles to bring it to a halt. The rider could twist the handlebars and a brake pressed against the rear wheel.

Macmillan, a high-spirited chap, raced stagecoaches, rode downhill standing up on the saddle, and carried pretty girls on his shoulders. Once he was arrested and fined for "furious driving."

A French blacksmith, Pierre Lallement, put the cranks up front in 1865. His machine, which had an iron frame and heavy iron tires, became the rage of France, England and the United States, for all its well-merited nickname, "Boneshaker."

Solid rubber tires were added in 1868, ball bearings and wire-spoked wheels in 1869. In 1874 James Starley of England brought out the first pedaled machines built for women. They had a so-called dropped frame that eliminated the backbone. No more embarrassing, leg-revealing gymnastics for ladies climbing aboard their machines.

The Ordinary was the next development, and a more misnamed vehicle has rarely been made. It had an enormous front wheel, 5 feet or more in diameter which placed the rider perched atop it as high as 8 or 9 feet from the ground. The bigger the drive wheel, the idea was, the farther the machine would go with one revolution of the cranks. The Ordinary was hard to mount, hard to keep upright, and falling off it could be as dangerous as tumbling from a horse, but it was vastly popular in both Europe and the United States.

Fortunately for limbs and lives, the Safety was introduced in 1876–1877 by H. T. Lawson in England and Colonel Albert A. Pope in America. It was the first real bicycle in that it had two wheels which were more or less the same reasonable size, it put the pedals between the wheels, and the driving power was transmitted to the rear wheel by a continuous chain.

During the 1880's, more than 200 varieties of pedaled machines were available including tricycles and quadricycles. Even in a century full of crazes, booms, and manias, the rise of the bicycle was astonishing. At one time, over 300 companies were manufacturing bicycles in the United States; one firm was putting them out at a rate of one a minute. More than a million cyclists were on the roads, especially on weekends and holidays. The bike, or the "wheel," didn't need to be fed or coddled like a horse. It didn't get tired. No ticket was required to ride it. It was marvelous for working up muscles and an appetite, for exploring, for tête-à-têtes.

Bicycles even made a difference in women's styles. Skirts got shorter.

"The discovery and progressive improvement of the bicycle," editorialized the New York *Tribune* in 1895, "is of more importance to mankind than all the victories and defeats of Napoleon, with the First and Second Punic Wars . . . thrown in."

The craze lasted until 1900 when it fell victim to the new intercity electric trolley lines and the oncoming automobiles.

Out in the Orient, another kind of wheeled vehicle was catching on. An American missionary, Jonathan Goble, invented a small, two-wheeled vehicle which could be pulled by a man on foot. It was named Jinrikisha, or rickshaw, it was first used as a taxi in 1871, and it rapidly spread throughout the Far East.

To get back to the Occident . . .

In 1800 an Italian genius, the physicist Alessandro Volta, put together a series of cups in which each cup held a brine or acid solution and two pieces of different metals. The pairs of metal pieces were linked, cup to cup, by metal strips, and they made history because when the two end cups were connected by a wire, a current of electricity flowed. This was the *couronne de tasses,* the "crown of cups," and it was the direct forerunner of the storage battery.

The English professor William Edward Ayrton and a colleague of his named Perry applied this great new energy source to a tricycle in 1882, and in no time battery-driven electric carriages were appearing on European streets. William Morrison designed the first one in America. It was driven in Chicago in September, 1892.

The electric carriages were relatively slow and their batteries had to be recharged every twenty-five to thirty miles, but they were silent, clean, and smooth-running. Furthermore, electricity was to be a vital part of the coming development and operation of the gasoline automobile, especially after the most inventive of all inventors, an American named Thomas Alva Edison, made the storage battery work better.

Came a second development: rubber.

A French explorer and geographer, Charles Marie de la Condamine, brought home to France in the 1730's samples of latex collected from trees in South America. He named the material *caoutchouc.* Before the eighteenth century was over, an English scientist, Joseph Priestley, had introduced draughtsmen to a use for *caoutchouc* which gave it its English name. When a piece of it was rubbed over a pencil mark, the mark erased. *Ergo,* the new eraser was called the rubber.

Rubber was also found to be useful for making waterproof clothes and boots, flexible tubes, elastic bands, and threads. Its value was limited, however, by a marked tendency to harden in cold weather and to melt on hot days. What was needed was a process of treating raw rubber that would make it stable.

The answer was provided by a young Connecticut Yankee, Charles Goodyear. While struggling to stay out of debtor's prison, Goodyear became fired by the dream of solving the rubber riddle. Early defeats in the project did not lessen his enthusiasm.

"If you meet a man who has on an India rubber cap, stock, coat, vest and shoes, with an India rubber money purse, without a cent of money in it," said a wit, "that is he."

After ten years of abject poverty and continuous experimentation, Goodyear accidentally made the discovery he was looking for.

In 1839, at the age of thirty-nine, Goodyear by chance allowed a combination of rubber, sulphur, and white lead to overheat on his pot-bellied stove. Instead of softening, the mixture grew hard, and the rubber produced by this method proved largely impervious to changes in temperature. Goodyear called the process vulcanization. It was the making of the world's rubber industry, though Goodyear himself never got much out of it except debts and lawsuits.

Solid rubber tires were soon cushioning carriage and bicycle rides. Within three decades, most bicycles and carriages were using them. Queen Victoria had them on her royal conveyance.

A different kind of tire that was hollow and filled with air, giving a much more comfortable ride, was invented in 1845 by an English civil engineer, Robert Thomson, but nobody was very interested then. It wanted the crescendoing surge of cycle wheels and an idea-rich veterinarian to establish the pneumatic tire.

John Boyd Dunlop, a Scottish-born veterinarian treating Irish animals in Belfast, was the man. His ten-year-old son wanted to compete in a tricycle race in 1888, so Dunlop joined some pieces of rubber garden hose end to end, and wrapped the tubing in canvas that he reinforced with rubber strips. He fastened it to the rim of each wheel by means of a rubber solution and tape.

It worked like a charm.

Young Master Dunlop won his race, and soon bicycles everywhere were switching to the pneumatic tire. It was ready for the oncoming automobile.

A third development was oil mining.

Whales were growing scarce in the middle of the nineteenth century and it looked as if the price of whale oil in the United States would exceed five dollars a gallon. That would have been enough to snuff out lamps throughout the country, and the demand for a cheaper lamp oil was loud. In response, a method for extracting kerosene from raw petroleum was developed in 1856. It was so successful that Abraham Gesner, the engineer who invented the process, predicted that "kerosene would make possible a long and lasting holiday . . . for . . . the finny monsters of the sea."

Initially, the oil men depended exclusively on surface seepage for their petroleum supplies. Colonel Edwin L. Drake had a different notion, and in 1857 he began drilling for oil in Pennsylvania. Many believed his project was ridiculous until August 27, 1859, when "Drake's Folly," near Titusville, came in at a depth of 691½ feet. That ended the last doubts and started the first oil rush. More than 2,000,000 barrels of oil were produced in Pennsylvania in 1864. Shortly, the drilling territory had spread into West Virginia and Ohio, and 40,000,000 barrels were being pumped out of the earth annually in those three states.

In refining the oil to get kerosene, a dangerous product known as gasoline was obtained. Some special apparatus like pressure stoves and soldering torches utilized it as fuel, but most of it was thrown away. There it was, set and waiting for the automobile.

A fourth development was the evolution of mass production techniques in the bicycle industry.

The fifth and last development was the invention of the internal combustion engine, one in which the burning fuel produced the power directly, not by creating steam to do the work. The fuel was exploded inside a cylinder, and as the hot gases expanded suddenly, the pressure pushed a piston in the cylinder. The motion of the piston could be harnessed to do work.

There were many pioneers in this field. In 1799 a French engineer, Philippe Lebon, constructed an internal combustion engine which employed illuminating gas as fuel, and in 1823 an Englishman, Samuel Brown, made another. Not that either of these engines did much. In 1859 a thirty-nine-year-old Frenchman, Étienne Lenoir, built one that was good enough to be hitched to a carriage. Lenoir drove it for fifteen miles. It wasn't very practical because it consumed colossal quantities of coal gas as fuel, but it showed the world the worth of internal combustion.

Nikolaus August Otto, an unschooled son of a Cologne, Germany, innkeeper, carried the idea much further. With the help of his friend, Eugene Langen, he built a gas engine that used only one-fifth as much coal gas as Lenoir's did. Then in 1876 the forty-four-year-old Otto invented a four-stroke compression engine whose principles are basic to the workings of internal combustion engines to this day. Briefly, Stroke One of the piston sucked fuel into the cylinder, Stroke Two came back to compress the fuel for ignition, Stroke Three was caused by the sudden expansion of gases in the cylinder, and the rebounding Stroke Four shoved the exhaust out of the cylinder.

Now it was merely a short step to the gasoline-powered internal combustion engine and the ubiquitous automobile.

The paternity of the modern, gasoline-powered automobile is the subject of passionate dispute. The arguments are many and they are clouded by conflicting dates, facts and opinions.

This much seems sure. Back in 1864 an Austrian engineer, Siegfried Marcus, applied a gasoline-burning engine to transportation. His first machine, a converted handcart, didn't perform well enough to please him, leading him to scrap it. Eleven years later, he ran a second version through the streets of Vienna at five miles an hour, only to be stopped by the police for making too much noise. Discouraged, he stopped making cars.

A fifty-one-year-old German engineer, Gottlieb Daimler, was a lot more successful. Fresh from the employ of Nikolaus Otto, he designed an improved version of Otto's engine in 1885. Impatient to test it on a vehicle and not having a carriage that could serve, he fitted the engine to a wooden bicycle. It was the world's first motorcycle and Daimler's son took it for a trail spin in November of 1885.

The following autumn, Daimler got hold of a four-wheel carriage and equipped it with a one-cylinder motor that produced one-and-a-half horsepower. He drove it happily through the suburbs of Stuttgart at a speed of eighteen miles per hour. Before the year was out, he had German and French patents on the machine.

Practically at the same moment, another German inventor was also bringing out a gasoline carriage. In the spring of 1886 Carl Benz, a forty-four-year-old mechanical wizard, installed a small Otto engine which put out all of three-quarters of a horsepower in a three-wheel carriage and made a test run around Munich. The local press reported that the test went well, except that Benz had some trouble steering his machine and plowed into a wall.

Still, Benz and his machine survived, and he got a German patent on it in 1886.

In short order both Daimler and Benz cars were being manufactured for sale in Germany and France. As Benz later remarked, "Germany was the father of the automoblie, but France its mother."

Early in the 1890's, a French firm, Roger, was making the trim Benz machines for sale. Another concern, Panhard et Levassor, was producing Daimler cars which were not so neat and much noisier. *"C'est brutal, mais ça marche"*—"It's brutal, but it runs," Émile Levassor consoled himself as he listened to the awful grinding sound of the gears. A third company, Peugeot, was building a Daimler car with a unique, new feature. Its engine was in the rear. Public opinion speedily forced Peugeot to move the motor up front.

Some American pioneers were equally hard at work on gasoline buggies, although they were well behind the Europeans.

A controversial character if ever there was one, George B. Selden applied for a patent on a gasoline-powered carriage in 1879, and it was eventually awarded to him in 1895, the first to be granted to an American gasoline car. Most authorities agree, though, that Selden never once constructed a car that ran.

The first Americans who did build a workable gasoline carriage were the two Duryea brothers, Charles and J. Frank, and the disputes as to what credit which of them deserved have lasted for decades. According to the most reliable testimony, Charles, a thirty-year-old bicycle maker, did the original designing and his younger brother Frank, who was a machinist, did the actual building. They completed their first car in April, 1892, and Frank drove it around the interior of their workshop in Springfield, Massachusetts.

The following year the brothers completed a second, better car. The Springfield *Evening Union* was rhapsodic about it. "If as successful as is expected, [it] will revolutionize the mode of travel on the highways, and do away with the horse as a means of transportation," the *Union* wrote on September 16, 1893. Six days later the paper reported an eminently successful road trial through the streets of Springfield.

Other Americans were following hot on the Duryeas' track. On July 4, 1894, Elwood Haynes, an erudite Indiana engineer, drove a gasoline carriage of his design on the Pumpkinville Pike in Kokomo. It did six miles an hour. Young Henry Ford, the chief engineer for a Detroit utility, was perfecting a gasoline engine in his spare time; Ransom Eli Olds, another Michiganite, was experimenting with a gasoline-burning car; and Edward Joel Pennington, a third Midwesterner, was dreaming up a gas buggy, and some of the slickest promotional schemes in financial history. Pennington may even have operated one of his cars in 1894, but apparently that was as far as he or the car got.

In any event, gasoline carriages were running on both sides of the Atlantic. It was the French who coined the name *automobiles*.

The gasoline-powered automobile had to fight hard for its right to existence. The steamers, which came back into vogue in the 1890's, and the electrics gave it a run for its money.

A number of historic races were to help decide the outcome, and very thrilling ones they were.

The first formal competition between mechanical carriages was held in France, from July 19 to July 22, in 1894. Twenty-five cars attempted to cover a seventy-nine-mile route between Paris and Rouen, and fifteen finished. The fastest time was turned in by a steam tractor pulling a two-wheel landau, but because the steamer needed both a stoker and a driver, the prizes went to the Peugeot and to the Panhard et Levassor—both gasoline carriages.

The success of this trial led a group of Frenchmen to sponsor a 732-mile race from Paris to Bordeaux and back in June, 1895. A Panhard et Levassor car covered the course in forty-eight hours, forty-seven minutes, and thirty seconds, an average of fifteen miles an hour. The driver was Émile Levassor himself, who took the car the entire 732 miles, making only brief stops and refreshing himself in Bordeaux with a glass of champagne.

America was not slow to pick up the idea. H. H. Kohlsaat, the publisher of the Chicago *Times-Herald,* sponsored a race that was run on Thanksgiving Day, 1895. The course was 52.4 snowy miles long, from Jackson Park, Illinois, to Evanston and back.

J. Frank Duryea participated in the race, and he gave a vivid description of it:

> A heavy snow had fallen during the night, and we experienced hard going as we drove out to Jackson Park. . . .
> Of nearly a hundred entries, only six cars lined up for the

1. Duryea, 1893–94, the first practical automobile using an internal combustion engine

THE HORSELESS CARRIAGE: some early models.

2. Roberts Electric, 1896

3. Henry Ford's first car, 1896

4. White Steamer, 1904

5. The Model "T" Ford, 1910

6. Hillman, 1919

7. Citroën, 1922

. The Smithsonian Institution; 2. Firestone Archives; 3. Ford Motor Company; . and 5. Firestone Archives.

start—two were electric vehicles entered by Morris and Salom of Philadelphia, and Sturgis of Chicago. Of the four gasoline-engined vehicles, H. Mueller & Co. of Decatur, Illinois, R. H. Macy and Co. of New York, and The De La Vergne Refrigerating Machine Co. of New York, each came to the start with an imported German Benz. . . .

The word "go" was given at 8:55, and the Duryea was the first car away (i.e., the start was staggered).

With me as umpire was Mr. Arthur W. White. The machine made good going of the soft unpacked snow in Jackson Park, but when we came to the busier part of the city, the street surface consisted of ruts and ice hummocks, in which the car slewed badly from side to side.

In its careening on the slippery road the Duryea hit a rut so hard that the steering arm broke, and Frank had to hunt up a blacksmith shop and repair the damage before going on. The R. H. Macy's Benz passed the Duryea and was not caught until Evanston. Then, a reporter noted, as the Macy car obeyed the rules and pulled over to let the Duryea go by, "The group of spectators along Forest Avenue applauded the unusual sight of one horseless carriage forging ahead of a rival." On chugged the Duryea. Suddenly, one of its two cylinders stopped firing. Put-putting along on one cylinder, Frank found a tinsmith's shop where the bad cylinder could be fixed. But the tinsmith was closed for the holiday. Duryea rushed to his home and found him fast asleep. The good man allowed himself to be routed from his warm bed out into the cold to open up shop.

By the time Frank was back on course, fifty-five minutes had been lost, and he fully expected that the Macy car would be leading him. But, wonder of wonders, the track ahead was unbroken. At 7:18 P.M., the Duryea crossed the finish line, victor in the first formal race staged in the United States.

Only one other car completed the course, the Mueller Company's Benz. Mueller collapsed from the cold and fatigue, but his umpire drove the car home. Macy's Benz encountered a string of horrible luck. It hit a horse cart, a sleigh, and a cab, and its engine broke down.

As a direct consequence of the race, the Barnum & Bailey Circus starred a Duryea gas buggy in its parade the next year, and in February, 1896, Duryea made the first sale of an American gasoline car, to a George H. Morrill, Jr. of Norwood, Massachusetts. Duryea cars finished one-two-three in a race held in New York in May, 1896. Another went to England to beat the best that Panhard et Levassor had to offer.

The struggle for supremacy among the gas buggies, the electrics, and the steamers was by no stretch of the imagination one-sided. When the first track race in American annals was held at Narragansett Park, Rhode Island, in September, 1896, a Riker Electric Stanhope won first prize, the second prize went to a Morris and Salom Electrobat, and the three Duryea gas buggies in the race got nothing.

Commercially, the battle seesawed. In 1898 electric cars were chosen for taxi service in New York City. New York and Boston department stores selected electric wagons for deliveries, and the U.S. Army bought electric vehicles. Increasingly, electrics like the Riker, the Woods, and the Waverley Electromobile, which featured a *two*-year guarantee on its battery, could be seen on the roads. Steamers, too. A time was to come when 125 different manufacturers would be making steam carriages in the United States! The names of some steamers were on the way to becoming household bywords, such as the Locomobile, the Gardner-Serpollet in England and France, the White Steamer, and, of course, the Stanley Steamer. In 1899 Freelan O. Stanley, one of the Maine twins who developed this fabulous performer, drove his quietly purring Stanley Steamer to the towering summit of Mount Washington, an incredible feat for the time.

Arguments over the merits of the three types of cars sizzled throughout America and Europe. The great Thomas A. Edison came out publicly in favor of the gasoline automobile. "The horse is doomed," he told a reporter for the New York *World* on November 17, 1895, and not by electricity, he said. When the newsman asked if future cars would be powered by electricity, Edison candidly replied, "I don't think so. As it looks at present, it would seem more likely that they would be run by a gasoline or naphtha motor of some kind. . . ."

The noted British engineer A. R. Sennett backed the steamer.

"The petroleum engine," he declared to the *Carriage Builders'*
Gazette, "has not yet attained the perfection for this class of work
that the steam engine has, and when the English know a little more
about this matter they will not be in such a hurry to discard their
old and faithful servant, steam, as the French have been. For example, you can't stop and start a petroleum engine. When you stop
your carriage your petroleum engine pegs away as merrily as ever,
or rather more so, which is very bad if you happen to have loose
teeth. . . . Then, again, the smell from the petroleum is decidedly
offensive. You will find the steam carriage will be far ahead of the
petroleum ones. They run very smoothly. . . "

It was anybody's guess as to which of the power systems would
come out on top.

Two things the gas buggy had working for it were courage and
imagination. Some of the most fertile, daring minds that any industry has known came into the gasoline automobile field during this
period, men like Olds, Ford, and Alexander Winton.

In 1893 Winton was a slender young man with a big mustache.
He was a bicycle builder, experimenting on the side with a gasoline
car. By the fall of 1896 he had tested a vehicle satisfactorily in
public, and the next summer set out on a trip that was startling by
American standards. He and W. A. Hatcher, superintendent of his
shop, drove from Cleveland to New York City via Rochester,
Utica, Syracuse, and Albany. Winton calculated that they traveled
800 miles. It was astounding not only because the American gas
buggy was so new, but because the roads over which they rode
were—to use Winton's word—"outrageous." Gasoline had to be
bought en route at drugstores. It was close to a miracle whenever
they found a druggist who had as much as one gallon of gasoline in
stock. Often they bought it by the pint. Since they consumed about
six gallons a day, they had to do considerable shopping around.

The trip began July 28 and ended August 7. The actual running
time was seventy-eight hours and forty-three minutes.

Winton began regular production in 1898. Twenty-five cars
rolled out of his shop that year and he made his first sale in March
to a Pennsylvania mechanical engineer, Robert Allison, for $1,000.
The Winton Motor Carriage Company pocketed a $400 profit.

COMES THE HORSELESS AGE

Ford was born in a two-story farmhouse near Dearborn, Michigan, on July 30, 1863. Some twelve or thirteen years later, the mechanically minded farm boy experienced what he always remembered as the biggest event of his youth, "meeting with a road engine about eight miles out of Detroit when we were driving to town." A steam engine, it was.

"I remember that engine," said Ford in the 1920's, "as though I had seen it only yesterday, for it was the first vehicle other than horse-drawn that I had ever seen. It was intended primarily for driving threshing machines and sawmills and was simply a portable engine and boiler mounted on wheels with a water tank and coal cart trailing behind. I had seen plenty of these engines hauled around by horse, but this one had a chain that made a connection between the engine and the rear wheels of the wagonlike frame on which the boiler was mounted. . . . One man standing on the platform shovelled coal, managed the throttle, and did the steering. . . . The engine had stopped to let us pass with our horses and I was off the wagon and talking to the engineer before my father, who was driving, knew what I was up to. The engineer was very glad to explain the whole affair.

"It was that engine," Ford stated, "which took me into automotive transportation."

By 1893, the year Ford was thirty, he was in Detroit, working at the Edison Illuminating Company as chief engineer. His face had the sharp, alert, half-amused look of a Yankee horsetrader who knew he couldn't lose. And he was on the track of his long-time ambition. At the very end of the year, he successfully tested an experimental gasoline engine.

Less than three years later, in the rainy predawn of June 4, 1896, his first gasoline-driven vehicle, a two-cylinder, four-horsepower car, set off on its test run with a friend of Ford's riding ahead on a bicycle to keep the road clear.

Ford sold the car to a Detroiter named Charles Ainsley for $200. He strongly believed in low prices. "A car that wasn't good for everybody wasn't any good at all," he felt.

Ainsley resold the car to a bicycle dealer, A. W. Hall, who was very pleased with it. He wrote to Ford in 1899:

". . . The little carriage is still doing its usual duty. I disposed of it this spring and the little rig was still in fair shape after all the banging around it has had and I guess you know that was considerable; I ran it almost two years as you know and about the only trouble I had was that one tire and the springs on the sparkers working loose. . . ."

To Olds went the distinction of founding an industry. An Ohio machinist, born in 1864, he started by building steamers, one of which was shipped to India for a maharajah, no less. The gasoline engine attracted him and in 1897 he formed a company to make automobiles in Lansing, Michigan. It foundered and he moved to Detroit. In 1899 he established the Olds Motor Works. It was to make him America's first successful automobile manufacturer.

Few other industries have ever been blessed with such technical maestros.

Gaily the curtain came down on the nineteenth and probably the greatest century in man's industrial development. Most of the world was at peace pro tem, economic conditions were prosperous, and the ordinary traveler, who had been given a new kind of freedom by the bicycle, was ready to exchange his bike pedals for a powered ride.

No one knew yet which route the horseless carriage would take, electricity, steam, or gasoline, but yearly the production of cars was increasing. In Europe, Benz alone had manufactured some 2,000 cars, and other concerns had turned out many thousands more. Just four cars had been registered in America in 1895; by the century's end, at least 8,000 cars were banging over America's dirt roads and cobblestone pavements. Some eighty companies with a total capitalization close to $400,000,000 had been established to build automobiles. Engineers were thinking up mass production techniques.

Demonstrating that automobiles were here to stay, the English Parliament had repealed the horrendous Red Flag Act in 1896. Now drivers could legally go twelve miles an hour without fear of arrest, provided their vehicles weighed less than one and one-half tons. Elsewhere, some drivers were going far faster. On April 2, 1899, the Belgian Camille Jenatzy set a world's record for speed on land of sixty-six miles an hour. He drove a cigar-shaped electric car.

Some big automotive tidings came from America, too. In the one year of 1899 the first automobile salesroom was opened; the first garage was started with "competent mechanics always on hand to make repairs when necessary"; and the first American woman driver was licensed. She was Mrs. John Howell Phillips of Chicago.

VIII

Fill 'Er Up, Please

HERE WAS THE twentieth century, the peripatetic century. In less than seven short decades, men were to travel faster, farther, and better than in all the thousands of years preceding. And more people were to go more places than ever before. Through new wonders of transportation, John Doe and hundreds of millions of his counterparts around the world were to become kings of all the landscape they beheld.

There was still some hard going before the horseless carriage came to be generally accepted. When it was suggested that President William McKinley might ride in an electric car during the District of Columbia's centennial parade in 1900, eyebrows were raised at the White House. Assuming that the thing was safe, which many of the President's advisers doubted, think of the damage to the Presidential dignity if the car should stall.

So President McKinley had to wait until the following summer to become the first president to ride in a horseless carriage. At home in Canton, Ohio, a friend drove him out in a Stanley Steamer. On September 6, 1901, the President took a sadder ride. An electric ambulance bore him to a hospital in Buffalo after he was mortally wounded by the anarchist Leon Czolgosz.

Many towns enacted special laws against automobiles. Some banned them from their streets. One stipulated that every motorist

156

had to halt his car and shoot off a Roman candle whenever he saw a horse-drawn vehicle approaching. The state of New Hampshire limited all cars to eight miles per hour. In Minnesota T. H. Shevlin was fined ten dollars in 1902 for exceeding ten miles an hour.

Out in the country, motor vehicles were called "devil wagons" and sulphurously cursed for running over chickens and scaring horses. Irate farmers used to bury rakes and crosscut saws just below the surface of roads, with the sharp ends up. Automobilists often found themselves with four flat tires at one time.

Miss Marie Comstock of Alpena, Michigan, had a beau from Cleveland who taught her to drive a Winton in the summer of 1901, the year she graduated from Vassar. "Talk about horses being frightened," she recalled. "Why, they weren't in it with people. Mothers advised their offspring to make for the nearest porch if they saw one of those gas buggies heading down the street."

A motorist had to be pretty enthusiastic, not to say dogged, to embark upon a twenty-five-mile Sunday drive. Besides the guerrilla warfare, he had to contend with motor breakdowns, mud holes and tire failures. A careful driver brought along extra gaskets, spark plugs, a grease gun, an ax, four or five feet of insulated wire, a block-and-tackle, a tow rope, several spare tires, and a portable vulcanizer.

Roads were seldom marked and no road maps were to be had. It took Dr. H. Nelson Jackson and his chauffeur Sewall K. Crocker sixty-three days to drive from San Francisco to New York in 1903, the first time anyone ever made it from coast to coast by automobile. One day, their Winton car got stuck eighteen times in buffalo wallows.

Among their more enlightening experiences was the occasion they asked a woman for directions. She told them and they chugged off. A few miles farther on, the road ended abruptly at a farmhouse where an old couple came out and stared unbelievingly at the contraption in their front yard. Exasperated, Dr. Jackson and Crocker retraced their path. They saw the same woman and Dr. Jackson asked her why in heaven she had done it.

"Oh," she blithely said, "I wanted Maw and Paw to see you. They've never seen an automobile before."

Bit by bit, the resistance to the "devil wagons" lessened. It had to. For one thing, country doctors discovered very early how useful a car was. It served as a fatigueless, if temperamental, conveyance for making their rounds, and it could double as an ambulance when necessary.

For another thing, auto clubs were springing up like weeds and motorists were banding together to go on tours. These excursions provided many communities with their first glimpse of an automobile and proved that the monsters weren't completely satanic.

Racing was a third factor. It was a continuous source of wonderful publicity. The racers took their horseless carriages into the tank towns and onto the big city dirt tracks, and they captured the public's heart everywhere.

The crowds used to go wild at races. The day that Henry Ford, driving in his first contest, raced the famous Alexander Winton at Grosse Pointe, Michigan, a woman in the stands got so excited that she jumped on her seat and yelled, "I'd bet fifty dollars on Ford if I had it." Her embarrassed husband had to whack her on the head to calm her down.

Happily for the lady, Ford won.

A racer like the cigar-smoking, devil-may-care "Barney" Oldfield had the entire country rooting for him. Ford gave Berner Eli "Barney" Oldfield his start. Correctly sensing that victorious racing would sell stock cars, Ford built two ultrapowerful racers, the *Arrow* and the *999*. "I put in four great big cylinders giving eighty H.P.—which up to that time had been unheard of," he wrote. "The roar of those cylinders alone was enough to half kill a man. There was only one seat."

Since Ford didn't choose to race the cars himself, he hired Oldfield, a professional bicycle racer, to do it. Oldfield had never driven a car before but he said he "would try anything once." He learned to drive the *999* in a week, no easy job inasmuch as the steering was done with a two-handled bar and the driver sat out in the open while the naked engine flung hot oil back at him.

Oldfield won his first race with the *999* in October, 1902, and went on to become an American folk hero. His name was synonymous with speed and glorious recklessness. For years, any American policeman who stopped a car for speeding was likely to start his tirade with, "Say, who do you think you are—Barney Oldfield?"

The whole world went wild when the Paris newspaper *Le Matin* and *The New York Times* cosponsored a race from New York to Paris—via Russia. It was the longest automobile race in history.

A crowd of 250,000 people saw the racers leave Times Square in New York on February 12, 1908. Headed for Albany on the first leg were three French contestants, a Motobloc, a De Dion Bouton, and a Sizaire-Naudin; an Italian Zust; a Protos from Germany; and a last-minute American entry, a Thomas *Flyer* driven by George Schuster and Montague Roberts.

After two hours the Sizaire-Nuadin was out with a broken axle. In Iowa the Motobloc withdrew, leaving the Thomas which had reached San Francisco, the Zust in Utah, and the Protos and the De Dion struggling through Wyoming.

The Americans set out on the second leg of the race: by ship to Alaska, north over dog sled tracks to the Yukon, and by ship across the Bering Strait to Russia. The day after they landed in Alaska, a telegram called them back to Seattle. The route had been changed.

By the time the Americans got to Russia, only they and the Germans were left in the race. Across Siberia slithered the two cars, weighted down with repair gear, extra tires, camping equipment, and food. And champagne for the Germans. It was brutal going. One day, the Protos got stuck wheel-deep in mud, and the Americans gallantly pulled it free. Another day, the Thomas was mired, and forty Russian soldiers dragged it loose. Tires shredded to nothing, four to every 150 miles, and both cars broke down almost as often. One morning, six teeth snapped off the driving pinion of the Thomas, and a 6-inch crack appeared in its transmission housing. Another day all the teeth were stripped off its gears. A third day its transmission died totally, and Schuster had to gallop 430 miles in a troika to get a new transmission. The Thomas would get the lead, the Protos would pass it, and the Thomas would pull ahead again. At the end, the Americans trailed the Germans into Paris by five days, but the triumph in the 22,000-mile marathon was theirs because the Germans had been given a fifteen-day penalty and the Americans a fifteen-day credit.

Automobile racing grew so popular that the Indianapolis speedway was built in 1909, and the first of its annual 500-mile races was held in 1911. Ray Harroun won it in six hours, forty-two minutes, eight seconds.

By the outset of World War I in 1914, the motor vehicle was a familiar part of the landscape in America and Europe. The 8,000 cars that had been listed in the United States in 1900 had multiplied twenty-five fold, to a registration of more than 200,000, and a variety of other events indicated the acceptance of motor vehicles. The first center line was painted on a highway, in Wayne County, Michigan, in 1911. The first stop sign was put up, in Detroit in 1912, the first electric traffic light in Cleveland. In Paris, honking taxis had replaced neighing horse-drawn fiacres along the boulevards. And fortunately so for the French. When invading German hordes reached the Marne in September, 1914, 600 requisitioned Paris taxis rushed to the front 6,000 Poilus who helped turn the tide.

One thing else had been decided as of 1914. The gas buggy reigned supreme in the motor vehicle field.

The steamer and the electric each put up a stiff fight. Seven of the thirty-four brands of cars displayed at the first National Automobile show at Madison Square Garden in 1900 were steamers. Four White Steamers—"Whistling Billies" was their nickname—made it successfully from New York to Buffalo in a 1901 endurance race, and three "Whistling Billies" won the Long Island Endurance Run in 1902. In 1905 a Stanley Steamer beat several gas buggies with time to spare at Denver, and a year later Fred Marriott broke every speed record in the world in a Stanley Steamer. He drove it 127.66 miles per hour at Daytona Beach, Florida. The steamers kept classy company. One headed the inauguration parade for President Theodore Roosevelt in 1905, and the late Queen Mary of England (then the Princess of Wales) had one. President William Howard Taft used to take his family for rides in a steamer while they were in the White House. It was an open-air seven-seater, chauffeur-driven and most impressive.

Electrics got to be extremely popular with women. Unlike the gas buggies, they were odorless, noiseless, and effortless to handle. There was no balky crank with which to vie. "The only car for a lady," an advertisement for them read, and a multitude of ladies concurred. When the prominent suffragettes, Nell Richardson and

Mrs. Alice Snitzer Burke, made a nationwide tour in 1912 to campaign for votes for women, they drove an electric roadster.

The gas buggies won out over the steamers because the steamers were heavy and needed frequent stops for water as well as for fuel. They vanquished the electrics because of the electrics' requirement for constant recharging. The gasoline-powered cars combined relative lightness with long range, and the leading auto makers of the period therefore chose to produce them. Before the steamer makers and electric makers could come up with improvements, the gas buggy men had picked up the ball and run away with it. Gas buggies began to be mass produced and were heavily promoted. The smart money went into internal combustion cars, and the steamers and electrics withered on the industrial vine.

The electrics had a bit of a comeback in the 1950's and 1960's. Thousands of them could be seen on golf courses, hauling golfers up and down the fairways.

But from the first years of the second decade, most main roads in most countries belonged to the gas buggy.

Europeans led the way in the invention and initial development of the gas buggy. Nobody may doubt that. They didn't hold their headstart long, though.

Some great automobiles and automobile empires were built in Europe—firms like Austin, Morris, Singer, Fiat, Citroen, and palatial cars like the Rolls Royce of Britain, the Hispano-Suiza, Bugatti, and Celage of France and Spain, the Horch, Mayback, and Mercedes Benz of Germany, the Isotta-Fraschini of Italy, and the Belgian Minerva, that ranged in price from $7,500 to $43,000.

Until the mid-1930's, the automobile was essentially a rich man's luxury in Europe, not the everyday necessity that it got to be in America. Production methods were archaic, the prices too high for the average man, and the demand inevitably low.

Hence, the focal point of the world's automobile industry left Europe early. It shifted first to the New England stamping grounds of the Duryea brothers, the Stanley twins, and Colonel Albert A. Pope. Production was soon ebbing there, though, and concentrating in the Midwest: in the south of Michigan, the north of Indiana, and in Ohio. Steel, coal, and other raw materials were nearby, rail and water transportation facilities were excellent, and, through some strange coincidence, many of the best automobile men happened to have been born or to be working in that region. For more than half a century these factors helped keep Detroit the automotive capital of the world.

Many men made the United States the Number One nation of automobile manufacturers and users. Of them all, Ransom Olds was pre-eminent.

A string of bad luck started Olds off well. His Olds Motor Works had a disastrous first year of production; it lost $80,000. Then, on March 9, 1901, the company staggered under what seemed the killing blow. Heat from a forge in the factory touched off a bag full of gas, and in minutes the place was a mass of spurting flames. Virtually everything was destroyed, including Olds' priceless designs.

All that was saved was one light, single-cylinder gasoline-powered runabout. Young James J. Brady, a timekeeper, dashed back into the blaze and emerged in a few seconds, pushing the little car before him. It was a silver lining to Olds' flaming cloud.

Olds had planned to sell merely a few cars of this runabout type. They were to be part of a diversified line. Now the runabout was all he had. To stay in business, he had to build and promote it exclusively.

New blueprints were drawn up from the surviving car, the company contracted out the making of the major components, and within a month after the fire the first of the new models had been assembled—and priced at $650. For the first time in history, a low-priced car was in quantity production.

To the modern motorist, the little "one-lunger" might have appeared ridiculous. It was shaped like a toboggan on wheels, and it had the driver's seat as high as an old buckboard. Yet with its curved dash, it was a snappy-looking vehicle all the same and a good little car for the age.

That autumn, an Olds' tester, Roy D. Chapin, who was destined to be Secretary of Commerce in the Hoover Administration, drove one from Detroit to the second annual Automobile Show in New York, covering the 820 miles in seven and a half days, at an average speed of fourteen miles an hour!

Chapin damaged a wheel coming down Fifth Avenue, but he managed anyway to wobble up to the Waldorf-Astoria where Ransom Olds was staying. Jumping down from the seat, he headed into the lobby, only to be intercepted by the doorman who was appalled at the idea of such a filthy, oil-spattered individual trying to get past him. Chapin had to sneak into the hotel through the back.

A New York dealer was so impressed with the little Oldsmobile's feat that he ordered 1,000, an unbelievable number at the time. By 1904 the company was producing and selling over 5,000 cars a year. Gus Edwards and Vincent Bryan even made the car the subject of a hit song, "In My Merry Oldsmobile." Everyone hummed it.

Unfortunately, Ransom Olds' financial backers decided that they wanted to diversify by moving into a higher price range, with a heavier car. Olds disagreed and he sadly left the company that bore his name.

A momentous legal war had to be fought to the bitter end before the newly born automobile industry could grow up safely. The sparks of the war were ignited in 1879 when the Rochester, New York, lawyer named George B. Selden filed an application for a patent on a vehicle powered by an internal combustion machine—and got it sixteen years later. He hadn't pursued it until 1895 because no one was sufficiently interested to back his idea. It was different after that because the patent, the first to be granted in the United States, apparently held for the whole burgeoning industry.

In 1900 the Electric Vehicle Company owned the patent rights and set out to enforce them. With much fanfare, it slapped a suit against the Winton Motor Carriage Company for infringement of its rights. After three years of fierce legal maneuvering, Winton gave in. Together with nine other companies it set up the Association of Licensed Automobile Manufacturers and agreed to pay heavy royalties.

Not so Henry Ford. He would have no part of any royalty deal.

Accordingly, a suit for infringement was brought against him in

1903. The case stayed in the courts for eight bitter years, with some of the top lawyers in the country lined up on each side. Thirty-six big volumes were filled with the testimony. The court of appeals finally overruled a lower court and decided in Ford's favor. The automotive field was free to move forward, the verdict meant.

Those first beginning decades saw many more colossi in the automobile industry. The early pioneer Alexander Winton went on to produce one of the very first eight-cylinder autos. John M. Studebaker and his brothers took their illustrious wagon-making firm and transformed it into a flourishing auto-making business. James W. Packard switched his attentions from electrics and designed a splendid gasoline-driven car that caught right on. David Dunbar Buick quit fabricating bathtubs to develop a new auto engine, and with it launched the Buick Motor Company. He didn't last in it, but his name did. Louis Chevrolet, the Swiss guide in a French wine cellar, invented a fine wine pump, sailed to the United States to sell it, and invented the first models of a splendid new car—the Chevrolet. William S. Knudsen—"Big Bill" to his friends—a Danish immigrant and production genius, rose from bicycle mechanic to be head of General Motors.

Blunt-speaking Walter P. Chrysler commenced his career as a mechanic and a railroad man. He bought his first car, a $5,000 Locomobile, while he had only $700 in the bank and a monthly paycheck from the Chicago Great Western of $350. He wanted so badly to study the car's innards that he borrowed the remaining $4,300. After he got home and told his wife what he'd done, he reported, "She did not scold me, but it did seem to me that when she closed the kitchen door, it made a little more noise than usual. . . ." Chrysler became president of Buick, first vice president of General Motors, saved both the Willys-Overland and the Maxwell-Chalmers companies from bankruptcy, and proceeded to build the mighty Chrysler Corporation.

William C. Durant founded the goliath General Motors Corporation and gathered into its corporate family such names as Oldsmobile, Buick, Cadillac, Oakland, Delco, Hyatt Roller Bearing and Champion Ignition. He was succeeded by another automotive great, Alfred P. Sloan, Jr. who took over the leadership of General

Motors from Durant and built it into one of the nation's greatest industrial enterprises.

Still another pioneer in the automotive field was the inventor Charles F. Kettering. An Ohio farmboy, born in 1876, he commenced a half-century of inventiveness by electrifying the cash register. Switching to the automotive arena, he developed a new ignition system for the Cadillac.

In 1910 "Uncle Henry" M. Leland, the white-bearded Cadillac head became infuriated when six of his workers broke their arms cranking Cadillacs, and a friend died after he got a broken jaw cranking a lady's stalled car.

"Something must be done about it," he said to Kettering. "I am breaking arms all over the country and it has got to stop."

At his behest, Kettering invented the first electric self-starter in 1912. It made the crank obsolete.

As research chief for General Motors, "Boss" Kettering helped develop Ethyl gasoline, quick-drying paint and many other improvements. He became an institution whose sharp mind and boundless optimism stimulated everyone around him.

"The future will be greater than the most fantastic story you can write," he once said. "You will always underrate it."

There was Henry Ford. Like most of the pioneers, Ford had trouble getting rolling. The first car-making concern with which he was associated, the Detroit Automobile Company, failed in 1901. The second, the Henry Ford Company, used Ford as an engineer; others ran the company. But in June, 1905, Ford established a company of his own that succeeded beyond all the hopes he'd had. He named it the Ford Motor Company and he aimed to build cheap, sturdy cars that farmers, workers, and salesmen could afford to buy and run. Certainly, he did that. In October, 1908, he brought out an automobile that, in the words of *The New York Times,* "revolutionized the automotive industry, and . . . changed the face of America"—the Model T.

Husky, vigorous, low-priced, simple to repair, the Model T could go almost anywhere and do practically anything. It could go on roads or crosscountry, through mudholes, sandtraps, and snow drifts. It could be hitched up to pump water, saw wood, chop silage, or generate electricity. With a special set of wheels it made a fine tractor. It was equally good as a pick-up truck, hay wagon, taxi, or fire engine. A typical joke of the period told of a dying farmer who asked that his Tin Lizzie be buried with him.

"Why?" he was asked.

"Because it has never gotten me into a hole it couldn't get me out of."

The Lizzie was operated with three foot pedals; a left-handed emergency brake; and a spark lever and a throttle lever on the steering wheel. The left pedal controlled the high, low and neutral friction drive gears; the center pedal worked the reverse; and the right pedal was the foot brake. Stepping down hard on the left pedal while the driver pulled at the throttle started the car moving in low. As the driver gradually lifted up on the pedal, the Lizzie went into high gear. To halt the car, the driver had to put the car into neutral and step on the brake. To stop it in a hurry, it was a good idea to jam down all three pedals at once and yank the emergency brake as far back as it would go.

Ford did all manner of things to speed production and cut costs. One was to confine his entire output to Model T's. Another was his introduction in 1913 of the continuously moving assembly line— bringing the part to the man rather than the man to the part. It was a stellar milestone in industrial history. With it mass production really became possible. Up to 1913 assembling a Ford consumed fourteen hours. In 1914 the process took ninety-three minutes.

Another startling innovation was Ford's decision in 1914 to raise the minimum wage for all nonsalaried employees over twenty-two years of age to five dollars a day. It set a pattern for the nation's industry.

The price of the "flivver" dropped in nine years from $850 to $360, while the car steadily improved. Later, the price was to go lower yet, to $290.

Sales soared—from 10,000 cars in the first year to more than 2,000,000 a year in 1925. For three years, half of all the cars manufactured in America were Model T's.

The 15,007,003 Tin Lizzies which Ford put on the road were a symbol of what happened to transportation in the first decades of the twentieth century. It was a revolution.

Man's mobility had for thousands of years been dependent on his wealth. The leisure class traveled, and the working class didn't, unless forced to by war, plague, or hard times. Now the working-man could reasonably hope that by carefully saving his pennies he would be able in the foreseeable future to afford a private means of transportation which performed about as well, all factors consid-ered, as the private means of transportation available to the man who employed him. An authentic equalizer, the mass produced automobile was a tremendous boon to democracy.

It was not just Fords that swept America off its feet in the early decades of the century. Thousands of other makes carried Ameri-cans around. There were cars like the Stutz Bearcat and the Mercer, the dreams of every young Romeo in the 1920's; the luxurious Pierce-Arrow; the Moon; the Chandler; the Deusenberg; the Willys; the Maxwell. "The Car of Contentment" was the Maxwell's dulcet advertising slogan. Altogether, some 3,000 different makes of cars were produced in America by 1,500 manufacturers between 1893 and the present. In 1965, 7 car manufacturers and 36 brands had survived.

The popularity of the automobile grew steadily. Seven thousand passenger cars were sold in 1901, 181,000 in 1910, and 1,905,560 in 1920. By the end of 1929 the number of cars sold in the United States exceeded 4,450,000 a year.

Another giant industry had to grow up to keep all those auto-mobiles rolling well. This was the rubber tire industry, and its pio-neers and progress were as striking as those of the automobile field.

Two far-sighted Frenchmen, André and Edouard Michelin, ignored the many pessimists who insisted that Dr. Dunlop's com-fortable new pneumatic tires might be excellent for bicycles but could not be used on motor vehicles. The pneumatics could not possibly hold the weight of a motor car, it was said. When the Michelin brothers couldn't get any automobile manufacturer to try their pneumatic tires, they purchased a car, equipped it with pneu-matics, and entered it in the Paris-Bordeaux Race in 1895. They had to use twenty-two inner tubes to reach the finish line, but they

1. Standard Oil Co. (N.J.)

Traffic jams—early variety, and today.

2. Ford Motor Company, Education Affairs.

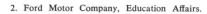

proved their point. Within three years most European car manufacturers had replaced solid tires with pneumatics.

The American automobile industry was full of doubters too. As late as 1907 an automotive trade magazine in the United States warned that automobiles could not be produced that weighed more than 3,000 pounds. "It is impossible to make pneumatic tires of any materials which will stand the strain," the magazine maintained.

American tire makers were not discouraged, though, and they convinced the American car manufacturers to shift to pneumatics.

Those early tire men were strong individuals, and daring. George T. Perkins of Akron, Ohio, was one. When Dr. Benjamin F. Goodrich wanted to establish a rubber factory in Akron in 1871 that would be the first rubber plant west of the Allegheny Mountains, Perkins aided in raising the money for him to do it. After Dr. Goodrich had to leave the area in 1880 for reasons of health, Perkins took over the management of the little B. F. Goodrich Company. Within ten years, he'd set Akron on the road to becoming the rubber capital of the world.

Doughty Frank A. Seiberling went into the tire business in 1896 and flopped. Undaunted, he and his family launched a new firm two years later which they named the Goodyear Tire & Rubber Company after Charles Goodyear, father of the vulcanization process. Defying all sorts of legal and financial pressure, the Seiberlings built Goodyear into one of America's industrial giants.

Third was an Ohio farm boy, Harvey S. Firestone. A short man, slim and agile, with shiny blue eyes, Firestone founded The Firestone Tire & Rubber Company in Akron in 1900 at the age of thirty-two. He began it with assets of $20,000 and his intention was to sell tires made by other firms. In three years he was making his own tires so he could control their quality. From one tiny plant in an abandoned foundry and a work force of twelve, his company was to mature into a concern with 88,000 employees, ninety-three plants in twenty-six countries, and sales topping $1,600,000,000 a year.

It was Harvey Firestone who developed the first low-pressure balloon tire in 1922—a remarkable innovation which used more air at about one-half the pressure that had been customary. The tire could, therefore, put more tread on the road at any moment inasmuch as it was softer and wider. It permitted automobiles to drive safely at much higher speeds on the bad, bumpy roads of the day.

Inventiveness was characteristic of the tire makers in the United States and Europe, as they kept pace with the automobile manufacturers. Faster, heavier cars demanded stronger, more heat resistant tires, and the tire makers produced them as needed. More and more of them. Some 2,400,000 a year in America in 1910; 37,400,000 a year in 1920; and over 51,600,000 a year in 1930. By 1966 the total was to top 148,000,000.

The revolution that had overtaken private transportation reached into the heart of popular life, rearranging it.

Instead of staying home all summer or renting a bungalow at the seashore for a week in July, people began to take advantage of their wheels to see America. As early as 1913 the *Motorist's Manual* of the Brooklyn *Daily Eagle* was fervently urging:

> It is difficult to imagine a more ideal way of spending a vacation than by touring through the country in an automobile. . . .
>
> Inns and cottages abound through the unfrequented sections, where food and lodging can be had at reasonable prices. . . . Now and then a mishap might occur and time must be taken for necessary repairs, but the memory of these fades when the vast amount of pleasure and experience that is gained is brought to mind. . . .

The rise of the suburbs was directly attributable to the automobile. During the 1920's building and population booms occurred on the outskirts of most major cities. The suburbanite no longer had to worry about proximity to trains, buses, or trolleys; his car would get him to and from his city job.

The impact on the industrial life was mountainous. By 1929 more than 23,100,000 cars were on the roads of the United States, one for every five Americans. The automobile industry was the biggest single customer for steel, rubber, plate glass, nickel, and dozens of other products. It consumed 15 percent of all the steel produced in the United States and was responsible for an enormous expansion of the oil industry. It had seeded countless other businesses.

If any question remained about the role the auto played in American life, it was answered in 1942. With the United States at war, studies were conducted to determine how much of a cut in passenger car use should be made. Of the approximately 28,000,000 cars in operation, America could spare 8,000,000, the experts decided. Less than 20,000,000, and America would have trouble getting to work, doing business, simply living.

The automotive industry helped immeasurably in the fight against Nazism. Back in 1940, for example, a group of automotive engineers visited Fort Benning, Georgia, to witness a demonstration of a small, four-wheel-drive vehicle designed and built by Captain Robert G. Howie. It was the jeep, and the automobile industry built them by the tens of thousands for the Armed Forces—and trucks and tanks and planes.

The final score showed that the automobile industry turned out over 55,000 tanks and armored cars and 2,400,000 military trucks in addition to 87 percent of all the aerial bombs, 85 percent of the steel helmets, and 75 percent of the airplane engines made in the United States.

Since World War II, the automobile march has continued unabated. As 1966 drew to a close more than 75,000,000 passenger cars dotted American roads, more than one car to every three people. Three out of every four American families owned at least one auto. In and around the big cities, the ratio was closer to one to one, and Los Angeles had more cars than families. Americans were driving over 2,000,000,000 miles each day.

The American automobile industry was breaking all records. Seven-and-a-half-million-car years were run-of-the-mill, and automobile men were predicting sales of more than 9,000,000 cars a year. The progress of the automobile was reflected across a wide spectrum of American enterprise. Thousands of drive-in theaters, drive-in banks, motels, shopping centers, and service stations, as well as the basic steel, rubber, and oil industries, were prospering.

It was a changed, more flexible automobile industry in the United States. Taking a leaf from the Europeans, it was manufacturing large numbers of compact cars that were small, neat and dextrous. A different type of man was running the industry: a broad-viewed managerial genius as distinguished from the rough-hewn inventor of yesteryear.

As a piece of machinery, the automobile had progressed prodigiously, too. Thirty miles an hour was hot speed for a gas buggy once. No more. During 1965, Craig Breedlove and Art Arfons, whizzing their jet-propelled racers across the Bonneville Salt Flats in Utah, were setting new world's land-speed records, in turn breaking each other's with speeds of more than 600 miles per hour. Jet automobiles those were, not jet planes. And no one doubted that these records had been made to be broken. Men would always want to go faster on wheels.

The automotive revolution came later to Europe, but when it did explode, the reverberations were loud.

The general view that the automobile was a luxury reserved for

1966 Cadillac CALAIS hardtop sedan.

General Motors Corporation.

the wealthy was long in passing. It was the late 1930's before the thought that automobiles were for everyone took hold in Europe. Then World War II prevented anyone from doing much about it.

Starting in the 1950's, it was a happier tale. Good, inexpensive cars became available, and with better economic conditions people had the money to buy them. Lots of them. The number of cars in the United Kingdom went from 5,000,000 to over 10,000,00 between 1954 and 1964. In 1956 France had 4,500,000 cars. In 1964 it had double that total. The Italian statistics were more dramatic yet, from 1,000,000 cars in 1956 to over 4,000,000 in 1964 plus 5,000,000 motor scooters.

Like the Americans, Europeans had come to think of automobiles as necessities to get to their work, to carry on their business, to travel their continent. Already one out of every ten Europeans owned an auto.

Elsewhere, the world was not so fortunate. People mostly had to move on foot, by animals, or by bicycles if move they did. The ratio was just one automobile to every 50 people in Peru, one to every 274 in Egypt. Among the Asians it was one to every 1,146 in Pakistan, one to every 3,084 in Red China. (In the Soviet Union, it was one to every 250.)

The automotive revolution that had swept the United States and Western Europe was bound to spread farther, though, and sooner rather than later. People had learned to want a better life for themselves and their children, and they knew that the automobile could drive them toward it. No other means of transportation had done so much for so many in so short a span of time.

IX

The Twentieth Century Unlimited

TRAVELERS OF THIS twentieth century have seen still other transportation wonderments. Road building, for instance.

At the outset of the century, only 141 of the 2,000,000 miles of roads in the United States were paved with any kind of hard surfacing. Some 150,000 other miles were classified as "improved," but in those days a road was labeled "improved" when most of the stumps had been pulled out and not much grass grew between the ruts.

The recorded experiences of motorists tell another portion of the story. On July 10, 1907, M. Worth Coldwell set out in his automobile along with eighty other cars on a driving tour from Cleveland to New York, via Toledo. The tourists got through the first day to Toledo all right, but that night it rained.

"The soft, pasty mud which that powdered dust made, was a study in physics and chemistry. . . ." Coldwell wrote in *The Outing Magazine*. "The roadbed itself was hard, and this covering of slime from a foot to two feet deep, made just the correct combination for fancy skidding. . . . The State road was full of great holes, the depth of which could not be ascertained until the car plunged right into them."

From Canton, Ohio, to Philadelphia, Coldwell said, the road was a series of road-wide bumps that had been built on purpose as water bars to steer rainwater off the roadway. They were nicknamed "thank-you-ma'ams," but they were nothing to be thankful for.

174

They stood 6 inches to 2 feet higher than the rest of the road, and they had to be crossed on the diagonal to save axles, springs, and tires. Some of the riders in rear seats were actually thrown out of their cars by "thank-you-ma'ams."

Only between Philadephia and New York were the roads paved. "The delightfully smooth macadam seemed too good to be true," Coldwell reported with a sigh of relief.

The American motorist was no man to accept conditions like these lying down, and a Good Roads movement was quick in gathering momentum led by such organizations as the newly born American Automobile Association, the National Grange, the National Association of Rural Letter Carriers and the Travelers Protective Association of America. Hundreds of local Good Roads groups joined in, from the Kennebunk Good Roads Association in Maine to the Contra Costa County Good Roads League in California.

By mid-1916 the campaign had achieved substantial results. President Woodrow Wilson signed the first Federal law to establish a countrywide system of interstate highways.

The construction gangs swung their pickaxes and in 1920 the United States could brag of 269,000 miles of surfaced road. As a wag pointed out, "It had taken self-propelled vehicles to bring it about, but at long last, America had roads as good as those of the ancient Roman empire."

One of the big problems was how best to build the roads to carry automobiles. All over the world, pneumatic tires were sucking the stones out of the macadam surfaces of those days, reducing them to the frightful shape of premacadam days. A new kind of surface was essential, something that would not be pulled apart by tires. And something that would eliminate the clouds of dust churned up by every car.

All sorts of things were tried in all sorts of places. The Scots paved a Glasgow street with rubber. In Geneva, New York, a road was made of steel. The State of Maryland built an attractive road of oyster shells, glistening white in the sunshine. Such surfaces were much too expensive, though, and not very practical.

Fortunately, some better ideas came along. The tiny principality of Monaco pioneered here. In 1902 it applied tar to an old-fashioned macadam road, a technique which turned out to be so successful that it was adopted universally. Other satisfactory solutions included the use of oil, asphalt, and Portland cement concrete. The first one-mile section of concrete rural road in the United States was laid on Woodward Avenue between Detroit and the Michigan State Fair Grounds. It was opened to traffic with due ceremony on the Fourth of July, 1909.

The Good Roads movement wasn't limited to the United States, by any means. As early as 1911 Canadian Good Roads enthusiasts were working for a transcontinental road to run from Halifax, Nova Scotia, to Alberni on Vancouver Island. Although Japan

MODERN ROADS:

1. Three-level highway intersection at West Englewood, N.J.

Standard Oil Co., (N.J.) photos.

2. *Los Angeles, Hollywood, and Airyo Seco Freeway*

3. *Harbor Freeway and Pasadena Freeway, looking north*

boasted an automobile population of less than 5,000 in 1919, it had a Good Roads movement. A similar movement was founded in China in 1921, and within five years an estimated 30,000 miles of Chinese roads had been built or improved.

The road builders were just getting going. Figures now can tell more of the story. By 1939 the United States had 1,063,000 miles of paved road; by 1950, 1,939,000 paved miles; by 1964, 2,730,-000 paved miles.

Some magnificent miles were included in these totals, like the famous Pennsylvania Turnpike whose first section was completed in 1940. This section was 160 miles long; it incorporated 7 tunnels and 288 bridges; and its construction necessitated the excavation of 66,406,586 cubic yards of rock and earth, the pouring of 10,419,-672 square yards of cement, and the use of 149,300 tons of steel. It has since been extended to a length of 360 miles, and dozens more expressways like it have been built throughout the United States. The Ohio Turnpike, for example, 241 miles across northern Ohio to Indiana. And the New York State Thruway, the longest toll road in the world: 559 miles from New York City via Buffalo, to the Pennsylvania State line.

After decades of hope, frustration, and incredibly hard work, a Pan American Highway System was open in 1966 for 7,700 miles, all the way from Fairbanks, Alaska, to Chepu, Panama, linking nine American nations. The noted journalist J. Frank Diggs drove over it as far as Panama City and found the road very exciting, what with 11,000-foot climbs, countless hairpin turns, fierce jaguars, and gun-toting bandits.

The road builders of other continents also were active. The Germans, in 1933, finished the first of their celebrated *Autobahnen,* a four-lane, divided highway running from Heidelberg to Frankfort. It was one of the very first high-speed roads in the world. The Italians built a 460-mile *Autostrada del Sole* from Milan to Naples that is among the world's great highways. This "Expressway of the Sun" covers the same route, for a while, as the historic old Via Flaminia. The Austrians constructed a road, the Gross Glockner Highway, which mounts to 7,433 feet and affords one of the most spectacular Alpine views imaginable. From one point, a motorist can see nineteen glaciers and thirty-seven Tyrolean peaks.

Of all nations, France has built the most roads in proportion to its population: 400,000 paved miles. Soviet Russia doesn't show up very well in this respect. For its vast territory, it had, according to a United Nations study, only 161,875 miles of paved roads in 1962. Japan is still worse off. At last report, it had merely 6,200 miles of paved road. Israel is the champion in the Middle East. It has built the most and the best roads. In 1958 it finished one 143-mile paved highway through unbelievably rugged desert land from Beersheba to the port of Elath on the Gulf of Aqaba that was truly an engineering coup. Because the road helps to connect the Mediterranean and the Red Sea, the Israelis refer to it fondly as their "Overland Suez Canal."

To advance all these new highways as well as the many new railways, the engineers have dug some superb new tunnels. Seven hard years of work went into it, but in 1906 the longest tunnel in the world was completed: the 12.06-mile-long Simplon railway tunnel under Monte Leone, between Brig, Switzerland, and Iselle, Italy. Forty-two men gave their lives to its construction, including two wealthy railway directors. (They collapsed from overwork.) Since then, such renowned tunnels have been dug as the 7.9-mile-long Cascade Tunnel in the state of Washington, the longest tunnel in the Western Hemisphere; the Holland and Lincoln Tunnels under the Hudson River to New York City; and, in 1964, the first automobile tunnel under the Alps, the 3.4-mile-long Great St. Bernard Tunnel between Cantine d'en Haute, Switzerland, and St. Rhemy, Italy. At the time it held the record of being the longest road tunnel in the world, but its championship didn't endure long. The very same year, the 7-mile-long Mont Blanc Tunnel under the Alps was opened.

That celebrated writer of wild-eyed science fiction, H. G. Wells, began a series of prophetic articles in 1901. The first was headlined, "Locomotion in the Twentieth Century," and in it Mr. Wells posed the rhetorical question, "In what direction are these new motor vehicles likely to develop?"

He answered himself with one of his more fantastic predictions,

MODERN   TUNNELS:

1. Entering the Tusca-
rora Mountain Tunnel,
Pennsylvania Turnpike

2. Lincoln Tunnel exit
at Midtown Manhattan

Standard Oil Co., (N.J.) photos.

"There will, first of all, be the motor truck for heavy traffic. . . . Sooner or later, no doubt the numerous advantages of such an arrangement will lead to the organization of large carrier companies using such motor trucks to carry goods in bulk or parcels on the high roads."

As usual, the imaginative Mr. Wells was proved to be quite right.

On May 20 and 21, 1903, the first American contest involving "commercial vehicles" was held in New York City. The eleven starters, comprising four gasoline-powered trucks, six steamers, and one electric, were expected to make two runs: the light trucks were to cover a forty-mile course, the heavy vehicles a thirty-mile route. The first route was to be as nonstop as the entrants could make it, and the second was intentionally full of starts and stops.

It was a vicious test, but truck drivers were as resourceful then as they are now. Going up a short, steep hill, one truck got stuck and its metal-tired wheels spun fruitlessly. The driver wasn't bothered. After several ineffectual runs at the slope, he simply swung the truck around and backed up the hill.

Though the two days were very warm for May, with temperatures in the blazing nineties, seven of the eleven starters managed to finish. Clanking and churning, they passed team after team of exhausted, resting horses.

The horse advocates fought tenaciously for their livelihoods, but the trucks couldn't be stopped. In March, 1911, the Saurer Motor Car Company sent the first across the continent. It started a truck with a seven-ton load and a four-man crew *west* from Denver. The truck needed sixty-six days to travel the 1,450 miles to San Francisco, but it made it. There it was put on a train for Colorado again. In Colorado, it took to the road once more, this time eastward.

It was June 12 when the truck departed from Colorado. On June 18 it arrived in Kansas City, Missouri, doing a 700-mile stretch in seventy hours' actual driving time despite an eight-hour halt because it crashed off a high wooden bridge. Several days more and it was in New York, "serving notice," as an historian put it, "that the freight motor carrier had grown in stature to economic importance."

Soon, trucks were making inroads into the province of four-footed hauling. The stamp of hoofs and the smell of hay began to disappear from firehouses and from the delivery departments of leading stores. By 1913 trucks were being used by progressive-minded meat packers, coal companies, brewers, contractors, furniture movers, and farmers. A Nebraska dairy farmer who used to employ four men and four horses to haul his milk to Omaha now did the job with one man and one truck.

The Great War gave trucking its biggest boost as soldiers traded in their wagons for lorries. At the Battle of Verdun, no less than 8,000 trucks were mobilized by the Allies to carry 190,000 troops and 22,000 tons of matériel to the front. In the United States, trucks eased the terrific pressure on the railroads. Thirty thousand trucks bound for eastern seaports and shipment to France were driven to the Atlantic coast instead of being carted by trains. En route they picked up food, guns, and other battle supplies destined for Europe. Encouraged by the Government, ordinary shippers turned to trucks, especially for short hauls.

Truck registrations zoomed. In 1910, 10,000 trucks were licensed in America. In 1919 the aggregate was up to 898,000.

But then the demand for trucking sagged to nothingness. The war was at an end, and nobody wanted any more trucks.

Convinced that trucking was vital to the economic well-being of

Modern trailer.

American trucking Associations.

the country, Harvey Firestone organized a national "Ship by Truck" movement that embraced parades, rallies, advertising, and the publication of hundreds of thousands of pamphlets designed to reawaken interest in trucks.

The backing of Chambers of Commerce, Boards of Trade, public officials, merchants, manufacturers, farmers, and truck dealers was enrolled in the campaign. Even the U.S. Army was enlisted. In the summer of 1919 the Army Transport Corps sent a convoy of sixty-five trucks and eight other vehicles from Washington, D.C., across the continent to San Francisco, no mean feat when one recalls the ghastly condition of the roads. Commanding the convoy was a Colonel Charles W. McClure. The second in command was a twenty-nine-year-old Regular Army lieutenant colonel named Dwight D. Eisenhower.

Mile by mile, the convoy was front page news. UNCLE SAM'S FLYING SQUADRON OF ARMY MOTORS RUMBLES THRU, headlined the La Porte (Indiana) *Daily Herald* on July 20, 1919. ARMY TRANSPORT CARAVAN PULLS OUT FOR COAST, the Chicago *Post* headlined on July 21. CITY GIVES MOTOR TRANSPORT TRAIN A SPLENDID RECEPTION, blared the Cedar Rapids (Iowa) *Daily Republican* on July 24. Said the subheads, "Dinner For Three Hundred and Fifty in Greene Square—Fried Chicken and Other Iowa Delicacies Make Military Men Forget Heat and Dust of the Day's Travel—Cedar Rapids Girls Danced With Them When Dinner Was Over." EPOCH MAKING CARAVAN WINS SUCCESS IN BATTLING ROADS ACROSS COUNTRY, reported the Salt Lake City *News* on August 16.

In spite of wrecked bridges and road washouts, the convoy reached California intact in sixty days.

Sparked by all the publicity, trucks grew popular anew. Registration started climbing again, to 2,500,000 in 1925, to 3,675,000 in 1930. Fearful of the competition, the railroads fought fiercely to choke off the spread of trucking through legislation restricting the size and usage of trucks. The effort was fruitless.

By 1965 there were more than 14,000,000 trucks rolling along American roads, and almost 21,000,000 more in other parts of the world, big and little, including trailer trucks, refrigerator trucks, dump trucks, tankers, trucks toting concrete mixers, as well as some sixteen-wheel trucks so big that they were utilized in England to deliver railroad locomotives.

Down on the farm it was a while before they felt the impact of the twentieth century.

Although many farmers shifted to mechanization, all they had to work with at the beginning of the century were absurd-looking steam traction engines mounted on wagons pulled by horses. A bit later, self-propelled steam traction engines became available, but they didn't represent much of an advance. They resembled antique railroad locomotives, and acted like them. Burning coal, wood, or straw, puffing out clouds of smoke and sparks, they crept along on wide, ribbed metal wheels, making loads of noise.

The first gasoline-fueled traction machines—perhaps half a dozen of them—were built in 1889 for farms in the northwestern United States, but they weren't much of a success. A pair of University of Wisconsin students, Charles W. Hart and Charles H. Parr, developed the first reasonably useful gas-burning machine in the infancy of this century. It was their firm which coined the word *tractor* to describe a gasoline traction engine. The Hart and Parr machine also had a hard time of it, though. As of 1910 scarcely 1,000 gasoline tractors of all makes had been sold in the United States.

Came the war, and with it an immediate demand for light, tough, inexpensive machines on the farm. That left the door open for Henry Ford.

Ford had been mulling over tractor ideas since his farm days, and began actively developing a tractor in 1907. By 1917 he had a model with which he was almost—but not quite—satisfied.

The British desperately needed tractors to help them cultivate new land for agriculture in their submarine-beleaguered islands, and they contracted with Ford at the end of June, 1917, for 6,000 of his tractors. He continued to tinker with them until autumn, however, and Britain's Lord Northcliffe finally hurried to Detroit to learn what was delaying delivery. Ford told him.

Never mind that, Lord Northcliffe entreated. "We can't wait for the perfect tractor, we need what's available. . . ."

Reluctantly, Ford agreed to ship them his tractors. By the following April, the original consignment of 6,000 had arrived in England—plus 1,000 extra. Two months afterward, Ford had American orders for more than 13,000, and the tractor was on the way to being a farm fixture.

It decreed the end of the 6,000-year supremacy of the four-footed farm animals. In 1920 there were 25,700,000 horses and mules on United States farms, and just 246,000 tractors. In 1963 there were 4,670,000 tractors, and the number of horses and mules had shrunk so low that the U.S. Department of Agriculture didn't census them any more.

Man's tractive power was growing in other directions. Road builders, construction crews, lumbermen, and others who had to work in roadless areas found a means of bringing their roads along with them.

The first tracklaying machines were built in the middle of the nineteenth century. By the start of the twentieth century—with the introduction of the Caterpillar tractor by inventor Benjamin Holt of California—they had achieved some utility. The combatants in World War I used the principle for tanks. These vehicles, initially called land ships, got their new names through chance when the British shipped them to battle in crates labeled "Tank" in order to fool German spies.

Now one sees tracked vehicles many places: waddling through Asian jungles carrying guns and soldiers; clearing Puerto Rican

Over rough terrain; the Canadair CL-91 DYNATRAC, a full-tracked, high mobility, utility carrier.

General Dynamics

slums to make room for the construction of fine housing projects; gnawing roads out of towering Andean mountainsides; snaking logs from German woodlands; crawling over trackless, snow-covered plains at the northern edge of Russia.

What was happening to the railroads all this while?

The years 1900–1966 watched railroad trains reach their heyday, and go into a sick decline—in the United States, at least.

Long-distance travel by train in the early years of the century had glamor. Trains were the fastest things on earth. The man at the throttle was an adventurer, a hero, and a little of his glory rubbed off on the passenger sitting snug in his seat, gazing out at the landscape whizzing by.

The railroads grew in mileage and munificence. By 1916 the United States had 254,037 miles of railroad. Many trains were luxury personified. They had library cars, barber shops, sleeping apartments done in brocade. When the crossword puzzle fad swept the country, the Baltimore & Ohio stocked all the trains on its main line with unabridged dictionaries. The dining cars rivaled the most elegant restaurants. The Louisville & Nashville served a pompano which would have been hailed at Antoine's, the Illinois Central had a shrimp creole that was nationally famous and the Southern Pacific had a chef named Bill Kurthy who could have graced the kitchens at the Waldorf-Astoria. In fact, he was trained there. He specialized in two-inch steaks. Nevada pheasants, Colorado brook trout, and whipped-cream desserts.

Some name trains became as famous as ocean liners. The New York Central's *Twentieth Century Limited,* which sped from New York to Chicago in twenty hours, the Pennsylvania's *Congressional Limited,* between New York and Washington, and the Santa Fe's *Chief* which toted movie stars by the carload from Chicago to Hollywood, were bywords for speed and opulence.

Mileage and magnificence were surging on European and Asian railways. The Russians completed the Trans-Siberian Railway clear to Vladivostok in 1903, neatly infiltrating northern Manchuria in the process. The Germans blithely embroiled half of Europe and most of the Middle East in near-war in their endeavors to grab off the concession for it, but they succeeded in building much of the

Baghdad Railway by 1911. World War I intervened and the rest of the 4,250-mile-long line was finished by other hands.

Historic trains like the *Orient Express*, the *Golden Arrow*, the *Blue Train*, the *Mistral*, settings for so many enthralling Hitchcock spy films, tore through the European and Asian landscapes with lush wagons-lits, mahogany-inlaid dining cars, and considerate continental service.

By 1900 some railroads were running on electricity rather than steam. A naturalized American, Nikola Tesla, a naturalized Englishman, Sir William Siemens, another Englishman by the name of Barlow, a Belgian, Zénobe Théophile Gramme, a German named Jacobi, and several other inventors helped to achieve the electric locomotive. The first of these worked on batteries. They didn't produce enough power so the inventors switched to overhead power lines and so-called third rails.

In most cities, the horse-car had to move aside for electrified trolleys. These trolleys were also used extensively outside of cities for short interurban trips. Ben Willens of Chicago even published an annual *Interurban Trolley Guide*. The 1915 issue informed its readers that it was possible to ride electric trolleys from Chicago to suburban Winnetka (17½ miles, 20 cents), to Amity, Indiana (289 miles, $5.35), to Chautauqua, Ohio (385 miles, $6.80), and to New York City ($19.62)—although the trolley traveler had to put up with a couple of brief rides on ordinary railroads.

The electrification of railroads made possible the spread of the subway to cities in all parts of the world. In America, New York, Chicago, and Philadelphia began studying subways. (Boston already had one.) As always, there was bitter-end opposition. Among other matters, it was charged in New York that the tunnels would be dangerous, unusable surely on foggy days.

"How," the critics demanded, "do you plan to keep fog out of the tunnels?"

The editor of *Engineering News* was so disturbed that he checked with both the Chief Engineer of the Boston Transit Commission and the General Manager of the Budapest Subway.

"I have been in the subway frequently, and have never noticed any fog," H. A. Carson answered reassuringly from Boston. "I beg leave to state," the Budapest executive replied, "that no fog has been observed in the tunnel of the Fr. Joseph's Underground Railway at Budapest even when fog prevailed on the surface."

The fog scare and other opposition to the subway in New York were overcome, and in 1904 nine miles of subway ran from New York's city hall north to 42nd Street and Lexington Avenue, west to Broadway, and north again to 145th Street and Lenox Avenue. Since then, the New York subway system has grown to 237 miles of track and 482 stations.

One after another, big cities went in for subways as the best solutions to their strangling problems of mass transit. London's was completed in 1863, and Glasgow and Budapest had them in operation before the end of the nineteenth century. The miraculously convenient Paris *métropolitain* opened in 1900, the Madrid subway in 1919, the Tokyo subway in 1927, the lavish Moscow subway with marble, mural-lined stations in 1935. Most recently, Canada completed its first subway in Toronto and started a second in Montreal, and Sweden installed a new subway system in Stockholm that was more decorative perhaps than Moscow's. One station, at Mariatorg, had a 470-square-yard wall made out of multi-colored stocks of ceramics. "To the commuter getting off his train," the *Scandinavian Times* reported, "it seems as if he has walked into a bamboo forest." In 1966 thirty-one cities in the world had subways in operation and under construction.

Regardless of the overpowering crushes, heat, dampness, and frequent tie-ups, subways have proven invaluable to metropolitan civilization. They have enabled urban industries to grow, have immensely enlarged the practical boundaries of cities, and have relieved city streets of unimaginable amounts of traffic.

The motor bus made its first appearance before the turn of the century, and within a very few years the horse was being laid off another job.

The Fifth Avenue Coach Company in New York City was typical. It tried out a double-decked thirty-four-passenger omnibus in 1905, and in 1908 the line was totally motorized. The bus companies of Greater London began the changeover in 1903. Inside of a decade, merely 142 horse-drawn buses were left to compete with 3,522 motor buses.

An early form of the urban bus was nicknamed "jitney." This was an automobile or a light truck driven by an enterprising young man who pulled up at trolley stops and offered anybody waiting there a ride for a "jitney," to wit, a nickel.

These jitneys pirated so much business that the indignant trolley magnates eventually got them outlawed from most North American streets. Not elsewhere. Thousands of jitney-types still offer cut-rate transportation in other lands. A common name for them in Latin America is *publicos*.

Initially, bus service in America and Europe was largely confined to small areas, usually a city or a town. This was for very understandable reasons. Beyond the towns, roads were so awful that no motor vehicle could run them regularly and survive.

However, the bus idea was much too valuable to be held back, roads or no roads. By 1909 two automobiles were covering the hundred miles between San Angelo and Big Spring, Texas, daily, carrying United States mail and passengers. Then, in 1912, a jobless miner named J. T. Hayes bought himself a secondhand Model T Ford and began driving people back and forth between San Diego and El Centro, California. He met his San Diego passengers in front of the Pickwick Theatre, so he called his little company Pickwick Stages. It was to become one of the biggest bus companies in America. In 1914 another miner, this one a Minnesotan named Carl Erie Wickman, went into the bus business. He'd put all his savings into a Hupmobile agency in Hibbing, Minnesota, and he'd been unable to sell his stock—one Hupmobile. So he made a bus out of it. He squeezed ten seats into the seven-seat touring car, and inaugurated a schedule of hourly trips from a saloon in Hibbing to the firehouse in the town of Alice, four miles away. A one-way trip cost fifteen cents, a round-trip twenty-five cents. This Wickman operation was also to grow into one of America's largest bus companies.

Riding a bus in Minnesota, or driving one, was not an unadulterated joy in those days. According to one bus company history, "In fierce weather the truck-chassis buses bucked and skidded, became mired in mud and snow, and iced by sleet. Drivers were equipped with light block and tackle and snow shovels. They provided passengers with lap robes and hot bricks for their feet.

Women viewed the trip as an extreme hazard. In fact, the woman passenger was a rarity."

Rough though bus travel was, new companies kept being hatched all around the country. In 1925 more than 6,500 bus companies were operating 7,800 different routes in the United States. Some of them were wild and woolly one-man shows with names like the Jack Rabbit Lines, the White Swan, the Tiger, and the Golden Eagle, but there were a lot of solid citizens among them and they made strides. By 1928 sleeper coaches were running at night, and transcontinental service had been introduced by Pickwick Stages. By 1930 the mammoth Greyhound Corporation, the first great consolidated bus system, had been established (absorbing, among others, the Wickman lines and Pickwick Stages), and soon thousands of its buses were streaking around the nation.

It was almost unbelievable how quickly bus transportation caught the public favor. By 1940 intercity lines were driving 188,-000 route-miles a year and carrying 380,000,000 passengers. By 1960 they were covering 238,000 route-miles and transporting 460,000,000 passengers, 35 percent more than the railroads.

Abroad, motor buses had captured foreign hearts also, stunning buses that had hostesses, "winecellars," and bars.

The railroads made progress for a while, too. After decades and decades of work, a powerful new kind of internal combustion engine, invented in 1892 by the mustachioed French engineer Dr. Rudolf Diesel, was brought down to a size useful for locomotives. That was in 1925, and nine years later a Diesel electric locomotive was hitched to the head of a new kind of passenger train, a streamliner, carefully designed to reduce wind resistance.

The first streamliner in America was the Union Pacific's *M-10,000*, and it debuted in February, 1934. Just two months after, the Chicago, Burlington & Quincy Railroad got a streamliner of its own, the *Zephyr,* and married a Diesel to it which dashed the 1,015 miles from Denver to Chicago in a shred over thirteen hours. The following October the Union Pacific did the Chicago, Burlington & Quincy one better as its Diesel-electric streamliner the *M-10,001* sped the 3,258 miles between Los Angeles and New York in fifty-six hours, fifty-five minutes, the fastest transcontinental passenger run made to that date by a single train, and ever since.

New posh comforts came in: "Vista-Dome" trains, two-deckers, roomettes, shower baths, air conditioning, radios, train telephones, movies.

Sad to state, they were largely in vain. Rail mileage shrank, from the 254,037 miles of 1916 to 216,440 in 1961; civilian passenger traffic sagged even more from 47,460,000,000 passenger miles in 1920 down to 18,300,000,000 in 1964. By 1958 passenger service wasn't available on 52 percent of the United States rail network. Railroad revenues were down from $10,200,000,000 a year in 1950 to $9,700,000,000 in 1964.

For a hundred years, the railroads had been "the coming thing," the challenger to existing modes of transport, never the challenged. Then came along the popular-priced automobile, the truck, the bus, the airplane, taking away the cream of the passenger business and much of the freight. To their horror, the railroads found that they were overbuilt for the automotive-aviation age. They tried manfully to keep their heads above water by cutting back on unprofitable runs while improving their long-haul service. They thought up many galvanic innovations: automated freight yards with remote-control switching devices; radar, television, and electronic computers; microwave radio communications; continuous welded rails as long as a mile; tri-level freight cars that could transport fifteen automobiles at a crack. They offered "piggyback" service to truckers allowing them to roll their loaded trailer trucks straight onto railroad cars for high-speed shipment to distant terminal points.

But, at best, it was a holding operation. Comparing percentages of traffic, American railroads handled 62.4 percent of all intercity freight traffic in 1939. In 1962 they had merely 43 percent; and their share of intercity passenger traffic was down to 2.29 percent, scarcely a third of what it was in 1950.

The outlook was happier on foreign railroads. French railroads carried an average of 12,700,000 freight tons a month in 1950. In 1960 they moved a monthly average of 18,900,000 tons. For West Germany, the contrasting figures were 19,400,000 tons for 1950 and 24,900,000 tons in 1960. Japan's totals went up from 9,700,-

000 tons in 1950 to 15,500,000, and Canada from 11,900,000, to 13,300,000. Rail passenger traffic was doing equally well overseas. The rail systems of Czechoslovakia, East Germany, West Germany, Hungary, Italy, Poland, the Soviet Union, and the United Kingdom *each* carried more passengers than all the railroads in the United States did in 1960. West Germany, the U.S.S.R., and the United Kingdom prided themselves that one year on carrying more than a billion rail passengers apiece.

Rail travel abroad grew increasingly comfortable and rapid. The *Mistral* zipped between Paris and Dijon, 195.2 miles, in 142 minutes. The *Sud Express* made the 359.8-mile-long run between Paris and Bordeaux nonstop at better than seventy-five miles an hour both ways. And those were nothing alongside the *New Tokaido Hitachi Superexpress* which went into operation in Japan late in 1965. It streaked from Tokyo to Osaka at an average speed of 103 miles an hour, 320 miles in 190 minutes including two stops at Kyoto and Nagoyo. That was faster than total airline time.

Best of all, glamor continued to surround foreign train travel. Riding the *Rheingold Express* through the lovely Rhine Valley of West Germany to Basel, Switzerland, afforded 450 miles of beautiful scenery, comfort, and efficiency. There was a multilingual stenographer aboard, at $1.50 an hour. It could be an unforgettable journey, traveling the Trans-Siberian Railway from Vladivostok to Moscow. A British journalist who made the trip in 1964 reported that he was overwhelmed by the friendliness of his fellow-passengers, the excellent service of the train personnel, and the food. A normal lunch consisted of borsch, steak, fried potatoes, eggs, tomato and cucumber salad, thick slabs of black and white bread, Russian cheeses, and no end of vodka, *peever* (beer), wines, and sweet champagne. Going on the Lima-Huancaya express in Peru could leave you gasping. The train climbed to an altitude of 15,685 feet, and, of necessity, was equipped with free oxygen. And the Kaohsiung-Taipei express in Formosa was a novel experience in punctuality and courtesy. If the train was so much as two minutes late on the ten-hour trip, the engineer lost face, and he used the train public address system to proffer his sincere apologies to the passengers for any inconvenience he might have caused them.

One of the oldest forms of transportation known to men came into its enormous own in the twentieth century—the pipeline.

Nearly 3,000 years ago, in 940 B.C., you will remember, the Chinese drilled wells and piped natural gas to salt plants through hollow bamboo poles. They utilized the gas to dehydrate brine, and they do it yet. These same pipelines are still in operation in China. Until the last century, however, pipes were used to carry little else but water in other parts of the world.

In 1821 the good citizens of Fredonia, New York, spotted gas seeping from the sides of Canadaway Creek. A shrewd group, they dug down 27 feet to tap the gas and ran it to their homes through a pipeline made of little hollow logs. They burned the gas to illuminate their homes. That was the first modern pipeline.

Samuel Van Syckel of Titusville, Pennsylvania, built the first commercial pipeline in 1865 to transport oil from the newly discovered oil fields around Titusville to a railhead five miles away. Teamsters had been charging four dollars a barrel to haul the oil out by wagon, and Van Syckel lowered the price with his pipeline to one dollar a barrel.

It must be said that Van Syckel and the other pipeline pioneers had to keep their guns at the ready. The angry teamsters cut the lines and set fire to the terminal tanks, and the railroads were as ugly. They employed thugs to rip up pipelines, barred pipelines from traversing their rights of way, and used their vast political influences with state legislatures to obstruct pipelines.

Nonetheless, a 60-mile-long pipeline from the oil fields reached Pittsburgh in 1875, and by 1879 pipelines were passing state boundaries.

The real spread of the pipelines came in the 1920's. The pipeline men took advantage of the development of electric welding and stronger steel to construct huge leakproof pipelines, hundreds of miles long, to carry natural gas and oil. By 1940, 117,000 miles of pipeline stretched across the country. Actually, the democracies might have lost World War II if it had not been for pipelines. When the ravages of the Nazi U-boats threatened to paralyze the Allied war effort because of a shortage of oil, pipeliners built the famous "Big Inch" and "Little Big Inch" pipelines in record-breaking time to move oil from the Southwest to defense plants and war ports in the East. By 1966 close to 500,000 miles of pipeline gridded the United States, and they were handling over 250,000,000,000 ton-miles of intercity freight. Outside of the United States, pipelines were also reaching in all directions. One giant pipeline stretched across Arabia from the Persian Gulf to the Mediterranean. Another extended 2,290 miles from the boundary between Alberta and Saskatchewan down across nearly two-thirds of the width of Canada to the city of Montreal, and the Russians were building the biggest pipeline in history—40 inches in diameter.

A lot more than natural gas and oil was flowing through pipelines. Copper, cement, nickel, sugar cane stalks, perfume, whiskey, milk, catsup, orange juice, maple syrup, and brewed tea were some of the substances going places by pipeline.

One wonderment of transportation rarely gets the credit due it. In one recent year, it is estimated, it safely carried 28 billion people 500,000,000 vertical miles. It is, of course, the elevator.

For 2,000 years, people had been concocting hoists of one sort or another, but they all had one unpleasant drawback. When the hoisting cable broke—as often it did—they crashed precipitously to the bottom. Then a forty-six-year-old Vermonter, Elisha Graves Otis, invented a hoist in 1852 that was different. It had an automatic safety device to keep the car from falling.

To prove its worth, he rode on top of the car at the Crystal Palace Exposition in New York City in 1854 and cut the cable. It didn't fall. Said the *Daily Tribune* on May 30, 1854, "We allude to an elevator, or machine for hoisting goods, which attracts attention both by its prominent position and the apparent daring of the inventor, who, as he rides up and down upon the platform occasionally cuts the rope by which it is supported."

The first of Otis' elevators was for freight alone. On March 22, 1857, he built the first passenger elevator. It was installed in a New York department store, had a speed of 40 feet a minute, and cost all of three hundred dollars. Architects were finally emancipated. They didn't have to hold their designs for hotels and stores down to four stories any more.

In 1900 the first moving staircase was put to public use at the Paris Exposition. An escalator, it was called.

Between them, elevators and escalators have broken all records for mass transportation on land.

X

The Seas Around Us

ON THE OCEANS, the twentieth century started out uglily.

Inward bound for New York through a blanket of dirty fog, the British liner, *Republic,* was stabbed amidships by another liner, the *Florida,* in the early morning hours of January 23, 1909. It was the *Republic's* death. Within minutes she was settling to the bottom of the Atlantic. Only the new miracle of Dr. Guglielmo Marconi's wireless kept the death toll to six. Three years and six weeks later, on March 5, 1912, the Spanish steamer, *Principe de Asturias,* hit a rock off Sebastien Point. This time no miracle helped and 500 persons were drowned.

Blacker hours were to follow. On the night of April 14, 1912, the biggest, newest ship in the world was racing westward through calm Atlantic seas on her maiden voyage. She had 2,207 festive people aboard.

All day her radio had been bringing messages about icebergs and pack ice near her path, but her officers were not much concerned. It was far south of the area where ice was normally seen in April. Besides, this was the *Titanic,* the ship that "God himself could not sink," as a Southampton dock hand had bragged before she sailed. She had a double bottom, and fifteen watertight bulkheads that divided her 880-foot length into sixteen compartments which could be sealed shut instantly by a man on the bridge. Her designers claimed that any two of her compartments could be completely

196

flooded and the *Titanic* would still float. Every one of the first four compartment's could be flooded and the *Titanic* would not founder, they said.

Between seven and nine o'clock that night the temperature of the ocean dropped sharply, from 43 degrees to 33 degrees. At ten-thirty, it fell further, to 31 degrees, below freezing.

No one on the bridge cared enough to reduce speed. The *Titanic* charged on at 22½ knots.

To the west, a small Boston-bound liner, the *Californian*, had to stop all her engines; her way was totally blocked by ice. The *Californian*'s wireless operator, Cyril Evans, began to tap out a message to that effect at eleven o'clock that night, but John Phillips, the wireless operator on the *Titanic*, irritably told him to keep quiet. Phillips was trying to get off a string of routine messages to a wireless station at Cape Race, Newfoundland.

Ten minutes later, a lookout in the *Titanic*'s crow's-nest spied a shape in the water dead ahead. Iceberg!

On the bridge, First Officer William Murdoch heard the clanging of the crow's-nest bell and picked up the phone. White-faced, he closed the watertight bulkheads, rang the engine room for full speed astern, and ordered the wheel spun hard to turn the *Titanic*'s prow to the left.

A 66,000-ton ship, making 22½ knots, cannot stop on a dime. Or turn. For the men on the bridge it is a truly terrible feeling. One has done everything possible to avoid an impending collision and yet the ship does not respond with anything like the urgency of her masters. Yard by yard, the *Titanic* ate up the distance between her

The TITANIC.

Wide World Photos.

and the iceberg, at the equivalent of the length of a football field every eight seconds.

When the iceberg was 100 yards ahead, the bow of the *Titanic* at last began to swing slowly left. Too slowly. The starboard side of the ship scraped the mammoth iceberg and below the waterline the jagged tines of ice peeled back the hull plating of five compartments and a portion of a sixth. Through the gaping rip, the seas poured.

The *Titanic* was done for, and at 12:15 A.M. Phillips was belatedly ordered to send out the distress call. "C-Q-D M-G-Y . . . C-Q-D M-G-Y . . ." Help. Help. *Titanic.*

Fifty-eight miles to the southeast, the steamer *Carpathia* wheeled and headed for the disaster. Her captain, Arthur H. Rostron, ordered the chief engineer to squeeze every bit of speed out of her old power plant. He even had the ship's heat and hot water systems shut off. He was almost four hours away, though.

The *Titanic*'s best hope was the *Californian*. She was lying only ten miles away. But the *Californian* didn't answer. Her wireless operator had turned in for the night, and a ship's officer made no attempt to investigate the distress flares that the dying *Titanic* was firing into the night skies.

At 12:45 A.M., Phillip's assistant suggested that they stop using C-Q-D and try the new code signal for help that had just been settled upon by an international convention. So Phillips tapped out the more easily recognized three dots, three dashes, three dots—S-O-S—the first one ever sent. They hoped that it might raise the nearby ship whose lights could be dimly seen from the *Titantic*'s bridge. It didn't.

At 2:20 A.M., the *Titanic* could struggle no more. The unsinkable ship sank into the Atlantic, taking with her some of the most illustrious citizens of the United States: John Jacob Astor, Benjamin Guggenheim, George and Harry Widener, Mr. and Mrs. Isidor Straus. Mrs. Straus wouldn't go into a lifeboat without her husband. "We have been living together for many years," she said. "Where you go, I go."

The ship had sixteen wooden lifeboats and four collapsible canvas boats that could hold at most 1,178 of the 2,207 passengers. More distressing yet, because of the utter confusion on the part of both passengers and crew (no boat drill had been held) many of the boats shoved off half full. The *Carpathia*, which arrived on the scene at 4 A.M., was able to save just 705 people. Some 1,572 of the *Titanic*'s passengers froze to death or died by drowning.

It was the worst disaster at sea in the peacetime history of man.

There were more horrors to come on water in this century, but they were to be outweighed by the luminous attainments of the shipwrights, the sailors, the canal diggers, the bridgebuilders and the many others concerned with transportation on, under, and over the earth's waters. Ships were to become bigger, more lushly comfortable, and much safer. Despite hot and cold wars, the merchant marine of the world was to grow amazingly in numbers and efficiency and was to strengthen mightily the maritime trade links between nations. A most formidable canal was to be completed, along with some of history's most memorable bridges.

The *Titanic* tragedy made shipbuilders and sailors sadder but wiser men. The first International Maritime Conference for Safety of Life at Sea was held in London in 1913 and 1914, and from then on all vessels were required by law to carry enough lifeboats for their passengers. Around-the-clock manning of passenger ship radios was instituted, and a common procedure evolved for all ships to follow after they received a distress call. An International Ice Patrol was created to locate and keep track of icebergs in the shipping lanes. As a result, the United States Coast Guard today patrols 45,000 square miles of the North Atlantic.

Many celebrated steamships were built as Great Britain, France, Germany, Italy, the United States, and other maritime powers jousted for supremacy on the rich Atlantic passenger run. Each ship was built to be more palatial than the others, with new accouterments like cabarets, sidewalk cafes, shops, stock brokerage offices, cinema theaters, tennis courts, outdoor and indoor swimming pools, dog kennels. And each ship was designed to be faster than the others.

First, and for long the greatest of all, was Britain's dashing, four funneled, 32,000-ton *Mauretania*. She was launched back in 1906 but it was almost a quarter of a century before any other ship could equal her record of four days, ten hours, forty-one minutes from Queenstown to New York. "The vessel with the proudest record in the whole history of the Atlantic service," the knowledgeable maritime historian H. P. Spratt rated her.

The Germans won the Blue Riband, symbol of the fastest crossing time, from the *Mauretania* with the *Bremen* in 1929. Rapidly, the title passed to her sister ship *Europa*, to the Italian *Rex*, next to the French *Normandie*—the first ship built longer than 1,000 feet and the first to cross in less than four days. Then in 1938 Britain's majestic *Queen Mary* lowered the time to three days, twenty hours, forty-two minutes. That record stood for fourteen years.

So much stress was placed on speed by the various shipping lines in the 1920's and 1930's that the ocean acquired a new nickname. Passengers who would have preferred a little less speed when the seas ran rough began to style it the "Frantic Atlantic."

Some fine innovations were achieved during this period that made ocean travel pleasanter, and surer. One piece of equipment, the stabilizer, did the near-impossible. It kept ships from rolling violently in stormy weather.

A very important discovery was sonar, a form of echo-ranging, done by bouncing electronic impulses off the sea bottom or off objects in the water. The United States Navy and the British Navy helped to develop sonar. As early as 1923 the U.S. Navy was experimenting with it. Over the years, sonar got to be quite accurate in calculating ocean depths, spotting uncharted reefs, detecting enemy submarines, tracing whales, and listening in on schools of whistling shrimp.

What with two devastating world wars that were fought in bloody part at sea, the century has witnessed some immense changes in naval mores.

In 1906 the British set a new fashion in battleships that lasted four decades. They launched a floating fortress that was bigger, faster, and packed more firepower than any ship before. Displacing 17,900 heavily armored tons, it could do twenty-one knots and carried ten 12-inch guns that could hurl 950-pound shells for many miles. An entire new class of battleships drew its name from hers: the *Dreadnought*.

Every big navy built itself some *Dreadnought* types and a fierce battle was fought with them by the British and Germans off the Norwegian coast, at Jutland, in May, 1916. It ended in a draw.

Germany set a new naval style during World War I by developing a flotilla of Diesel-powered submarines (U-boats) and turning them loose for unrestricted warfare upon Allied and neutral shipping. These submarines proved one of the most deadly of naval weapons, sinking 5,708 ships. In World War II, they were almost the deciding factor. Axis submarines sunk 23,350,000 gross tons of shipping, and came perilously near to starving the British Isles to death.

A still greater change in naval warfare was to occur in World War II. It was the emergence of the aircraft carrier as the backbone of most navies and the writing of *finis* to 5,000 years of naval predominance by the battleships.

The carrier made her first appearance in World War I when the British converted an old 22,000-ton ocean liner, the *Campania,* into a carrier as an experiment in 1916. Two years later, they remade the cruiser *Furious* into another one. The first American flattop was the *Langley,* commissioned in 1922. By the outbreak of World War II, every navy, with the exception of the Germans and the Italians, had large contingents of these floating airdromes.

Practically without exception, the "battleship admirals" fought to maintain the starring role of their battlewagons. History was against them; the battleship was too vulnerable. The British lost the *Royal Oak* to a Nazi U-boat; the *Repulse* and the *Prince of Wales* to Japanese planes. The Germans had the giant *Bismarck* and four other battleships sunk, crippled, or trapped. The United States had almost all its Pacific fleet wiped out by Japanese carrier planes at Pearl Harbor, and the Japanese, in turn, had virtually their entire battleship fleet sunk by United States planes and submarines—and the rest of their navy as well.

Air power became supreme at sea. At the crucial Battle of the Coral Sea in May, 1942, not one American or Japanese warship saw an enemy vessel. All the fighting was done by carrier planes. That was the first time such a thing had ever happened, and no navy man missed its meaning. Afterward, battleships were good only for a supporting role in sea fighting, if that much.

Since the war, carriers have become goliath in size. The U.S.

The carrier, USS FORRESTAL, launched in 1954.

Navy's *Forrestal*-type supercarriers displace 60,000 tons and can launch thirty-two fighting planes in four minutes. And this is small stuff by comparison with a newer U.S. Navy carrier, the *Enterprise*. She is 1,253 feet long, displaces 85,000 tons, has a crew of 4,600 sailors and airmen, and can carry 100 planes.

One result of World War II was more constructive—the perfection of radar, a splendid system of transmitting short radio waves so that they hit an object in the air, or water, or out in space, and send back echoes which can be readily computed to determine the object's precise location. The pioneer research on this idea was done by the U.S. Army scientists at Fort Monmouth, New Jersey, but a brilliant Britisher, Professor Robert Watson-Watts, perfected it. More than any other invention, it helped the Royal Air Force drive off the Luftwaffe during the Nazi blitz of London in the fall of 1940. Beyond that, it quickly showed itself to be a remarkable aid to marine and aeronautical navigation.

This, too, should be recorded of radar. It made the first contact between the earth and its satellite, the moon, in 1946.

The smell of gunpowder had scarcely faded out of the salt air before shipwrights and seamen were at it to move people and cargoes across the oceans.

Americans again entered the transatlantic sweepstakes, and for the first time in one hundred years, won it. In 1952 a sparkling new American liner, the 51,821-ton *United States,* headed eastward from New York to Bishop Rock Light, off England's Scilly Isles, 3,144 nautical miles away, on her maiden voyage, and got there in three days, ten hours, forty minutes. She swung about and won a second Blue Riband by racing back to New York in three days, twelve hours, twelve minutes. As of 1966, no other ship had equalled either of her records.

The shipping lines piled luxury upon luxury. The giant *Queen Mary* and her sister ship *Queen Elizabeth* had Turkish baths, gymnasiums, beauty salons, nurseries for the children, first-run movies, as much caviar as one desired, and nine English secretaries for conscientious executives who'd brought along their briefcases. The *United States* was air conditioned throughout, had several heated swimming pools, a night club with Broadway entertainers, and dictating machines as well as live secretaries for the hard-working businessmen.

A dinner menu on the posh P & O liner *Canberra* included such fare as Indian curries (chicken, beef, lamb, and fish) with the correct accompaniments of chutney, popadams, and Bombay duck; Scottish salmon; Australian lobster; New Zealand mutton; a Welsh goat cheese called *Caerphilly;* fresh mangoes, papaya, and other Pacific island fruits. For breakfast, the *Canberra* served poached smoked haddock, pan-fried calves' liver and "a small steak with *bubble* and *squeak."*

Even the dogs of passengers were treated regally. On the exquisite, 66,000-ton French liner *France* dogs were put up in separate, wall-to-wall-carpeted compartments behind the captain's cabin, and had three different exercise rings for sniffing, comingling, and exchanging gossip.

Naturally, the canine passengers got a new printed menu daily. A sample one read: *"Le Plat de Tayant (Consommé de Boeuf— Toasts—Légumes); Le Régal de Sweeney (Carottes—Viande Hachée—Épinards—Toasts); La Gâtene "France" (Haricots Verts—Poulet Haché—Riz Nature Arrosé de Jus de Viande et de*

Biscottes en Poudre); La Préférence du Danois (Os de Cote de Boeuf, de Jambon et de Veau): Le Régime Végétarien des Dogs (sic). (Tous les Légumes Frais et Toutes les Pâtes Alimentaires.) Biscuit—Ken'l."

Despite all these sybaritic pleasures, the great ocean liners began to have their difficulties in the 1950's attracting passengers of the human variety. Yearly, the faster airlines took more passengers away from the seagoing liners, particularly after the development of jet planes which could whisk a person from New York to London in six hours. In 1956 the steamship lines operating in the North Atlantic sailed 740,000 passengers from the United States to Europe, and the airlines flew over 692,000. By the end of 1957, air traffic had surpassed sea traffic, and in the mid-1960's it was three times as much.

The big liners had to go into the cruise business to offset the loss of the transatlantic passenger trade. This was no new idea, to be sure, among shipping men. Britain's venerable P & O (Peninsular and Oriental Steam Navigation Company) was running holiday cruises in the 1840's. It invited William Makepeace Thackeray to sail on a cruise free in 1844, and on his return he gratefully wrote a book about it, *From Cornhill to Cairo*. In the roaring 1920's, cruises were very popular with thirsty Americans anxious to escape the arid regions of Prohibition. But it took the post World War II passenger dropoff to switch the really big liners from their devotion to the North Atlantic run. In 1957 the shipping lines had an income of about $55,000,000 from cruise business. By 1965 that figure was nearer to $125,000,000.

Ship owners were hoping for a recovery on the North Atlantic passenger run, though. They believed that travelers always would want to smell salt in the air and feel the invigorating sting of ocean spray. They were so optimistic that they were wagering hundreds of millions of dollars on their faith in seagoing ships. The Italians, alone, launched two luxury 43,000-ton superliners, the *Michelangelo* and the *Raffaelo*, in 1963.

In the freight field, nothing altered the hoary superiority of ships for moving substantial cargoes across water. Since World War II, the world fleet of merchant ships has virtually doubled in tonnage, from 70,000,000 gross tons in 1945 to more than 132,000,000

THREE MODERN
SUPERLINERS:

1. QUEEN
   ELIZABETH

2. QUEEN MARY

3. LEONARDO
   DA VINCI

1. Cunard Line
2. Cunard Line
3. Italian Line

gross tons in 1963. That year, 17,861 seagoing ships were plying the five oceans. They had a lifting capacity of over 185,000,000 deadweight tons.

On one typical day, June 30, 1962, according to a report in *Life* magazine, 6,392 passenger ships, freighters, and tramp steamers involved in intercontinental trade were at sea. The figure did not include coastal or most intracontinental trade, nor did it include tankers, which on that day made up more than a third of the tonnage afloat and en route. "The vessels of some eighty nations," *Life* reported, "carry a billion tons of goods every year" on the shipping lanes of the world.

The most surprising fact about the postwar growth of merchant shipping was the development of gigantic tankers to transport oil. Before the war, a tanker with a deadweight capacity of 16,000 tons was considered large. In 1966, a 150,000-ton tanker was at sea, and a 205,000-ton tanker was under construction in Japan.

One new United States tanker, the *Manhattan*, could carry 910,000 barrels of oil. She was so big that she couldn't dock in most ports. Oil centers were digging deeper harbors to accommodate the likes of her.

The United States had the largest merchant fleet, but it was far from being a leader in shipbuilding anymore. At one time during World War II, United States shipyards were turning out five ships a day. In 1965 American shipyards had orders for only sixty-four commercial ships totaling 368,200 gross tons, and the United States was in tenth place on the roster of shipbuilding nations, far behind its chief World War II adversaries. Japan with 5,363,000 gross tons abuilding led the world, and Swedish shipbuilders were at work on 1,170,000 tons to put Sweden in second place, some 97,000 tons ahead of the United Kingdom. Two-thirds of United States trade was carried in United States ships during 1946; at last report, a mere 10.5 percent of American trade was sailing in vessels flying the American flag.

To counter the adverse trend, American shipbuilders had come up with some excellent innovations in freight ships—speed, for one, in the traditionally slow-sailing cargo arena. A new United States freighter, the *American Challenger,* could cross the North Atlantic in less than five days. And with her triple hatches and multiple cranes, she could handle cargo at an unprecedented rate. She even had eight individual, temperature-controlled liquid cargo tanks in her hold.

Several big U.S. tankers had been converted into "piggyback" service. They each could carry nearly 500 truck trailers, loaded down with freight. At the port of debarkation, the trailers were derricked onto truck chassis, and away they rolled with a substantial saving in unloading time. The Japanese were doing something like this too, but with loaded barges. These were floated into the freighter's hull and the water pumped out. At the destination, the hull was filled again, and the barges deftly hauled out and away by tugs.

The nautical story would be incomplete without a mention of the popularity that yachts and motor boats suddenly won after World War II. Although pleasure boating harks back to antiquity, the sailing yacht is much newer. King Charles II of England introduced it; he had twenty-six *jachts* (as the Dutch called them) which he sailed and raced for fun. The first motor boat designed as a pleasure craft probably was the one invented by an American, F. W. Ofeldt, in 1885. It had a two-horsepower engine that worked on naphtha. The notable automobile inventor, Gottlieb Daimler, was motor-boat-minded. He demonstrated a boat with a one-horsepower gasoline engine, at Kannstatt, Würtemberg, in 1887. The first outboard motor, called the *Motogodille* for some strange reason, made its debut in France in 1902. Seven years later the American Ole Evinrude produced his outboard. The first race for motorboats was held in 1903 at Queenstown, Ireland, and the winning speed was all of 19.53 miles per hour. In 1959 Donald Campbell of Britain set a jet speedboat record of 260.35 miles per hour. At one point, he was roaring along at 275.12 miles per hour.

It used to be said that only the very rich could afford yachts. The United States Census reported 2,811,000 outboard motors in use in 1950. In 1963 there were 6,390,000. Boating in all its forms had become one of the ten most popular outdoor sports in America, almost twice as popular as horseback riding, and more than five times more popular than outdoor concerts and drama.

Nor would the nautical story be fully told without a sadder note. Shrewd as men are as sailors and shipwrights, the sea continues a

Draconian foe, ready to take its toll in corpses. It was so on January 27, 1949, when the Chinese liner *Taiping* collided with a collier, and both sank, drowning 600 people; on September 17 of that same year when the Canadian Great Lakes cruise ship *Noronic* caught fire, killing 130; on August 1, 1953, when the French *Monique* disappeared, with 120 passengers in the South Pacific; on July 25, 1956, when the beautiful, new Italian liner *Andrea Doria* collided with the Swedish liner *Stockholm* and sank off Nantucket Island, 52 dying that night; and it was true on April 10, 1963, when the U.S. Navy submarine *Thresher,* with 123 men aboard, dived deep into the Atlantic and never came up. And it was tragically true again on November 13, 1965, when the cruise ship *Yarmouth* burned between Miami and Nassau with a death toll of 89.

Not that men stopped for a minute building ships and taking them to sea.

Nor did danger and hardship halt men from widening their seas by linking them with sturdy artificial waterways.

The Panama Canal was an example. The United States' interest in a canal across the Isthmus of Panama between the Atlantic and Pacific Oceans went back a long way. As far back as 1825, Secretary of State Henry Clay sent a message to an Inter-American Conference held under the aegis of the illustrious Simón Bolívar, recommending that thought be given to an isthmian canal which would be of benefit to all nations.

In 1903, fourteen years after Ferdinand De Lesseps and his pathetic, corrupt associates went bankrupt trying to dig a sea level canal across the Isthmus of Panama, the United States government acted. The Republic of Panama seceded from Colombia in a pleasant revolution that cost the lives of one man and one mule, and the dynamic President Teddy Roosevelt recognized the new nation within seventy-five minutes. He agreed to guarantee Panama's independence, to pay it $10,000,000 at once, and $250,000 a year *ad infinitum* in return for which the Panamanians promised to grant the United States "in perpetuity all the rights, powers and authority" over a 10-mile-wide strip of their isthmus. (The United States raised the rent to $1,930,000 a year in 1955, and was preparing to lift it again in 1966.)

Few construction jobs have been as frustrating. One hundred million cubic yards of earth had to be hacked out of jungles, wild rivers and the unstable mountainsides of the Continental Divide. There were poisonous snakes, tarantulas, and crocodiles to contend with, plus rain and steaming heat. The yellow fever, malaria, and dysentery that struck down 50,000 of De Lesseps' workers were waiting.

In ten years the job was done at an expenditure of $366,000,000. Two men largely did it: Colonel William Crawford Gorgas, a resourceful U.S. Army doctor who eliminated the mosquitoes and the yellow fever they spread, and a U.S. Army engineering wizard, Major George Washington Goethals, who let no obstacle interposed by nature or man slow his progress. He lifted the canal by water steps 85 feet above the level of the Atlantic, and took it down again by other water steps to the Pacific. He dammed the treacherous Chagres River and made a cut 9 miles long—the Culebra Cut—through the Continental Divide.

This Culebra Cut was the meanest enemy. One October night in 1907 a landslide dumped 500,000 cubic yards of earth and rock in the diggers' way there. In January, 1913, a whole mountainside—the *Cucaracha* (the Cockroach)—fell into the canal, 2,500,000 cubic yards of earth to move.

But Goethals finished the "Big Ditch" ahead of schedule, 50 miles long, 110 feet wide, 41 feet deep, with twelve sets of locks. On August 15, 1914, the canal was declared officially open as a decrepit French cement carrier, the *Ancon,* steamed through in less than ten hours.

More than 11,800 ships with 64,000,000 tons of cargo made use of this one canal in the year 1964.

The busiest canal in the world, Germany's Kiel Canal, was opened in 1914, too. A ship enters it every eight minutes. The Netherlands' Amsterdam-Rhine Canal was completed in 1952, and the St. Lawrence Seaway, from Montreal to Duluth, Minnesota, a 2,400-mile combination of canal, river, and Great Lakes waters, went into full operation in 1961. It was built jointly by the United States and Canada.

A modern bridge: Taconic State Parkway over Croton Reservoir, N. Y.

Incidentally, inland canals and other waterways continued to be a prime transportation medium. In 1963, 235,000,000,000 ton-miles of intercity freight were moved on inland waterways in the United States. That was more than 16 percent of the international total, and in Europe inland waterways were as popular. In 1961 nineteen European nations, ranging from Austria to Yugoslavia, moved 246,292,000 tons of freight on their inland waterways.

The bridge builders also outdid themselves in this century. They spanned the Baltic Sea, the wide Derwent River in Australia, the St. Lawrence near Quebec, the Straits of Mackinac in Michigan, the Hudson River in New York.

The kind of superdifficulties they had to overcome can be shown by just one project: the construction of the Golden Gate Bridge over San Francisco Bay, for almost three decades the longest suspension bridge in the world.

One of the two piers which were to support the 4,200-foot span had to be built more than 1,000 feet from the shore, in 90 feet of water, on a spot beset by fog, high winds, four fearsome tides a day, ground swells, and underwater surges that were akin to submarine tidal waves.

In one of San Francisco's pea-soup fogs, a freighter plowed into the trestle that had been built to the site of the pier and tore a 300-foot gash in it. No sooner was this repaired than a storm carried away another 800 feet of the trestle. An enormous steel caisson that was to hold the pier had to be abandoned. The ground swell tossed it around like a chip of wood.

It was no use, people said to Charles Swigert, the pier contractor. The job just couldn't be done.

"Can't be done?", old Charley Swigert snorted. "Heck, I haven't even started trying yet."

He went ahead and built the pier regardless of the fogs, tides, winds, and all else. (The job took its toll, though. When the Golden Gate Bridge was dedicated on May 27, 1937, Swigert was not there to see it. His heart had given out.)

A suspension bridge larger than the Golden Gate was completed in 1964: the Verrazano-Narrows Bridge between Brooklyn and Staten Island, New York. The longest suspension bridge in the world, with a channel span of 4,260 feet, its two decks carried twelve lanes of motor traffic high over New York Harbor.

Down the East Coast a bit, a project was finished in 1964 that rivaled the Verrazano Bridge for magnificence and greatly exceeded it in length: a 17.6-mile-long bridge-causeway-tunnel complex across the entrance to Chesapeake Bay.

A bridge and causeway arrangement might have been built the entire distance from Cape Charles to the Virginia Beach-Norfolk area except for one thing. The U.S. Navy with its large installation at Hampton Roads did not relish the prospect of a bombed-out bridge someday possibly blocking the Navy's way to and from the Atlantic.

The engineers obligingly hyphenated the overwater road. Twice

USS NAUTILUS goes to sea—Jan. 17, 1965, powered by the first atomic engine ever to propel a ship.

Westinghouse photo.

it dips down under the channels into mile-long tunnels—tunnels prefabricated on land, towed in sections to the proper spots, and sunk into place; tunnels that have their entrances and exits on islands the builders made themselves.

So while the cars are going over the ships in New York Harbor, the ships are going over the cars in Chesapeake Bay.

For thousands of years, all the seas heard were the creaking of oars and the rattle-snap of full sails. Then, in the last century, arrived in short order wonderful new sources of power: steam, electricity, internal combustion by gasoline, and, early in this century, the Diesel engine. But something greater, stronger, better by far than any of these, still was coming.

On September 30, 1954, a terse radio message was transmitted by a brand-new U.S. Navy submarine, *Nautilus*. "UNDERWAY ON NUCLEAR POWER," it said. The atomic age had reached transportation.

A determined little band of men in the U.S. Navy's Bureau of Ships, under the driving leadership of Admiral Hyman George

The 6,900-ton ETHAN ALLEN, the first Polaris-firing nuclear submarine designed as such.

General Dynamics.

Rickover who had beaten back all kinds of opposition in and out of the Navy—produced the *Nautilus*. It was not only the first seagoing craft powered by the atom, but also the first true submarine. With its nuclear reactor, it did not need to surface for months at a time. One United States submarine, the *Triton*, circumnavigated the earth entirely submerged in 1960, following the 30,708-mile-long path of Magellan's sixteenth-century voyage.

By 1966 many nuclear-powered submarines were in operation as well as a nuclear-powered aircraft carrier, the *Enterprise*, and a guided missile cruiser, *Long Beach*. Happier news was that ships were powered by the atom for peaceful purposes. The Soviets had a 16,000-ton nuclear ice-breaker, the *Lenin*, which could grind a path through ice 8 feet thick at two knots, and the United States had built the world's first nuclear-powered merchant ship, the 22,000-ton *Savannah*. She made her first transatlantic crossing with sixty passengers in the summer of 1964, and a good time reportedly was had by all.

The atom was working well at sea.

XI

"If I Had Wings, Like Noah's Dove..."

FROM HIS VERY FIRST DAYS, man envied the birds that flew above him. Then it came to pass that the birds had cause to envy man.

The dreams men dreamed ages ago of unshackling themselves from the earth can be discerned in their ancient legends. Almost always their deities could fly. "Therewith grey-eyed Athene departed in the semblance of a sea-eagle. . . ." Homer wrote. Or he lyrically told how she "bound beneath her feet her lovely golden sandals, that . . . bore her alike over the wet sea and over the limitless land, swift as the breath of the wind."

Man himself could fly on occasion. Daedalus, so went another Greek myth, made wings of feathers, wax, and thread for himself and his son Icarus, in order that they might escape the wrath of King Minos of Crete. It was a sad voyage to freedom. Vainly, Daedalus cautioned the boy not to fly too close to the sun. Exultant over gaining the power of flight, Icarus soared higher, higher, higher, until the heat of the sun melted the wax in his new wings. They disintegrated and he plunged into the sea. Daedalus alone achieved safety.

Kai Kawaus, a Persian king, it was written, had a carriage built with cornerposts fabricated of spears. Hunks of meat were impaled on the spears, just out of the reach of four young eagles that were harnessed to the frame. As the eagles beat upward in their futile attempts to seize the meat, the carriage rose after them into the sky.

In Japan, so the story goes, a bold bandit named Ishikawa sought to steal a pair of solid gold fishes from a temple tower by having himself flown over its minarets on a bamboo kite.

Yet these legends long remained merely legends.

Century trailed century in antiquity, and flying continued in the province of birds, gods, angels, and myths.

Science only began to approach flying in the thirteenth century. The "Admirable Doctor," that English philosopher and man of all sciences, Roger Bacon, seriously wrote of "instruments to flye withall, so that one sitting in the middle of the Instrument, and turning about an Engine, by which the wings being artificially composed may beate the ayre after the manner of a flying bird." He definitely foresaw the possibilities of balloons. He proposed filling a large globe of thin copper sheet with rarified air or "liquid fire." This was to be launched from some high place, like the top of a mountain, and would "float like a vessel on water."

Even then it was the sixteenth century before anyone is absolutely known to have tried to fly. He was the Italian mathematician Giovanni Batista Danti. In January of 1503 he carried a glider of some sort up the tower of a church in Perugia and attempted to fly off the ramparts. The machine fouled on the building and crashed to the roof, Danti suffering a broken leg.

The most versatile of all men—painter beyond compare, sculptor, architect, engineer, and scientist—Italy's Leonardo da Vinci, tried to fly shortly after.

Leonardo was obsessed by birds. He spent hours, days, watching them, and he maintained that "A bird is an instrument working according to mathematical law which instrument it is within the capacity of man to reproduce with all its movements." He designed several ornithopters (wing-flapping machines), as well as a species of a helicopter, a practical parachute, and a lifejacket for a flier downed in water. By 1505 or 1506 he was ready to try his hand at flying. He apparently settled on a bat-winged ornithopter for the venture, and he chose Swan Mountain in Tuscany for the place. Exuberantly, he wrote in his notebook, "From the mountain that bears the name of the great bird, the famous bird will take its flight and fill the world with its great fame."

That was all, though. Leonardo never referred to the subject again. The son of a friend wrote, many years after, "Leonardo da Vinci . . . tried to fly, but he, too, failed," adding dryly, "He was a magnificent painter."

For nearly three more centuries, most of the men who dreamed about flying and tried to figure out how to do it used or copied birds. Flapping wings was the rage. Either the aeronaut was theoretically hauled into space by a flock of well-trained birds, or flapped his own wings, or rode in a machine that utilized flapping wings.

Some scientists were on the right track. The Italian physicist Giovanni Alfonso Borelli pointed out in 1680 that while the weight of the muscles a bird used for flight equaled about one-sixth of its total poundage, man could call upon a far smaller percentage of his bulk to flap his mechanical wings. If man were going to fly, Borelli concluded in a notable thesis, *De Motu Animalium,* it would not be that way.

But men continued to build wings and to flap them. As late as 1742 the Marquis de Bacqueville jumped from a riverside Paris building, hoping to soar across the Seine and land in glory in the Tuileries. Instead, he fell in a heap on a washerwoman's barge.

Two brilliant French brothers straightened out the world's thinking and got it flying. Forty-two-year-old Joseph Montgolfier and thirty-seven-year-old Étienne were papermakers in the small town of Annonay, near Lyon, but they were more interested in studying the nature of air than in manufacturing paper. One November day in 1782 in Avignon, Joseph had an inspiration. Smoke rises, he said to himself. So, why not . . .

He asked his landlady for a scrap of silk, cut it, and sewed it into an oblong bag. Crouched over his fireplace, he held the bag mouth-down to catch the smoke from the fire. It began to swell. When it looked full, he took it away from the fire and let go of it. It shot to the ceiling, startling his landlady and exciting him.

"Prepare promptly a supply of taffeta and ropes, and you will see one of the most astonishing things in the world!", he immediately wrote to his brother at Annonay.

The Montgolfiers were careful scientific workers. They were hot on the trail of a discovery that they knew would make them world-famous, yet they took their time. Their first outdoor experiment, made secretly, was a success. A balloon rose 70 feet before it settled down to earth. But they made two more private tests anyway, with bigger aerostats and thicker smoke. They seemed to have felt that the denser the smoke in the bag, the better its levitating properties. (They believed that a mysterious, unknown gas was raising their balloons; they never did realize that it was the hotter, more rarified air that was lifting the bags.) Eventually, they settled on burning a mixture of straw and chopped wool, and in their third, unpublicized test the balloon ascended 1,000 feet and drifted a good mile before coming down again. That was proof enough, the Montgolfiers felt at last, to warrant a public demonstration.

The people of Annonay were gathered in the marketplace on June 4, 1783, and they saw a great linen-and-paper bag rise 6,000 feet after it had been filled with smoke.

Startled, the Academy of Sciences invited the Montgolfiers to exhibit their invention in Paris. The demonstration was so successful that King Louis XVI and Queen Marie Antoinette commanded a royal performance at Versailles on September 19, 1783. Thrilled, the brothers Montgolfier determined to try something extra. For the ascension at Versailles, they attached a basket to their balloon and loaded it with the world's first aerial passengers: a rooster, a duck, and a sheep.

After a one and a half mile flight, the trio of animal aeronauts landed dizzy but unharmed.

Man would be next.

Meanwhile, the filling of balloons was being studied from a different angle. Back in 1766 an English scientist, Henry Cavendish, had sent a paper to the Royal Society on the subject of *factitious air,* air that was made chemically in the laboratory. He had discovered that by mixing acids and certain metals he could concoct something he called "inflammable air" which was much lighter than natural air. Hydrogen, it is called now.

An Italian, Tiberius Cavallo, tried to use this gas for getting off the ground, but he gave up in disgust. He couldn't make any container light enough to rise when full of hydrogen and still nonporous enough to keep the gas from escaping.

However, a French physicist, J. A. C. Charles, was acquainted with a couple of brothers, Anne-Jean and M.-N. Robert, who had a process for coating silk with rubber that they hoped would hold in the hydrogen. He got them to make him a "flying globe," 13 feet in diameter, that he filled with the "inflammable air" and, late in the afternoon of August 27, 1783, he sent up the world's first hydrogen balloon in front of an excited crowd of 50,000 Parisians who had been waiting in the rain all day.

In the crowd was the American diplomat, Ben Franklin. As the balloon rose through the drizzle, a French Army officer turned to him and remarked, "Interesting. But of what use is it?"

"What use," Franklin replied succinctly, "is a newborn baby?"

Less than a year after Joseph Montgolfier's fireside experiment, a young French doctor named Jean-François Pilâtre de Rozier became the first man in the history of the world to fly. The King had wanted to assign two condemned criminals to this dangerous task, but it caused an uproar. Was the honor of France to ride with two convicts? Was the glory of the first balloon ascent to go to two criminals? Pilâtre de Rozier was the leader in this opposition, and when the King graciously backed down, he was awarded the mission.

Twice Pilâtre de Rozier made ascents in a Montgolfier-type hot-air balloon that was tethered securely to the ground. Then on November 21, 1783, he and the Marquis d'Arlandes, a French infantry major, made man's first balloon flight.

The balloon used for the occasion looked like a gaudy, upside-down Christmas tree ball. Seventy feet high and 46 feet in diameter, it was embroidered all over in gold, and it carried its smoke-making source with it, on a grate suspended beneath the open neck.

Pilâtre de Rozier and the Marquis d'Arlandes took off in it from the gardens of La Muette outside of Paris. What a flight they had! The Marquis d'Arlandes wrote afterward:

I was surprised at the silence and the absence of movement which our departure caused among the spectators, and believed them to be astonished and perhaps awed at the strange spectacle; they might well have reassured themselves. I was still gazing when M. Rozier cried to me—

"You are doing nothing, and the balloon is scarcely rising a fathom."

"Pardon me," I answered, as I placed a bundle of straw upon the fire and slightly stirred it. Then I turned quickly, but already we had passed out of sight of La Muette.

Suddenly, the Marquis discovered that sparks from the fire were burning holes in the ropes that held the balloon. More alarming, sparks were burning the balloon itself. Hastily, he sponged the bottom of the balloon and the ropes with water.

After a five-mile ride the balloonists headed for a landing. Wrote the Marquis:

As soon as we came near the earth I raised myself over the gallery, and leaning there with my two hands, I felt the balloon pressing softly against my head. I pushed it back, and leaped down to the ground. Looking around . . . I was astonished to find [the balloon] . . . quite empty and flattened. On looking for Rozier I saw him in his shirt sleeves creeping from under the mass of canvas that had fallen over him.

The age of flight had been born.

Ten days later, J. A. C. Charles and the younger Robert brother made the first hydrogen balloon ascent from the Gardens of the Tuileries. Four hundred thousand Parisians shouted, *"Vive le Roi!"* as the pair took off on a flight that lasted more than two hours and covered twenty-seven miles to the village of Nesle.

"Mon cher ami," Charles reveled, "how happy we are . . . the sky belongs to us! What a breathtaking scene!"

Charles was so happy that he went up again, alone, the same afternoon, attaining the giddy altitude of 9,000 feet. It made him the first person to see two sunsets in a single day.

These two flights did it. Europe became balloon wild. Everyone thought, talked, dreamed, balloons. They were woven into tablecloths, painted on fans, used as clock designs. Hairdressers modeled ladies' coiffeurs on them. And everyone who could went up in a balloon. Women, too. A Mme. Thimble was the first woman to fly, in France, in June 1784, declaiming poetry as she did. An Italian, Vicenzo Lunardi, was the first man to fly in England, in September, 1784, and a Mrs. L. A. Sage, became the first woman to fly there, in 1785. She was a rather Junoesque belle who weighed approximately 200 pounds.

Then as now there were airmen frightened of nothing, ready to try anything. Scarcely a year after Charles' first flight, the English Channel was crossed in a hydrogen balloon by a daring French-man, Jean-Pierre François Blanchard, and Dr. John Jeffries, his English sponsor. They had a hair-raising trip from Dover, England, to France during which they had to throw almost everything they had overboard to lighten the load, including a bottle of old brandy and Blanchard's trousers, but they landed safely in a clearing near Calais.

That was in January, 1785, and in June the gallant Pilâtre de Rozier attempted to fly the channel. It was his last flight.

Rashly, he decided to combine the virtues of the hydrogen bal-loon and the hot-air balloon in a single machine; the two types would be used in tandem, the hydrogen-filled sphere on top. Too late he realized that this was begging for trouble; a spark from the fire heating the lower balloon could set off the inflammable hydro-gen in the balloon above it. But his pride and reputation were at stake, and he began his ascension from Boulogne on June 15 with the builder of the balloon, Pierre Romain, as a passenger.

In half an hour, the hydrogen balloon exploded and both men were killed, the first recorded deaths in an aviation accident.

The daring, and money-minded, Blanchard was the first man to fly in the United States. He went up from the prison yard of the Walnut Street Jail in Philadelphia at ten minutes past ten on the morning of January 9, 1793, first selling one hundred two-dollar and five-dollar tickets to the public. President George Washington was among those who came. After a forty-six-minute flight, M. Blanchard descended fifteen miles away near Woodbury, New Jersey, with his co-passenger, a small black dog.

Some of the deeds of these early aeronauts were extraordinary. One Englishman, Charles Green, made over 500 ascensions and took up thousands of people without a mishap. In 1836 he made the first long crosscountry (and crosswater) flight, from London to Weilburg, Germany, in a beautiful red-and-white-striped balloon, 480 miles in eighteen hours. Two other Englishmen, Henry Coxwell and James Glaisher, reputedly got up 37,000 feet in a balloon. The French aeronaut, Eugène Godard, performed such phenomenal feats that the name *Godard* became a synonym for balloon in France.

Of course, ballooning was not always the most comfortable activity. When the winds were rough, aeronauts had their problems. William Lloyd Garrison's newspaper the *Liberator* bore witness to that in a news dispatch on January 31, 1835:

> Mr. Elliot, the Aeronaut, has attempted to make an ascension in New-Orleans, but the wind proved to be too strong. After seating himself in his balloon, and cutting loose, he was swept violently across the arena, knocking down several persons in his passage. The balloon next encountered a chimney top, which was overthrown by the concussion, and Mr. Elliot's thigh was broken. Part of the bricks of the chimney falling into the car, prevented the balloon from rising higher, and it was afterwards dragged over house tops and walls, and dashed against windows, till the aeronaut's hands, face and head, were shockingly cut and mangled. At length the cords of the balloon became entangled on the masts of two vessels in the river, and fortunately for Mr. Elliot, his farther flight was checked. In his passage over the buildings in the city, some of the cords by which the car was attached to the balloon, were sundered, and the aeronaut afterwards sailed with his head nearly downwards.

Control of a balloon, making it *dirigible* or directable, was a concern of the aeronauts from the very first. Some people proposed to equip balloons with various combinations of oars, paddlewheels, trained eagles, and sails. It was soon seen that the two things primarily needed to give the aeronaut control over his balloon were a more easily directed shape and a mechanical source of power.

The shape he could have. A French physicist, M.-J. Brisson, suggested a cigar-shaped balloon in 1784 and that summer M.-N. Robert built one. A Dr. Solomon Andrews of Perth Amboy, New Jersey, even developed an elongated balloon in the 1860's that could fly against the wind *without power*. The United States gov-

ernment was disinterested, and Dr. Andrews' company went bankrupt despite an astonishing number of successful flights.

The main problem was the mechanical source of power. All
known types were tested. In 1852 the famous French balloonist,
Henri Giffard, built a 132-foot, cigar-shaped dirigible with a three-
horsepower steam engine hung beneath it that turned a propeller. If
the winds were not too bad, it could do six miles per hour and steer
a little. In 1883 Gaston Tissandier, also a Frenchman, constructed
a dirigible with an electric engine that flew some and steered some,
too.

Alas, the steam engine and the electric motor were both too
heavy for any real use. Dirigibility had to wait for the internal
combustion engine.

Not that balloons weren't useful in their own way during this
period. Professor Thaddeus S. C. Lowe of New Hampshire persuaded President Abraham Lincoln to authorize a balloon corps for
the Union Army in the Civil War and captive balloons were used to
observe Confederate positions in Virginia for about two years before the Union Army brass hats lost interest in them.

When the Prussian Army besieged Paris for four months in the
Franco-Prussian War of 1870–71, the French government and
the Paris citizenry kept in contact with unoccupied France by send-
ing men, mail, and passenger pigeons soaring over the enemy lines
in balloons to friendly territory fifty-five miles northwest of the
capital. The passenger pigeons returned to Paris with messages
from the unoccupied areas.

Fifty-eight of the sixty-six balloons that attempted the flight made
it. Six were captured by the Prussians and two drifted out to sea.
Considering that these balloonists had to depend upon a favoring
wind to blow them to safety and that many of them took off at
night, their record was nothing short of incredible.

One American balloonist, John Wise, had bigger aspirations.
Twice he tried to cross the Atlantic by balloon. His latter and better
attempt was in 1873 when he crashed forty miles from New York.

Some deep thinking and high experimentation on heavier-than-
air-flights were going on by now, and their outcome was to alter the
dimensions of the world.

The man who really started this was a marvelously brainy York-shireman by the name of George Cayley. Sir George Cayley, he became. As a child he experimented with paper balloons; as a teen-ager, he built a toy helicopter; in his twenties, he did pioneering research on the nature of air, air pressure, and the importance of wing angles. It was he who discovered that shaping an airplane's wings into a shallow V increased its stability. And in 1809, at the age of thirty-five, he published a scientific paper that laid the basis for all present-day aerodynamics. "The whole problem," he saw, "is confined within these limits, *viz.*—to make a surface support a given weight by the application of power to the resistance of the air."

Cayley built the first true steerable glider. "It was very beauti-ful," he said, "to see this noble white *bird* sail majestically from the top of a hill to any given point of the plain below it, according to the set of its rudder. . . ." That was in 1804, and during the next half-century he built many more gliders: monoplanes, biplanes, and triplanes. He constructed a glider in 1849 that was so big that it carried a ten-year-old boy "off the ground for several yards." He built one in 1854 that was as large as a World War II fighter craft, and he cajoled his unwilling coachman into going up for a flight in it.

"Please, Sir George," the frightened servant said after he'd flown across a little valley. "I wish to give notice. I was hired to drive and not to fly."

Cayley himself never gave notice. To the end of his four score and seven years, he thought, researched, and invented things aero-nautical that had enormous influence in the aviation field.

Before Cayley died, one of his countrymen, William Samuel Henson, was working out an idea of his for a powered, fixed-wing airplane. He designed a mammoth monoplane with a 150-foot wing span that was to have a twenty-five-horsepower steam engine and two 20-foot pusher propellers, inset close to the fuselage in the trailing edge of each wing. It was a remarkably prophetic design and with the help of a mechanic, John Stringfellow, Henson built a 20-foot model of it.

A tremendous amount of publicity was given to the machine and to Henson's plans for organizing an "Aerial Steam Transit Company" to fly it all over the world on set airlanes. Not enough was known about building such an aircraft to enable it to withstand the stresses of flight, though. The model proved too weak to fly in 1847, and Henson was so humiliated that he gave up the project. He married and went to the United States where he vanished into anonymity. Stringfellow got a smaller model with a midget-sized steam engine to fly the following year. It went 120 feet. Not far enough to impress anyone, so "finding nothing but pecuniary loss and little honour," Stringfellow quit, too.

The effort to fly divided itself into two approaches: one was to develop a power plant capable of driving a lifting surface through the air; the second was to develop a strong, stable craft that could glide through the air under the control of a man before any worrying was done about an engine to push it along.

Into the first class fell a young French genius, Alphonse Pénaud, who carried further Cayley's research. Pénaud showed that there were two other prime problems to flight in addition to air resistance: the resistance of the plane itself, and the need for a light engine. In 1870 he invented the twisted rubber band motor for powering model planes and built a little model plane, the *Planophore,* that flew 180 feet, proving beyond question the feasibility of sustained flight.

Pénaud's masterpiece was a design he made in 1876 for a superb amphibian plane with the first joy stick, the first retractable landing gear, and the first glass cockpit canopy. It was never built. The appropriate engine could never be gotten to power it, and Pénaud received a disgraceful amount of ridicule. So much so that he stored away all his papers in a small coffin and, at the age of thirty, killed himself with a bullet through his handsome head.

Clément Ader of France was another in this group. He claimed to have flown his steam-driven, bat-winged plane, *Éole,* for 164 feet in 1890. The French Army took him seriously enough to help him build two more planes but neither was successful.

Britain's noted Sir Hiram Maxim, the man who invented the machine gun, was another power proponent. And a most impressive one who did big things in a very big way.

Sir Hiram commenced by designing a pair of steam engines that would turn propellers. Next he figured out the weight of the water and fuel that would have to be carried. Then he estimated the amount of lifting area needed to get all this load, plus pilot, passengers, and its own weight, into the air. Thereafter he drew up plans for an enormous craft called the *Multiplane* that had a wing area of 4,000 square feet, had a 360-horsepower steam engine, and weighed four tons.

Maxim put his machine on a half-mile stretch of railroad track at his fashionable estate in Kent, and rigged the track in such a way that the craft could go no higher than one inch above the rails. He gunned the monster's engines and down the track it went, picking up speed rapidly. It began to rise, ripping away the restraining gear. Deliberately, Sir Hiram shut off the power and his creation crashed.

It was the only test Maxim made of the machine. As far as he was concerned he had proven that flight was possible. Other people could worry about the details.

In the United States, a distinguished scientist named Samuel Pierpont Langley was at work on power. Langley, a Massachusetts boy who never went beyond high school, had risen to be Secretary of the Smithsonian Institution in Washington, D.C. Late in his life, he became interested in aviation, made laboratory tests on lifting surfaces and air resistance, and in 1891 published the results in *Experiments in Aerodynamics*. He went on to build model aircraft, and in 1896 he built a steam-driven model plane that flew three-quarters of a mile over the Potomac River. It was a remarkable achievement. In September, 1903, he was ready to try out a full-scale machine, this one with a gasoline engine developed by Charles M. Manly. Manly was to be the pilot.

The plane was set up on a catapult on a barge in the middle of the Potomac. With numerous reporters looking on, the engine was revved up, turning the two propellers at a rate of 1,000 revolutions per minute, and the signal was given to release the catapult.

What happened next has been a source of controversy. Some agree with Langley that the plane fouled on the catapult. Others say that the craft was too lightly constructed to fly, and collapsed under the sudden stress. In any event, it is certain that the machine plunged off the end of the barge into the river.

Manly was rescued, wet but unhurt, and three months later, on December 8, 1903, Langley tried anew. Again the plane was torn

Wilbur Wright in his 1902 glider. The motor came later.

Original Wright Brothers aeroplane of 1903.

apart by an undetermined force and dove ignominiously into the water. Langley, a fine scientist, became the laughingstock of the country, a tragic fate he did not deserve.

The great pioneers of the glider group were Jean-Marie Le Bris of France, Otto Lilienthal of Germany, Percy Pilcher of Scotland, and Octave Chanute of the United States.

Using the albatross as a model, Le Bris built a glider with graceful, down-curved wings that measured 50 feet from tip to tip. When he was ready to test his craft in 1855, it was placed on a farm cart hauled by a horse. Le Bris gave the go-ahead, and the driver urged the horse forward into the wind. As the cart picked up speed, Le

Bris twisted the wings of the glider to catch the air, and the glider rose to a height of 300 feet. After he had flown about 200 yards, Le Bris noticed that the driver of the cart had become tangled in a rope trailing from the glider and was swinging, terrified, beneath him. Very carefully Le Bris descended until the man was securely on the ground again. Then he safely landed his glider.

Subsequent tests by Le Bris were not so felicitous. He broke a leg and wrecked the glider. A second machine cracked up, too. He never flew again as well as he did the first time.

Following years of study, research, and writing on the subject of flight, Lilienthal began making gliders in 1891 and flying them from a 50-foot, cone-shaped hill he'd built himself so that he could take off into the wind regardless of what direction it was blowing. He used a monoplane to start, with his head and shoulders protruding above the wings and the lower part of his body dangling below them to provide equilibrium. He controlled the glider simply by moving his weight around. He was forty-three years old at the time.

He quickly became the topmost glider pilot of all the world. Between 1891 and 1896 he made more than 2,000 glider flights off roof edges and hillslopes, and attained such skill that he could make turns in the air though he had no rudder, and could zoom up to altitudes higher than his launching site. He was the idol of fliers everywhere, and he inspired countless others to try flying.

His dream was to learn everything there was to know about the art of flying to help prepare man for powered flight when it came. At last in 1896 he felt that he'd advanced sufficiently to try powered flying, and he fitted out a glider with a small internal combustion engine.

He never got to fly it. While the machine was being completed, he lost control of another glider and crashed down to his death.

In Britain, Pilcher, an ardent and successful follower of Lilienthal, was on the verge of attaching a motor to a glider in 1899 when he was fatally injured in a gliding accident.

The American, Chanute, was best known for his experiments with stabilizing devices for gliders, and for his splendid history *Progress in Flying*, published in 1894, that collected in one volume all the known facts about aviation. It was an aviation milestone. A kindly, warm-hearted man, Chanute was the mentor of the American aviation world. Newcomers to the field turned to him for advice and he was generous in giving it.

It was to Chanute that a thirty-three-year-old Ohioan who was interested both in the gliding and the power aspects of aviation went for counsel in 1900. In May of that year, Chanute received a letter that said,

"For some years I have been afflicted with the belief that flight is possible to man. . . ."

The letter was signed "Wilbur Wright."

Wilbur Wright and his younger brother Orville were the sons of Bishop Milton Wright of the United Brethren Church. Neither of them had much formal education or scientific background, but each had a magnificent imagination, a brilliant engineering mind, patience, and full integrity, enough so that they were able to do what no other man ever had been able to do before—make a piloted flight in a powered airplane.

When Wilbur was eleven and Orville seven, their father gave them a toy helicopter, and that did it. The two become aviation devotees who went in succession from toy helicopters to kites to gliders.

They began their experiment with gliders openmindedly. In writing to the Smithsonian Institution in 1899 to ask for a list of aeronautical books, Wilbur said that he planned to "devote what time I can spare from my regular business"—a little bicycle manufacturing and repair shop that his brother and he operated in Dayton, Ohio—and added characteristically, "I am an enthusiast, but not a crank in the sense that I have some pet theories as to the proper construction of a flying machine. I wish to avail myself of all that is already known and then if possible add my mite to help on the future worker who will attain final success."

In September, 1900, when the bicycle business slacked off as it usually did in the autumn, Wilbur headed for Kitty Hawk, North Carolina, a spot he and Orville had selected with the help of information on prevailing weather conditions supplied to them by the U.S. Weather Bureau.

The idea the two wanted to test with glider number one was whether they could control the craft and give it stability by twisting the tips of the wings as buzzards did. They chose the sand dunes of Kitty Hawk because historically the winds were consistently strong in the area, and there were no hills or trees to stir the air into serious turbulence.

Wilbur left Dayton first and worked on the glider for several weeks before Orville joined him. "I was glad to get Orv. off," their sister, Katherine, wrote to Bishop Wright. "He had worked so hard and was so run down. They never have had a trip anywhere since the World's Fair."

Most of that first session at Kitty Hawk was spent flying the glider simply as a big kite, often loaded with chains—"to give it work to do," Orville explained. But they were able to test the wing-warping idea by controls on the ground, and were very satisfied with what they saw. The next year they returned to Kitty Hawk to try a larger version with wings shaped to conform to air pressure tables composed by Lilienthal. They were dismayed to find that this glider was not as good as the previous model. Worse, the figures of the great German pioneer differed substantially from their own observations.

Encouraged by Chanute, the brothers built a small wind tunnel that fall, and in it they tested hundreds of different kinds of model wings set at varying angles to their manufactured wind. Out of this came glider number three, whose wings were narrower in relation to length than on the earlier versions. For the first time the Wrights added a rudder and hooked it up with the wing-warping controls to increase the plane's stability.

Their trials were so successful that they decided the next step was to build a powered flying machine. No lightweight gasoline engine was to be had, so they designed and built one themselves—a twelve-horsepower, water-cooled engine with four cylinders.

They left for Kitty Hawk in late September, 1903, and three weeks were consumed in putting together the big new biplane that they hoped to fly under power. One thing after another cropped up then to plague them. In the first ground test of the motorized plane, a propeller shaft was twisted. After the shafts had been strengthened in Dayton, the strain on the propeller-shaft sprockets kept loosening them. Then a shaft was cracked and Orville himself had to rush home to make a replacement.

Finally, on December 14, they moved the aircraft out to the top of a 60-foot monorail track that had been laid to guide the plane down a dune on a truck.

The plane had fabric-covered wings, 40 feet of them, one above the other. The pilot had to lie flat on the lower wing. In front of him was the front rudder, or elevator—two horizontal vanes with which he could control the rising and falling of the machine. Behind him were two vertical rudders, linked to the wingtip controls to steer right or left. On either side of his feet were the propellers.

They flipped a coin, and Wilbur won first try.

It was only a middling day for flying. The wind was light and not coming from quite the right direction. However, Wilbur was later to blame his failure to fly that day not on the conditions but on his error of judgment in trying to get the plane into the air too quickly. It stalled and crashed. With merely minor damage.

By December 17, they were ready to try again. This time it was Orville's turn. The wind was blowing at more than twenty miles an hour from the north, and the monorail track was laid on flat land. The sole onlookers were five men from a nearby lifesaving station.

Just after ten-thirty in the morning, the plane began to move along the track into the wind, with Wilbur running beside it, steadying the right wing. Both he and Orville were wearing starched collars and neckties; they always did. Near the end of the track the plane rose into the air, and one of the lifesaving men snapped what

"The Flying Dude," a military scout plane with Glenn L. Martin, 1913.

was to become aviation's most thrilling photograph: the first controlled, powered plane to fly, with its wings 5 feet off the ground.

Orville had a little trouble with the elevator, and the plane flew merely twelve seconds, leaping through the air like a drunken woodpecker, before it came down. But three better flights were made that day, by both brothers. "At just 12 o'clock Will started on the fourth and last trip," Orville recorded in his diary. "The machine started off with its ups and downs as it had before, but by the time he had gone three or four hundred feet he had it under much better control, and was traveling on a fairly even course. It proceeded in this manner till it reached a small hummock out about 800 feet from the starting ways, when it began its pitching again and suddenly darted into the ground. . . . The distance over the ground was 852 feet in 59 seconds."

Late that afternoon in Dayton, as the Wright housekeeper was getting supper started, a telegram arrived for Bishop Wright. It had a few typographical errors in it, but its import was clear.

SUCCESS FOUR FLIGHTS THURSDAY MORNING ALL AGAINST TWENTY ONE MILE WIND STARTED FROM LEVEL WITH ENGINE POWER ALONE AVERAGE SPEED THROUGH AIR THIRTY ONE MILES LONGEST 57 SECONDS INFORM PRESS HOME CHRISTMAS.

OREVELLE WRIGHT

Fred C. Kelly, the Wrights' authorized biographer, records that the Wright household was delighted not as much by the triumphant flights as by the knowledge that the brothers would be in Dayton for the holidays. As always, Wilbur, who was known for his culinary talents, would stuff the Christmas turkey.

A rich Brazilian playboy made the first powered flight in Europe. He was Alberto Santos-Dumont and he'd been meandering around the skies of France in small dirigibles for years until he resolved to try wings. The craft he built was almost ludicrously different from the trim Wright machine. Its wings were like big box kites set in a wide V. At the point of the V the pilot stood to the controls. In front of him a long, cloth-covered neck drooped to support another box kite. Still Santos-Dumont flew this plane nearly 200 feet at Bagatelle, in Paris, on October 23, 1906.

There were numerous other aerial pioneers. The United States had Glenn Curtiss, Glenn L. Martin, Alexander Graham Bell. France had Henri Farman, Léon Levasseur, Louis Blériot, Gabriel Voisin, Robert Esnault-Pelterie. Britain had S. F. Cody, A. V. Roe, Geoffrey de Havilland, Frederick Handley Page, T. O. M. Sopwith. Russia had Igor Sikorsky, the Netherlands had Anthony Fokker.

Along with the pioneer builders came pioneer pilots. Often, like the Wrights, they were embodied in the same person. Curtiss built and flew. In 1908 he won the *Scientific American* trophy for the first public airplane flight of a mile. In 1909 Blériot thrilled the world by flying the English Channel, the first time it was crossed in a heavier-than-air machine. But a breed of fliers who were exclusively fliers also emerged. It included daredevils like Galbraith P. Rodgers who made the first coast-to-coast flight in the United States in 1911. He did it in forty-nine days in spite of nineteen crashes along the route from New York City to Pasadena, California. And Lincoln Beachey who thought nothing of flying under the railroad bridge at Niagara Falls, or skimming the ground and tipping a wing just enough to hook a handkerchief from the grass. And the beautiful American Harriet Quimby, the first woman to fly the English Channel. In 1915 she tumbled out of a cockpit over Dorchester Bay in Massachusetts and died.

Like their earth-bound brothers-in-speed, the auto racers, these early-day fliers barnstormed from town to town, wildly vying with each other for altitude, distance, speed, and endurance records, and taking all manner of chances with their lives and everyone else's.

The initial public reaction may be surmised from a city ordinance passed in Jacksonville, Florida, in 1908. This forbade airplanes to fly over the city faster than fifty miles an hour. The lower a plane flew, the slower it was required to fly: at an altitude of 10 feet, the speed limit was eight miles an hour; at 20 feet, fifteen miles an hour; at 50 feet, thirty miles per hour. Jacksonville's lawmakers further required that every passing aircraft have a horn, brakes, and a parachute with which to lower itself in case of engine failure.

Winged aircraft were hardly ten years old when the first Great War started and they were most often frail, wood-and-cloth machines, carriages only for daredevils. They came of age in the new battlefield of the air.

The engine-powered balloon had already matured. In July, 1900, Count Ferdinand von Zeppelin, a retired Prussian general in his sixties, flew his first dirigible, the 425-foot-long *Luftschiff Zeppelin Number 1*. Its performance was encouraging enough to induce the Count to build another, the LZ-2. This one was forced down on its maiden flight in 1906 by a variety of mechanical difficulties. It landed safely, but that night, moored in a swamp, it was buffeted by severe winds and badly damaged. Undaunted, the old man tried again, and in the fall of 1906, an LZ-3 soared upward on a test flight. It flew well, even in the teeth of a twenty-five-mile-an-hour wind, and overnight Count von Zeppelin became the toast of Germany. So he started building the LZ-4 which the German Army agreed to buy if it could fly 435 miles in twenty-four hours.

Misfortune fell into step with the Count once more. On its run for the money in August, 1908, the LZ-4 was troubled by engine failure and had to land for repairs. While it was on the ground, a squall boiled up and the Zeppelin was torn from the hands of the men detailed to hold it down. After a hectic half-mile run-away, it dove into trees and exploded.

The Count was ruined.

Or so it seemed until the mail began arriving at his hotel in Friedrichshaven the next morning. It held money from all over a patriotically aroused Germany. Some 6,096,555 marks poured in, nearly $1,500,000.

In 1909 Zeppelin and a colleague formed the first passenger airline whose long German name was shortened to DELAG. By 1913 DELAG Zeppelins had carried thousands of passengers, sitting in wicker chairs and drinking wine, between Berlin, Frankfort, Hamburg, and Dresden. Some 1,600 commercial flights had been made in the hydrogen-filled balloons, covering 100,000 miles, without a serious mishap involving a passenger.

The call to arms in August, 1914, found the Zeppelin ready and anxious to inaugurate a radical new method of fighting: bombardment of unarmed enemy cities from the air. However, the tangible results of these raids were limited. They cost England only 557 lives and $7,500,000 in property damage.

Airplanes were much more effective. They may have entered the

Great War as flimsy scout craft, but they ended it as full-fledged fighters and bombers.

The early weapons carried by the scout planes included carbines, shotguns, and bricks. The first machine gun to take to the air for hostile purposes was a Lewis gun that a duo of enterprising British fliers swiped from their squadron supplies. The first time they tried it out, the gun was so heavy they couldn't get the plane up within range of their target. The gunner let go a burst anyway and scared the pilot so badly that he almost lost control of the plane.

"If you two must stir up strife in the air," the commanding officer of the squadron said, "Please use a rifle. Machine guns are for the infantry, not airplanes."

Progress, so-called, was rapid. In the period between September 12 and 15, 1918, close to 1,500 aircraft were marshaled by Brigadier General William Mitchell of the U.S. Army for a concerted bomber attack on German positions around St.-Mihiel.

How sad seemed the Wrights' hope, as expressed by Orville.

"When my brother and I built and flew the first man-carrying flying machine, we thought that we were introducing into the world an invention which would make further wars practically impossible."

Yet these same weapons of aerial war were soon to breed glorious instruments for peace and civilized advancement.

"If I had wings, like Noah's dove," went the old song, "I'd fly up the river to the girl I love." Man could.

XII

Sky High

AFTER WORLD WAR I many pilots felt uprooted, disoriented by the horror of war. Some of them stayed in the military. For others barnstorming provided a home—stunting, racing, or taking intrepid passengers aloft on short hops. New frills and thrills had been added to stunting now, like walking on a wing thousands of feet up in the air, or hanging by one's teeth from a trapeze at one hundred miles an hour.

Riskiest of all was flying the mails. Winged postal service was introduced first in India on February 18, 1911, when Henri Pequet flew a package of letters and postal cards six miles from Allahabad to Naini Junction. Postal service via wings came to the United States during the latter part of World War I when the U.S. Army inaugurated an airmail service between New York, Philadelphia and Washington. The Post Office took it over late in 1918.

That the U.S. Post Office has lived down its first days in the airmail business is fortunate. About everything that could have gone wrong did. The department printed the airmail stamps upside-down. The three Curtiss Jennies supplied by the Army arrived in crates, disassembled. With President Wilson watching, the plane detailed for the first flight from Washington to New York wouldn't start. The Chief Executive got very restless before someone could diagnose why the engine didn't catch: no gas. After that was rectified, the plane took off and headed in the wrong direction. The first airmail landed in a remote part of Maryland, came back to Washington in an automobile, and went to New York on a train.

However, the run between New York and Washington was soon being made regularly by Post Office fliers, and it was so successful that Postmaster General Arthur S. Burleson decided to open a service between New York and Chicago. Flying the mail the 205 level miles between the nation's capital and New York was within the capabilities of the planes the Post Office was operating, and the pilots had the Atlantic Ocean as a navigating point. But between New York and Chicago were the Allegheny Mountains, a stiff challenge for the flimsy DH-4s which were used on the route. Furthermore, there were no radio beacons, no weather stations, no equipment for flying blind. Thirty-one of the first forty fliers hired by the U.S. Post Office were killed by 1934.

New pilots signed up in droves anyway and one way or another the mail got through. The pilots used to mail bricks to each other, since the heavier the airmail load, the greater was their pay.

Another thing an ex-military flier could do was to start an airline. The first, Deutsche Luft Reederie, began operations between Berlin and Weimar, Germany, on February 5, 1919, followed a few days later by the Lignes Aériennes Farman which flew from Paris to London, serving luncheon and champagne en route. Other airlines were started in England and Holland.

America's first real airline, Aero Limited, began life in August, 1919, with a New York to Atlantic City run, and grew up with the times (i.e., Prohibition), flying passengers from dry Miami to the wet Bahamas.

Thus, a new age of flying was launched.

It was a period when aerial milestones followed fast upon one another. On May 16 and 17, 1919, a U.S. Navy Curtiss flying boat, the NC-4, piloted by Lieutenant Commander Albert C. Read, returned Columbus' compliment to the New World by discovering the Old World from the air. It flew the Atlantic nonstop from Newfoundland to the Azores, 1,380 ocean miles, and proceeded proudly on through Old World skies to Portugal and England.

On June 14, 1919, two nonchalant British RAF officers, Captain John Alcock and Lieutenant Arthur Whitten Brown, took off from

Newfoundland in a twin-engine Vickers-Vimy biplane bound east across the Atlantic nonstop to Britain. A stuffed cat named Twinkletoes accompanied them as a mascot.

Four hours out over the cruel North Atlantic, their radio went dead. "Wireless out; unable to repair," Brown hastily scribbled on a piece of paper that he passed up to Alcock in the front cockpit.

Jack Alcock just grinned. "How about opening a bottle of ale?" he wrote in reply.

A piece of an inner exhaust pipe broke off and the plane nearly caught fire. A miserable snow and sleet storm struck, throwing the plane into an almost uncontrollable dive. The carburetors began to ice up and six times Brown had to crawl far onto the wings and hack away at the air intakes with a penknife to keep the engines running. The pair won out, though. After sixteen hours and twenty-seven minutes in the air, Alcock crash-landed the Vimy safely into a bog at Clifden, Ireland.

Less than a month later, lighter-than-air craft got into the act. The British dirigible R-34 flew the Atlantic from East Fortune, Scotland, to New York. Because of the headwinds, it took her four days, twelve hours, and twelve minutes. Heading home to England, she did it in three days and three hours. That November, a husky Aussie war pilot, Captain Ross Smith, with a crew of three in a Vickers-Vimy biplane, made the longest flight yet, from London to Australia, an 11,000-mile route, thousands of miles of which had never been flown before. They did it in twenty-seven days and twenty hours.

There were technical advances. A German designer, Hugo Junkers, had produced an all-metal plane toward the end of the war. Now, Adolph Rohrback, another German, carried the idea further, making the metal skin of the plane a smooth surface. This was bravissimo engineering from two points of view. It lessened resistance to the air and allowed the skin to be used to add strength to the craft.

In 1924, two Douglas-Liberty 400 bombers flown by U.S. Army officers circled the earth by air—the first time that had been done. The trip was made in 174 days, touched down in twenty-one countries, and included the first transpacific flight and the first westward flight across the Atlantic.

What was flying like in those years?

Byron Moore, a senior pilot for American Airlines, described an everyday experience:

> Fighting my way to the old Detroit City Airport . . . . I got down on Telegraph Road, just above the high tension wires. Where Telegraph Road peters out, I'd angle right and pick up Oakwood Boulevard. By hugging it I missed a tall gas tank. When I came to an electric sign of a peculiar shade of blue, spelling BIJOU THEATRE, I'd angle farther right, missing some stacks on Woodward Avenue. Another sign indicated Six Mile Road, which I had to keep on my right to avoid the four-hundred-foot gas tank standing smack in the middle of City Airport. This tank had a characteristic pattern of lights on it; when I saw them go by my right wing, I'd bend that old Fokker around, groping for a certain line of street lights that I knew led to the south runway.

The poet of the air, Antoine de Saint-Exupery, wrote of a friend of his named Mermoz who was given the job of scouting a route for a South American airline. Flying through the Andes, Mermoz made a forced landing on a 12,000-foot-high plateau. He and his mechanic spent two days trying to find a way off it, but on every side were precipices. In the end, they got back into the plane, started the engine, and headed for the nearest drop off into space. Once over the edge the craft plummeted, picked up speed, and Mermoz was able to nose it up over a mountain before the motor quit. Below him were plains and safety.

A curious fight was raging then among military men over the future of military aviation. In Italy, a hot-tempered officer by the name of Giulio Douhet, who had been sent to prison during World War I for daring to criticize Italy's bumbling conduct of military operations, was arguing that future wars would be won in the air. Destroy the enemy cities by heavy aerial bombardment, break the morale of the civilians, and victory would be assured: that was his thesis. It was the origin of the mass-bombing strategies of World War II. No one would listen to him then, though.

A similarly air-minded prophet was largely without honor in the United States—Brigadier General William "Billy" Mitchell, the dashing, handsome flier who had commanded the air arm of the

American Expeditionary Forces in France so brilliantly. After the war, he was appalled by the way the United States' military air power was being allowed to molder under the influence of the post-hostility isolationism and economy. The Army Air Service had to fly the obsolete DH-4s, and daily they were proving more and more to be "Flaming Coffins." Between the summers of 1920 and 1921 the Air Service had 330 crashes with sixty-nine dead. The fact was that neither the Army nor the Navy brass had much use for aviation.

Loudly, Mitchell shouted in speeches, articles, and statements to the press that the United States had to have an air arm second to none. Air power was the key to future victories, he insisted, and he warned that the nation could not depend on battleships to protect it against attack. Airplanes could sink any battleships anywhere, he said, and to prove his assertion he demanded a chance to bomb some captured German warships.

A test was held seventy-five miles off the entrance to Chesapeake Bay in the summer of 1921, and a German submarine, a destroyer, and a light cruiser were sunk in short order.

The most important target the airmen were given was a heavily armored, supposedly indestructable battleship, the *Ostfriesland*. Battleship admirals sneered at the idea of an airplane hitting a ship with bombs, never mind sinking it, and Secretary of the Navy Josephus Daniels offered to stand "bareheaded" on the German dreadnought while the Army, Navy, and Marine Corps fliers attacked her. Fortunately for him, he was dissuaded from this gesture inasmuch as Mitchell's Army fliers hammered her with 2,000-pound bombs and sank her in precisely twenty-five minutes.

The admirals still wouldn't give up their old-fashioned battleships.

Mitchell kept up his crusade for air power, and President Calvin Coolidge had him demoted and exiled to an obscure post in Texas. When the Navy dirigible *Shenandoah* was torn apart in a September, 1925, storm, Mitchell rashly accused the Navy and the Army high commands of "incompetency, criminal negligence, and almost treasonable administration of national defense." He was court-martialled, found guilty, and suspended from the Army for talking truth.

Another fearful world war was needed to demonstrate how far-sighted he and Giulio Douhet had been.

Fliers continued to chart marvelous new highways through the skies. A tall, curly-haired, shy Midwesterner got into an automobile in New York City on the rainy, misty night of May 19, 1927, and drove across town to a theatre where he had tickets for the musical comedy *Rio Rita*.

On the way the car stopped; a companion got out and went to telephone the Weather Bureau. In a few minutes he came back and stuck his head in the window of the car.

No passerby could have known what a momentous scene that was: the man standing in the rain beside the car, bent over, talking; the lights of 42nd Street bearing faint haloes and casting blurred scribbles of reflections on the street. The man was telling his pilot friend from the Midwest that although the weather was bad in the city, out over the Atlantic it was unexpectedly showing signs of clearing. The man at last got back in the car, which turned and headed for Long Island.

Twenty-four-year-old Charles Lindbergh would take off all alone at dawn. The destination: Le Bourget Field, Paris. He was hoping to be the first man to fly the Atlantic solo.

Loaded with 425 gallons of gasoline and weighing 5,135 pounds, the little Ryan monoplane the *Spirit of St. Louis* felt logy to her pilot as she warmed up at the end of the runway on Roosevelt Field. Recalled Lindbergh, "I'm conscious of the great weight pressing tires into ground, of the fragility of wings, of the fullness of oversize tanks of fuel. There is in my plane this morning, more of earth and less of air than I've ever felt before."

Into the foggy gray dawn of May 20 the single-engined craft lumbered and rose slowly, just enough to clear the telephone lines at the end of the runway by 20 feet. Long Island Sound was smooth as glass, and the thirty-five miles Lindbergh flew to cross it was the longest distance over water he'd flown in his life. For that matter, he had only been out of sight of land once before, at the age of eleven, when he and his mother had taken a boat trip south to the Panama Canal.

Cape Cod . . . Nova Scotia . . . Newfoundland. A small speck in the empty sky over the North Atlantic, and in that speck was a young man desperately fighting weariness. He had not slept the night before he left, and his body was dragging him down toward sleep. He bounced around in his seat, shook himself, banged his feet on the floor, sang at the top of his lungs, put his hand out the window to steer cold air onto his face; and, still, on that night over the Atlantic, when he wasn't coping with fog and icing and navigation problems, he kept dozing off. A sixth sense woke him whenever dozing became dangerous, but each time he came to he found himself off course.

It was with amazement that when he sighted the Irish Coast—two and a half hours ahead of schedule due to a tailwind—he discovered he had made his landfall only three miles from where he had planned. Now he was over Cornwall, now over Cherbourg, now over Deauville at dusk, "in this long twilight of late spring." Now he was over Paris, unsuspecting that a delirious reception by thousands of Frenchmen awaited him below while he searched for the poorly lit Le Bourget airport.

He touched down. His 3,605-mile flight had lasted thirty-three hours and thirty-nine minutes, averaging over 107 miles an hour, and its impact on aviation was fantastic. With this one heroic feat, aviation grew up.

On the heels of Lindbergh's success, hundreds of fliers started taking off for distant places. Thirty-one crossings of the Atlantic were attempted in the following year.

Tousle-haired, lanky, grinning Amelia Earhart—some thought her the female counterpart of Lindbergh—became the first woman to fly across the Atlantic in June, 1928. She only went as a passenger in a plane Wilmer Stultz flew from Newfoundland to Wales, and she shrugged off the praise heaped on her, preferring to earn it. Which she did in 1932, becoming the first woman to fly the Atlantic alone. Miss Earhart was to disappear mysteriously in July, 1937, on a flight across the Pacific. Some reports had it that she was executed by the Japanese as a spy.

Captain Dieudonné Coste and Maurice Bellonte, two Frenchmen, flew from Paris to New York nonstop in 1930. In 1931, drawling, Texas-born Wiley Post, blind eye and all, flew around the world in eight days, fifteen hours, fifty-one minutes, with Harold Gatty, an Australian, doing the navigating for their Lockheed monoplane, the *Winnie Mae*. Flying alone, Post cut his round-the-world time to 7¼ days two years later. He was to crash to his death in Alaska with the beloved comedian Will Rogers in 1935.

The most unusual record, perhaps, was set in July, 1938, by a thirty-one-year-old transport pilot and airplane mechanic named Douglas G. "Wrong Way" Corrigan. He flew the Atlantic by error, or so he claimed. He took off from New York City alone in a rickety, one-engine plane without official permission and landed in Dublin, Ireland, without a permit twenty-eight hours and thirteen minutes later. He said he was heading for California but had made a mistake in his navigation.

To help fliers came technical improvements, such as the radio beam. On June 28, 1927, Lieutenants Lester Maitland and Albert Hegenberger of the U.S. Army Air Corps took off from Oakland, California in a Fokker trimotored plane and pointed its nose out over the Pacific. They were the first fliers over an ocean to have the aid of radio beacons in navigation. They didn't ride beams throughout, but electronics helped in their achievement: the first nonstop flight from the United States to Hawaii, 2,407 miles away. The automatic pilot, which could be employed as a relief for the human pilot, was developed. Wiley Post used one on his solo trip around the world.

Lieutenant Apollo Soucek, a U.S. Navy pilot, set a different sort of record in 1930. He soared to an altitude of 43,166 feet in a Wright Apache. A Swiss physicist, Auguste Piccard, went higher, in a balloon, in 1934, to 57,979 feet.

Little more than a quarter-century had elapsed since the Wrights first flew, and man was beginning to fly around in that hitherto dangerous element, air, almost as if he owned it. He was even commencing to make the air satisfy his wants for faster mass transport. In 1919 all the airlines in the world (save those of Russia and China) carried a total of 5,000 passengers. By 1929 they were carrying 434,000 passengers a year, and by 1938 American airlines alone were moving more than 1,350,000 revenue passengers a year.

The Transcontinental Air Transport originated crosscountry

passenger service in the United States in 1929—with the help of the railroads. TAT passengers flew during the day and rode in Pullman sleepers at night. The next year TAT became TWA (then the abbreviation for Transcontinental and Western Air, ancestor of Trans World Airlines) and began flying passengers all the way in trimotor Ford planes. Passengers sat in the plane for two days with a blessed overnight rest stop in Kansas City.

Soon airlines were knitting the whole world together. Pan American Airways, which began flying from Key West to Havana in 1927, was spreading over Central and South America by 1934. The Dutch KLM had routes throughout Europe and on to the Middle East, India, the Malay Peninsula, Java, and the Dutch East Indies. French lines connected Europe and Africa and French Indo-China. The British flew to Bombay, Hong Kong, and Australia.

Pan Am introduced transpacific service, in luxurious, four-engined flying boats. On November 22, 1935, its *China Clipper* took off from San Francisco Bay with eighteen pampered passengers and winged out over the unfinished Golden Gate Bridge for the Philippines. In 1939 Pan Am and British Imperial Airways started transatlantic service. They would have done it earlier if the American and British governments had not been so long wrangling over air rights.

Both in America and abroad, government subsidies were needed to keep the airlines running. In the United States, a majority of airlines got their subsidies in the form of payment for carrying airmail. The Post Office began turning over the job of hauling airmail to private airlines in 1925, and routes were opened that tied together such cities as New York, Chicago, St. Louis, Dallas, Los Angeles, San Francisco, and Seattle. All these domestic airmail contracts were canceled by Postmaster General James A. Farley in February, 1934, on the grounds of collusion in rate setting, and the task of flying the mails was given to the Army Air Corps. The Air Corps wasn't up to it. After ten pilots had been killed in plane accidents, the mail mission was returned to the airlines in May, 1934.

By 1939 airplanes had grown vastly in size and safety, and had changed in style. From the wood and fabric biplanes that dominated the years following World War I—all sharp edges and wing struts and open cockpits—they became single-winged, streamlined, and all-metal. Their cabins were enclosed and their furnishings got to be as lush as the old-time railroads. The Pan Am Clippers had walnut-paneled walls, silk draperies, and curtained berths with downy mattresses. The French Farman airliners had soft lighting, ultracomfortable upholstered armchairs, and a mahogany bar with a shoulder-high brass rail for the passenger to grasp in the event that he or the weather got bouncy.

*"The Flying Banana"
—the twin-engined
Piasecki HRP-2
helicopter.*

Many notable aircraft were produced in this period. Among them were the Clippers of Sikorsky and Martin; the twelve-engine Dornier flying boat; and the champion of them all, the Douglas DC-3. The "Workhorse of the Skies," the DC-3 was first built in three types: The Skysleeper, which could leave New York at sunset, fly across the country while its fourteen passengers slept in berths, and land in California the next morning; the fourteen-passenger Skylounge, a luxury plane; and the twenty-one-passenger day coach, the model that prevailed. Tough, strong, and cheap to operate, the DC-3 was first produced in 1935 and it was still flying on the airlines of every inhabited continent in 1966.

Helicopters came a long distance during this period. The first workable rotary wing machine had been built by Paul Cornu in France in 1907, but though it could raise itself and a passenger off the ground with its two horizontal propellers, it was not much more than a gadget. The Spanish aeronautical engineer, Juan de la Cierva came up with an improvement in 1923, the "Autogiro," that lifted itself into the air by means of four long, whirling blades. In 1936 the Germans produced the first truly workable helicopter, the Foch-Achgelis FW-61 which could fly forward as fast as seventy-six miles per hour. It was lifted into the air—where it could stay for an hour and twenty minutes at a hop—by twin rotors, one on either side of the fuselage. Igor Sikorsky improved the species in 1939 with a single-rotor machine that had as its rudder a vertical propeller set on the tail.

In one aspect aviation did not progress during the years between the big wars. The great dirigibles, the graceful, quiet-riding Zeppelins, were *Kaput.*

The handwriting had been on the wall for years. It was obvious that as soon as winged machines could cross the oceans regularly, safely, and much more speedily, the greatest number of airship passengers would switch to them. But the airplane wasn't the instrument that truly killed dirigibles. What slew them was the stubborn insistence of the Germans on using hydrogen to float their Zeppelins.

As early as 1922 after one of its hydrogen-filled dirigibles had blown up, the U.S. Navy had switched to nonburnable helium. The British dirigible R-101 had crashed and blown up in France in 1930 with the loss of forty-eight lives and the British stopped building dirigibles. But the Germans kept on flying with explosive hydrogen overhead.

On May 6, 1937, it all came to an end. The Zeppelin *Hindenburg,* 803 feet long and 146 feet high, settling beside a mooring mast at Lakehurst, New Jersey, after a flight from Germany, exploded in an awesome burst of orange, red, and black. Why, no one knows. Thirty-six people were killed and so were the prospects of rigid airships.

World War II accelerated the development of aviation in the same way that World War I had done. Greater range was one legacy; the operational jet plane was another.

The long-range bomber became more and more important as the

combatants tried to knock each other out on the home front. The Boeing Company of Seattle, which had built the doughty B-17 "Flying Fortress" for the Air Corps, was assigned the job of constructing a bomber that could minimize the great distances of the Pacific. Its XB-29 was the result. This experimental "Superfort" was first flown in September, 1942. After one early flight, Colonel (later Lieutenant General) Donald L. Putt dashed off some notes to himself: "Unbelievable for such large plane to be so easy on controls . . . easier to fly than B-17 . . . faster than any previous bombers. . . ."

The Superforts set a torch to sixty-nine Japanese cities with their fire raids. Brigadier General Thomas S. Power, who was to become Commanding General of the Strategic Air Command, led more than 300 of these B-29s on a fire raid against Tokyo on March 9, 1945, and called it "the most destructive single military action in the history of the world." The raid, Power noted, "caused more casualties than the atom bomb attacks on Hiroshima and Nagasaki."

"The best way to describe what it looks like when these fire bombs come out of the bomb bay," Power said, ". . . is to compare it to a giant pouring a big shovelful of white-hot coals all over the ground. . . . They started fires everywhere. . . . Tokyo was a highly inflammable city, and as the fire swathes widened and came together they built up into one vast fire."

One hundred and eighty square miles of built-up city areas were burned to the ground in Japan by fire raids like that between March and August, 1945.

Two Superforts, the *Enola Gay* and *Bock's Car,* carried the atomic bombs that flattened Hiroshima and Nagasaki on August 6 and 9, and brought to an end history's most hellish war.

As Mitchell and Douhet had predicted, it was a war in which air power played a leading role, perhaps *the* leading role. The side which dominated the air dominated the action, and when the Axis air forces became inferior to those of the Allies, the tide of battle clearly turned.

Had Adolf Hitler, the megalomaniacal Nazi *Führer,* been more prescient, he might never have lost the advantage in the air with which he began. One of the leading examples of this lack of farsightedness was his failure to capitalize on the tremendous jump German aeronautical engineers had gotten in the area of jet propulsion. This was a radical new form of propulsion that did away with pistons and propellers. The principle is the same principle according to which a toy balloon jumps forward when the air is released from it. Push compressed air, highly expanded by an ignited fuel, out of jet nozzles in the rear of an engine, and an enormous thrust forward can be achieved that will move a plane at a tremendous speed.

A junior-size—he was five feet, three inches tall—RAF pilot named Frank Whittle invented the jet engine. He took out patents on it in England in 1930 when he was twenty-three years old. However, the Germans beat the British, and all the other Allies, into the air with jets. A Dr. Hans von Ohain designed a turbojet engine based on Whittle's idea that was test-flown in a Heinkel He-178 in August, 1939, almost two years before the British got a jet up. By 1942 the Germans had flown a twin-engined jet fighter, the Messerschmitt Me-262 that could do 530 miles an hour—faster by far than anything the Allies could put in the air.

The Luftwaffe Major General Adolf Galland described a test flight in a Me-262: "It was [as] though angels were pushing."

That was where Hitler interfered. He decided that the Me-262 would not do as a fighter. "We shall call it a medium bomber," he said, thereby delaying its appearance in combat by a year at the least. It flew as a bomber in 1944, did not perform well in that capacity, and had to be turned into a fighter again. By the close of the war, 1,500 of the Me-262s had been produced, but they were too few and too late.

The only Allied jet to fly in combat was the British Gloster Meteor which came into service late in the conflict and was used principally to knock down the lethal Nazi buzz bombs. The United States had a flyable jet fighter by the beginning of 1944, the Lockheed P-80, but it did not go to war.

America and her Allies won the war because they had many more planes and much better pilots.   (

War's end found fliers reaching for more speed and greater distances. In October, 1946, a U.S. Navy P2V Neptune, the *Truculent*

Turtle, built by Lockheed, flew from Perth, Australia, to Columbus, Ohio—11,236 miles—nonstop, without once being refueled in
the air, taking just fifty-five hours and seventeen minutes to complete the hop.

In the realm of speed, a P-80 jet flown by Colonel William H.
Council raced across the United States in four hours, thirteen minutes, twenty-six seconds, in 1946, averaging 584 miles an hour. A
hundred years earlier, four months would have been good time for
the overland trip.

The first successful assault on the sound barrier (the shock-wave
that piles up in front of a plane as it approaches the speed of
sound) was made in 1947, and a frightening thing it was to try,
since no one knew exactly what would happen to a plane going
through it. Young Geoffrey de Havilland and his DH-108 had liter-
ally vanished during an attempt to blast through it in 1946.

In October, 1947, in California, a stocky, twenty-five-year-old
West Virginian, Captain Charles E. Yeager of the U.S. Air Force
climbed down a ladder dangling from the belly of a B-29 bomber
flying at 7,000 feet; wedged himself into the cockpit of a stubby
Bell X-1 rocket plane that was hooked under the Superfort; closed
the door with a stab of pain—he had broken two ribs the night
before in a fall from a horse, but had told nobody about it—and
got set for a flight faster than sound.

He was frightened. "I was always scared when I flew the X-1,"
he said later, "but nobody believed it." Before he and the X-1 were
carried aloft, he quipped, "I'll be back all right—in one piece or a
whole lot of little pieces."

The Superfort hoisted him in his X-1 to about 25,000 feet.
Yeager related:

> You are sitting there; it is quite dark, and the bomber pilot . . .
> says: "I'll give you a five-minute warning here and you can set
> all your knobs the way they are supposed to be set . . . and get a
> death grip on the stick." He gives you about a minute warning
> and then he starts counting down to five seconds and he says
> five seconds, four, three, two, one, drop, and about a minute later
> the copilot finally releases you. As with all bomber crews I think
> he sits there asleep until the pilot nudges him and says, "You
> were supposed to drop him."

The X-1 was dropped, Yeager fired its rockets, and took it up to 37,000 feet. There, where the speed of sound was approximately 100 miles an hour less than the 760 miles per hour it would have been at sea level, he accelerated past the magic number, Mach 1, and through the sound barrier.

"I was kind of disappointed that it wasn't more of a big charge than it was," he said. He did land all in one piece.

There come tense moments when a nation must stand up for what it believes, regardless of the risks, or abandon its ideals and slink off into the dark corners of history.

The United States faced such a choice in 1948. A deeply moving account of what happened was prepared by a *Reader's Digest* correspondent:

Late in June, 1948, Russian soldiers blockaded West Berlin. Unless the three big Western democracies, America, Britain, and France, withdrew their occupation troops from the city and permitted a Communist dictatorship to take power, the Kremlin threatened to reduce the 2,100,000 Berliners to starvation and death.

The highways, the railroads, and canals were blocked. Only one route was left open—the air. But how could a huge metropolis be supplied with coal, food, and all its other wants by plane?

General Lucius D. Clay, the gentle-voiced but steely U.S. Commander in Germany, telephoned Major General Curtis E. LeMay, the U.S. Air Force chief in Europe. "Curt," he asked, "can you deliver coal by air?"

LeMay swallowed hard. "Will you repeat that question, please," he said.

"Can you deliver coal by air?"

"Sir," LeMay replied, "the Air Force can deliver anything."

So started the epic of Berlin Airlift. The next morning, a thin line of warworn C-47 "Gooney Birds" took off from West Germany for Tempelhof Airfield in Berlin. By evening they had flown in eighty tons of flour, milk, and medicine.

June 26 it was. By June 28 the RAF was in on the airlift, too.

Some U.S. Air Force men didn't have faith. At a staff meeting in the Pentagon on June 29, Major Edward Willerford was asked to forecast the airlift's potential capacity. He bravely estimated 1,500 tons a day by July 20.

The reaction was fantastic, he said.

"Everyone was studying me in consternation. You could read it in their faces: 'Old Willerford is tetched in the head. Grab the strait jacket, boys, before he gets violent!' "

But before the airlift was over, the Allies were flying not 1,500 tons, but 8,000 tons a day into Berlin. One Sunday they carried in nearly 13,000 tons.

From all over the world, the U.S. Air Force rushed 147 big, four-engined C-54 transports and four giant C-82s to West Germany, and, by the fall of 1948, planes were taking off from West Germany for Berlin every three minutes, like clockwork. They flew up one corridor to Berlin, unloaded, and flew out another corridor. One-way traffic throughout. In the words of the *Reader's Digest* correspondent, "It was a flying conveyor belt with each pilot following exactly the same rhythmic routine. The pilot had to pass over each check point exactly on time, keep the exact distance behind the preceding plane, maintain exactly the prescribed altitude." The fliers worked fourteen, sixteen, eighteen hours a day.

Talk about Yankee ingenuity. A rush order came from General Clay for several titan-sized steamrollers. They were needed for building a new airfield.

"Impossible," the pilots said. "You can't get a steamroller on an airplane. It's too big."

"Horsefeathers," said Major General Bill Tunner, the hard-driving commander of the airlift. "You can get anything on an airplane."

He ordered that the steamrollers be cut apart with an acetylene torch, flown to Berlin in pieces, and welded together again. It worked.

With winter came icy blizzards and black fog, the worst in years. "Soup I can take," remarked the movie star, Bob Hope, when he came over to entertain the airlift men, "but this stuff has noodles in it." Snow fell on nine separate days in a month and the temperature dropped far below freezing. The airlift kept on flying, though. Not a day passed that some planes didn't make it to Berlin.

The Red Army tried its utmost to foul up the airlift. Russian fighters buzzed the unarmed cargo planes; barrage balloons were let loose in the airlanes.

"What do we do about it?" Bill Tunner was asked.

"We keep on flying regardless of what those b—ds do," he said. "That's what we're paid for."

A top-secret Pentagon report recorded 733 instances of hostile Russian actions, including 54 cases of anti-aircraft fire at Allied planes, 42 cases of air-to-ground fire, 37 cases of bombing, 77 cases of vicious buzzing, and 103 cases in which Russian searchlights blinded Allied pilots on takeoff.

"We lived each day as if it might be our last," Lieutenant Colonel Robert Hogg has recalled.

In fifteen months, United States and British transport planes toted 2,323,067 tons of coal, food, petroleum, and other supplies to Berlin until the Soviet Union finally called off the blockade on the Allies' terms.

Canadair CL-84—a V/STOL airplane, combining many properties of conventional airplanes with those of helicopters.

General Dynamics Photo.

The cost of the airlift to the United States and British governments exceeded $200,000,000. Plus seventy-five lives, lost in plane crashes.

But it was worth it. Europe saw Allied planes rescue the freedom-loving Berliners, and took courage.

Now all the aeronautical advances began to pay off in the area where it counted most—moving ordinary travelers where they wanted to go safely, comfortably, and much more speedily.

In 1952 the jet age arrived for civilian passengers. The first jet airliner went into service that year in Britain. On October 4, 1958, the British pulled off another first. That day, the British Overseas Airways Corporation took another giant step and opened transatlantic jet passenger service. Twenty-two days later, Pan American followed suit. By the early 1960's, jet airliners, flying seven miles up and carrying their passengers in pleasantly pressurized cabins, were speeding across the Atlantic in six hours, crossing the breadth of the United States in four or five.

Magnificent planes they were. The most popular of them, the Boeing 707, was 145 feet long, and had a wing span of 131 feet and a tail that was, at rest, 42 feet off the ground. It could fly nonstop from coast to coast at more than 600 miles per hour and still have ample fuel reserves to remain in the air for extra hours. The Convair 990, the Douglas DC-8, the British Comet, the Russian TU-108, and the French Caravelle with its twin engines in its tail were also big, powerful, and lovely to see zooming up into the sky, vapor trails stringing out behind. The new three-engined Boeing-727, too. Its wonderfully quick takeoff made jet travel practicable for short intercity hops.

Travel by air had come to be as luxurious as anything the sea had to offer (and far more plush than the railroads). Chic, charming stewardesses—good-looking girls, twenty to twenty-seven years of age—were at the passengers' beck and call. Magazines, newspapers, electric razors, souvenir rings for youngsters, and bottles for the babies were to be had free. On the best-run lines, food was ambrosial. American Airlines served its transcontinental passengers filet mignon with a Bordelaise sauce made, according to the menu, of "a slowly simmered rich beef sauce, given unusual character

U.S. Air Force version of the variable-wing F-111 fighter bomber.

with shallots, mushrooms and the proper accent of select, full-bodied red wine." Air India regaled its New York to London passengers with a choice, to commence, of "fresh fruit Calypso in Kirsch," glazed artichokes with asparagus tips, salpicon of venison, stuffed clams, or caviar on ice. Then they were given their pick of *filets de soles Caprice, poulet grillée à la Tandoor* (very spicy it was), or filet mignon Albert I, accompanied by rice, spiced vegetables, tomatoes stuffed with mixed vegetables, and Berny potatoes, and a green salad. Afterwards followed a pastry, assorted cheeses, fresh fruit, coffee or tea, bonbons, and *Mignardises Indiennes,* translatable as Indian sweetmeats. Naturally, there were cocktails at the start, followed by vintage French champagne, a dry white wine and two red wines to go with the meal, and a cognac or liqueur to close it. All served by beautiful stewardesses in saris.

Some airlines were even offering their passengers movies in flight and television pictures of their own takeoffs and landings made by a camera in the nose of the plane.

Most comfortable of all were the fares. Between 1951 and 1963 the lowest transatlantic rate was sliced nearly in half, and in 1964 it

English Electric Lightning Mark/2, can fly at speeds up to twice those of sound.

was cut 14 percent more. At the end of World War II, it cost $515 to fly from New York to London one-way. In 1966 it could be done in half the time by jet for $300 round trip.

Joining the airline and military planes in the air in the 1960's was an immense fleet of private aircraft. About 60 percent of all arrivals and departures in the United States were in this category. They involved planes used for business, instruction, charter lines, air taxi service, farming, and fun. As of 1966 there were more than 80,000 of these private planes in the United States, including such craft as the Lockheed JetStar, costing a mere $1,500,000 to buy and $650 an hour to operate.

It is an incredible picture. Tens of thousands of airline planes, private planes, and military planes fill the air day and night where sixty-five years ago only birds, bats, insects, and an occasional balloon navigated. Faster and faster, farther and farther, planes go. In 1957 three U.S. Air Force B-52 bombers flew around the entire world nonstop, from and back to California, 24,325 miles in forty-five hours, nineteen minutes, with a few casual refuelings in mid-air enroute. In 1965 an American, Colonel R. L. Stephens, set a world speed record for jets of 2,063 miles per hour in the new YF-12A; another American, Major Robert M. White, set a world altitude record of 314,750 feet—fifty-nine miles—in an X15-1; and an American rocket plane, the X-15, flew 4,093 miles per hour.

The skies are getting crowded with stunning new helicopters, too. Big ones that can carry as many as 180 passengers. And fast, powerful ones. Jean Boulet of France flew one at 212 miles per hour in 1963, and Commander J. R. Williford of the U.S. Navy took one 2,105 miles nonstop from California to Florida in 1965. The U.S. Army has made aerial jeeps of "choppers" in Vietnam, and airlines have been turning them into flying buses for local service in many parts of America and Europe.

The revolution has been enough to make one gasp. As Lindbergh, full of wonder, wrote,

"Flying has torn apart the relationship of space and time; it uses our old clock but with new yardsticks."

XIII

Journey into Tomorrow

ALL MANNER of new transportation marvels were in the making in the mid-1960's on land, at sea, and in the air.

One of the biggest surprises occurred on land. The wheel, which got history rolling, underwent a radical change. Its shape was remade.

The round wheel, as its keen British historian A. J. Poulton wrote, "is the one thing man has invented by himself, with no help from anything found in nature. . . . Without it, transport as we know it would have been impossible." However, round wheels have always had a serious disadvantage. On soft ground, they can become hopelessly mired. When they spin without traction, they can dig themselves deeper into the mud and make their motive job even more difficult.

The solution: make wheels less circular.

Early in 1963 Poulton reported from England that "a revolutionary idea" had been patented for a set of elliptic wheels, which looked somewhat like longitudinal cross-sections of eggs. Four of them were arranged in pairs under the chassis of an ordinary truck, and the traction they achieved was astonishing; they could move the heaviest loads across the worst ground. Because of a novel axle structure, the vehicle could run as level as any other truck.

And that was nothing by comparison with a truck that was designed for the U.S. Army in 1966. It was 10 feet long, four feet

255

wide, and it had four manlike legs that, it was hoped, would walk it through swamps, jungles, and snow drifts.

Many revolutionary ideas on passenger car design were being tested. By 1966 Detroit engineers had developed three devices that did away with steering wheels. One system allowed a driver to pilot his car simply by manipulating a pair of small dials, the way you tune a radio. A second system utilized two plastic rings, one on each end of a crossbar that was attached to an adjustable column. The third system was more versatile yet. A short control stick, very much like the traditional airplane joy stick, was placed at the left side of the driver and he could use it not only for steering, but for accelerating and braking as well.

Radar was being put into cars. One company was experimenting with a miniature radar device fixed to a car's grille that could alert the driver to objects in his path.

But to see something far out of the norm, one had to be on hand at a specially built oval track, a quarter of a mile long, in New Jersey one day in 1960. There the car and the road of the future were demonstrated.

A road around the track had a continuous guidance cable buried beneath the pavement, plus other electronic gear. On the road were two cars equipped with electronic controls—in effect, automatic pilots.

The cars were braked, accelerated, and steered electronically, and their passengers were informed of hazards, intersections, and driving problems by messages beamed to the car radios from the guidance cable—which also held them in the proper lane. If either car on the road exceeded the speed limit, it activated roadside signs that said so. Other roadside signs flashed on to warn of the presence of a car ahead—cautions that could be lifesavers in a dense fog.

It all performed excellently, establishing that on this kind of road a driver with such a car need merely "lock on" his blind-driving controls when he entered the highway and the equipment would take over. He could sit, read a book, play bridge, watch television, or sleep while the car sped to its destination.

According to one designer, the insides of these cars of the future would have "the look of a comfortable, colorful, well-decorated room which is going somewhere." They would be furnished with air conditioning, television sets, and cooking gear, he predicted.

Exotic new fuel sources were under development. Scientists had an electrochemical system in the laboratory that converted liquid fuel into electric energy for powering an automobile. U.S. Army scientists were working on a system that produced enough electric energy to power a truck by adding a little cheap liquid hydrogen to a small fuel cell.

A passenger car with a brand-new kind of engine was on the road—a turbine engine car which ran on inexpensive fuel oil or kerosene, and required no carburetor, no piston rings, no radiator, and only one spark plug.

Some of these turbine engine cars, each of which cost a half-million dollars to produce, were loaned to motorists throughout the United States to test under average driving conditions. The first of the test drivers, an editor of *Look* magazine, reported that the car started up instantly in subzero temperatures, and that it could do 120 miles per hour, or better. "On start-up," he wrote, "the engine emits a shrill, jet-like whistle. It sounds a bit scary, but is completely safe. Turbine-whistle vanishes at fifty miles per hour, and at eighty, the car's speed seems like forty. Come to a halt, turn the key, and the turbine whines down—like a dying vacuum cleaner."

By April, 1966, 203 volunteers had driven turbine-powered cars 1,100,000 miles. Should they work out as their designers hope, they could save motorists big sums on operating and maintenance costs.

Railroad planners had some tingling tricks up their sleeves. They came forward with a dramatic plan in 1962 for a completely automated aerial transit expressway that could, it was said, provide large cities with fast commuter service every two minutes of the day and night. Under this plan, light aluminum cars, each seating twenty people, would roll on rubber-tired wheels along an elevated roadway. Electronic computers would manage everything, from assembling the trains to selling tickets. Each train would number anywhere from one to twelve cars; the computers would decide how many.

A demonstration project, underwritten in appreciable part by United States government funds, was under construction near Pittsburgh.

Swift new monorails—those sleek railroads that ride on or are suspended from a single track—were extending in all directions.

These monorails were not a new means of transportation. A monorail, three-quarters of a mile long, intrigued visitors to the Exposition at Lyon, France, in 1872, and a monorail at Wuppertal, Germany, had carried more than a billion passengers from 1901 to 1966 without a single serious mishap. A 1.2-mile-long monorail was one of the most outstanding and profitable attractions at the Seattle World's Fair in 1962. The trains went fifty-five miles per hour.

Only very lately, though, were monorails being seriously considered as a means of mass metropolitan transit. Tokyo opened a $45,500,000 monorail, linking its airport with the center of the city, 8.2 miles away, in September, 1964. And the Kremlin announced plans in the summer of 1964 for the world's largest monorail, to stretch twenty-two miles from the Avtozavodskaya subway station, on the southeast edge of Moscow, to Domodedovo Airport, Moscow's biggest. The monorail was to ride 16 feet above the ground and leap the curling Moscow River twice.

Some transportation experts had bigger concepts. They were taking vast areas like the East Coast section between Washington and Boston, the Detroit-Cleveland-Pittsburgh district, and the Los Angeles-San Diego zone, treating them as superregions, and planning self-contained rapid transit facilities for them. Thus, one ultra-rapid transit network would connect Washington, Philadelphia, New York, and Boston. Superexpresses would sprint at speeds of 160 miles an hour over redesigned roadbeds and deliver passengers from downtown Washington to downtown New York in less than two hours. As forecast by an eminent transportation engineer, Henry D. Quinby, trains with wide, comfortable seats and broad aisles would stop just for the briefest intervals in a few principal cities. Station platforms, Mr. Quinby said, would be fully enclosed with automatic sliding doors at the entrances to the cars.

And that was small stuff in comparison with a plan conceived by Dr. Joseph V. Foa, chairman of the Department of Aeronautical Engineering and Astronautics of Rensselaer Polytechnic Institute, under a research grant from the Federal Government. It proposed the development of a 130-foot, torpedo-shaped vehicle propelled by turbofan jets which would ride on six giant air-cushion pods through steel tubes 500 feet underground, with 104 passengers. It would go 400 miles an hour and easily zoom from New York to Washington in forty-five minutes.

Pipeliners were also looking ahead. They were experimenting with techniques for shipping parcel post by vacuum-powered pipelines. To guard against damage, they were trying to prevent packages from bunching and crunching at the terminals. The U.S. Post Office Department was sufficiently impressed to negotiate an experimental project for handling letters in the same fashion.

The poor pedestrian was not entirely neglected. Moving sidewalks were being installed in many airports and railroad stations.

The U.S. Army was doing things for its weary foot-sloggers. It was field-testing a rocket belt for infantrymen that propelled a man as high as 30 feet and as far as 360 feet at a clip. "You might say it's like having a big person . . . a giant . . . pick you up by the arms," a reporter declared.

Some things novel were being added to the waterways of the world, like hydrofoils.

Wings work in water the way they work in air. When they attain certain speeds, they provide a lift and support weight. If a set of such wings is attached under a boat by stilts, they will lift the boat's hull clear of the water as soon as it gets moving fast enough. At that point, all the resistance that the hull presents to the water vanishes. There, capsulized, is the principle of the hydrofoil. It is as though a boat were riding on a pair of giant water skis.

Since the small, thin surfaces of the foils give the water little to grab at, a hydrofoil boat can whiz along at a speed of more than one hundred miles an hour.

Like the monorail, the hydrofoil is far from being a recent invention. An Italian, Enrico Forlanini, built the first hydrofoil and drove it across Lake Maggiore in Italy in 1906 at a snappy pace of forty-four miles per hour. Orville Wright and his brother Wilbur played around with the hydrofoil for a spell in 1907, but jilted it in favor of their true love, the airplane. Captain H. C. Richardson of the U.S. Navy built America's first, and skittered it down the Potomac in 1909. In 1918 seventy-one-year-old Alexander Graham

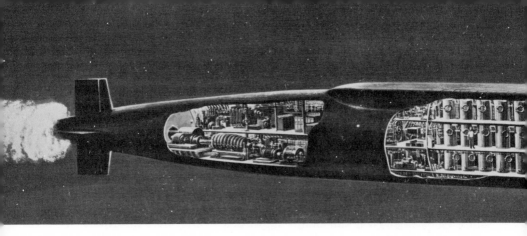

Typical Polaris Fleet

Bell, the inventor of the telephone, became interested in hydrofoils and teamed with Casey Baldwin to develop one that reached sixty knots an hour on ladder-shaped foils. But Messrs. Bell and Baldwin couldn't get anyone to finance them, and the hydrofoil idea went into hibernation for the next several decades.

Then it came awake and started going lots of places.

By the mid-1960's, Volga boatmen were sweeping up and down the historic Russian river in 150-passenger Meteorclass hydrofoils, and Sputnik-class hydrofoils were carrying 300 passengers on the Black Sea. A jet-propelled Soviet hydrofoil had racked up a sixty-eight-mile-an-hour record. Italians were skidding across the Straits of Messina in hydrofoils and devotees of *la dolce vita* were riding them between Riviera towns. Trieste and Venice were bonded by a hydrofoil run on the Adriatic, and a Spanish company was scheduled to start a ferry service between Barcelona, Valencia, and the island of Majorca with an eighty-eight-passenger hydrofoil in the late summer of 1966. It was to do fifty knots an hour.

In the United States, hydrofoils promised to help solve commuting problems for cities bordering on navigable waters. New York City got its first commuter service of this waterborne genre in 1963 when a twenty-four-passenger hydrofoil named the *Albatross* began shuttling between midtown Manhattan and suburban Port Washington on Long Island. A *New York Times* account said, "The passenger feels nothing unusual until the boat reaches eighteen miles an hour, at which point the hydrofoils develop enough lift to raise the hull about four feet above the water.

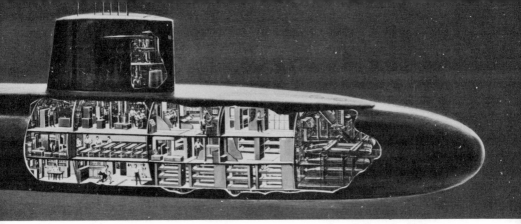

ballistic missile submarine.

"The passenger has to concentrate to be aware of the moment when the boat lifts itself up onto its water wings," the *Times* went on. "There is a slight elevation of the bow, the boat seems to hunch itself slightly forward and upward, in a motion less noticeable than that in a slow-moving elevator. And then it hangs firmly in its new position, racing blithely along over the arching spray from its underwater wings."

A flotilla of these hydrofoils carried thousands of gay visitors up the East River to the New York World's Fair in 1964.

Both the U.S. and the Soviet Navies were enthralled with hydrofoils as possible submarine chasers. It was the only species of ship afloat that could keep up with the new high-speed nuclear submarines.

Underwater, fuel cells were being tested for powering submarines, and U.S. Navy researchers were working on a propulsion system that might eliminate the traditional screw and rudder on submarines. In their place, they were employing "some twenty narrow blades mounted on a sort of band encircling the submarine's hull and rotating at controlled speeds." Each blade could alter its pitch at need.

The Navy said that such a system, placed both at the bow and the stern, would let its submarines carry out any kind of maneuvers.

Submarine men were predicting wide use of their craft by civilians. The time was coming, they said, when submarines would ply the underseas as regularly as today's surface ships breast the waves. As they foresee it, submarines will carry cargo and passengers safely out of range of the storms that toss the surface. They say that submarines will serve as underwater jeeps, trucks, and tractors for underwater fish ranches where measureless numbers of finny creatures will be bred, raised, and herded to nets. The United States government anticipates harvests of 220,000,000 tons of fish a year from these ranches. The submariners predict that their craft will also be used to plant and reap marine vegetables, and for underwater mining operations. They say that the ocean floor is thick with copper, cobalt, manganese, nickel, and other metals that submarines could easily scoop up. The *Diving Saucer,* a highly maneuverable research submarine, designed by the eminent French oceanographer Jacques-Yves Cousteau, showed in 1965 that this was more than an idle dream. It put in a stint at the bottom of the North Pacific and brought up a load of precious rocks from the ocean bed. The U.S. Bureau of Mines demonstrated its faith in the concept by contracting for the construction of a submarine to explore the mineral riches of the oceans.

Prospecting for oil is another mission that the submariners foresee, and a very lucrative one when you consider that there is probably far more oil under water than under land. It is a safe bet, petroleum experts say, that 25 percent of new oil and gas finds during the next quarter-century will be made underwater, and will be worked by submarines. Four unmanned robot submarines were tending underwater oil wells off the California coast in 1966. They were controlled from the surface by operators who watched over them through television cameras.

An incredible variety of bizarre new craft for investigating the ocean's depths was in the works. At the Woods Hole Oceanographic Institution on Cape Cod, a 22-foot-long underwater vehicle was making test dives in 1966. Named the *Alvin,* it could carry two men on ten-hour trips 6,000 feet below the surface at a speed of three miles per hour. A 40-foot submarine named *Deep Quest* with the capability of taking four men and a 3½-ton payload down 6,000 feet was under construction on the West Coast. A strange underseas vessel called the *Aluminaut* was cruising at the bottom of the Gulf Stream off Miami. Made of an aluminum alloy, it looked like nothing so much as "a big roll of foil." It was 51 feet long, had a diameter inside of 7 feet, and its 6½-inch thick walls could with-

General Dynamics Photo.

Research submarines STAR II and STAR III now active in oceanographic research surveys.

stand pressures of 50,000 pounds per square inch! It could carry twelve men 15,000 feet down, and make three-day tours, roving about the depths of the ocean at a speed of four miles per hour, picking up anything on the ocean floor that seemed interesting.

(The record for deep sea diving was held by the U.S. Navy bathyscaphe *Trieste*. Dr. Jacques Piccard, the famous underwater explorer, and Lieutenant Don Walsh of the U.S. Navy took this deep sea diving craft down 35,800 feet in the Pacific southwest of Guam on January 23, 1960.)

A different function for submarines was unveiled in Switzerland in the summer of 1964—sightseeing. Dr. Piccard started sailing sightseers down to the bottom of Lake Geneva in his forty-passenger, $1,500,000 submarine, the *Auguste Piccard*. It had large windows through which the passengers could look out at marine life on the bottom of the lake, and there was a television screen over every four seats that let passengers see through the craft's periscope. A forty-minute ride cost ten dollars per person.

Submarine travel was increasing so much that the U.S. Navy was developing a network of special weather stations to provide trustworthy forecasts of underwater conditions.

Some people were going in for submarining as a sport and special submarines were being built for them. A chic Texas department store even advertised "His" and "Her" submarines for sale in its Christmas gift catalogues. They were priced at $18,700 apiece.

Another type of underwater project was due to start in 1966—the greatest of its kind in history. After an eighty-two-year lapse, tunneling was to recommence 160 feet below the rough waves of the English Channel.

In 1878 French engineers began tunneling westward from a point near Calais. Three years later, British engineers set out to meet them boring eastward from Dover. Then, the British government changed its mind and revoked its authorization for a tunnel under the Channel. An enemy might use it to invade England, the Cabinet feared. Lieutenant General St. Garnet Wolseley shrilly warned, "Surely John Bull will not endanger all that man can hold most dear, simply in order that men and women may cross to and fro between England and France without running the risk of sea-sickness." By 1884 all work was halted.

In 1966 the two governments finally agreed to let it be resumed by a group of British, French, and American companies.

The longest tunnel in the world, it will stretch thirty-two miles from Folkestone to Calais with twenty-three of these miles under water, and it will cost about $500,000,000. It is to be a railroad tunnel for automotive vehicles. Double-decker "piggyback" trains will carry automobiles and trucks through in sixty-five minutes, nearly two-and-a-half hours less than the time a ferry takes. The motorists will see television shows en route. When the tunnel is completed in 1971, it will be able to handle as many cars in a week as can cross the channel by ferry in a year: 600,000.

Serious planning was going on in 1966 for a new canal between the Atlantic and Pacific Oceans. A sea level canal across Colombia, Nicaragua, or Panama was most favored, and the talk was of using nuclear explosives to do the digging. Dr. Gerald W. Johnson, Assistant to the U.S. Secretary of Defense, estimated that a canal could be dug with nuclear explosives for one-seventh of the cost of conventional methods; for $750,000,000 with "nukes," that is, as against $5,000,000,000 or more with ordinary dynamiting techniques.

So the atom could truly be working for peace, and saving a mint of money.

It was once said that the airplane would not be worth much until it could back up. That day may be approaching. By the mid-1960's, airplanes were able to do something quite as extraordinary—take off and land vertically. The U.S. Navy had test-flown one model that went straight up off a carrier deck like an elevator, and descended straight down again.

A 1966 report by the Massachusetts Institute of Technology predicted that by the mid-1970's 400-mile-an-hour VTOL (Vertical Takeoff and Landing) planes would be able to take off and land with passengers on the roofs of office buildings right in the heart of town, thereby avoiding the agonizing ground transit between urban centers and their far-off airports.

In the light of this accomplishment, backing up a plane in midair should certainly be feasible.

Something else that could make aeronautical history was in prospect. A new wing design that could eventually allow aircraft to stay in the air three to four days without refueling was test-flown at Edwards Air Force Base in California in 1963. The design, the split wing, was termed "the most promising innovation" since the jet engine. For substantial reasons.

Four-fifths of the friction drag on a wing is caused by a phenomenon known as the boundary layer turbulence, in other words, the boiling flow of air over the wing's surface. The split wing does away with this problem. It has a series of tiny lengthwise slits, each no more than 0.008 inch thick, along both its sides. Special pumps breathe in the air through these slits as it passes over the wing and shoot it out behind, eliminating the turbulence and a good 80 percent of the drag. A great deal less work is required of the plane's engines, and the consequent savings in fuel can extend its range by thousands of miles.

With it, nonstop passenger flights would be possible from key cities in the United States to almost every point in the world.

A lot more speed was in the offing for air passengers, too. The British and French governments were collaborating on the production of a supersonic jet airliner, the *Concorde,* in 1966, that was expected to do 1,450 miles per hour. This plane was to have a passenger capacity of 140 and a range of 4,000 miles. The multinational designers planned to have it in passenger service in 1970. They wanted it to be the world's first supersonic airliner.

The Soviet Union's airline, Aeroflot, had its own ideas on the subject. Reportedly, it was test-flying an airliner in 1966 that could carry 150 passengers at a speed of 1,800 miles an hour. It was said to be a copy of the Russian Air Force's bomber *Bounder*.

The United States was a strong entry in the air speed sweepstakes. Spurred by the Federal Government, two great American aviation companies were designing an airliner that they hoped would do 2,000 miles per hour in the early 1970's. Unlike the French and British engineers who were using an aluminum skin and "souped-up current jet engines" that were presently accessible

The Boeing B-52,
powered by eight
Pratt & Whitney J-57
Turbo-Wasp Engines.

The Boeing Company.

to them, the Americans were gambling on the evolution of new, infinitely more powerful engines and the perfection of a titanium skin that could endure 400-degree temperatures.

The designs called for a plane that would be 271 feet long, nearly as long as a football field. It would carry 255 passengers from New York to Paris in less than three hours. Each plane would cost $30,000,000.

The feasibility of the design was demonstrated in April, 1966, when the U.S. Air Force's XB-70, the forerunner of the SST (Supersonic Transport) easily did 2,000 miles an hour at an altitude of 70,000 feet.

With such speed, air travel will be nigh-unbelievable. In 1918 the average single-engine wooden biplane went 90 miles per hour. In 1925 the new all-metal transport did 100 miles an hour. In 1930 the two-engine airliner cruised at 158 miles per hour, and in 1940, the first four-engine airliners got up to 200 miles per hour. When the first American jet airliners went into service in 1958, 600 miles an hour was a good speed. But with Mach 2 and Mach 3 planes, a traveler can anticipate airline schedules that read: New York to Paris—two hours, thirty minutes; New York to Rome—two hours, fifty-one minutes; New York to Buenos Aires—three hours, forty-six minutes; New York to Anchorage, Alaska—one hour, forty-nine minutes; New York to Tokyo—three hours, forty-five minutes.

A United States Senate aviation subcommittee was told that a passenger in a Mach 2 or Mach 3 aircraft "could leave London at eight A.M., refuel, be in Los Angeles before eight A.M., there refuel and be in Hawaii at eight A.M., Hawaii time."

Why should anyone want to travel so fast? A journalist put that question to Najeeb E. Halaby, when he was Administrator of the Federal Aviation Agency, and he had a straightforward answer:

> To save time. Why did we go from propellers to jets? Why did we go from the horse to the Ford? Why do we want to get more speed out of our ocean liners? Man is always trying to conquer matter. . . .
>
> Cutting the time between New York and Sydney, Australia, to a third of what it takes now—or the time saving between Washington and Tokyo—with a supersonic transport will have a great value to the businessman, to the Government official, maybe later to the military man.
>
> It will bring these nations closer together. It will enable scarce items like serum and plans and special things that need to move very rapidly to be more within reach.

Meanwhile, the American airline industry was not standing still awaiting the arrival of the SST. The biggest airliner in history, one that could carry 490 passengers, was in production. It was sched-

Sikorsky Aircraft photos.

Helicopters in action: 1. A Sikorsky CH-53A aboard a carrier;

uled to make its debut on the airlanes in September, 1969, and, if its designs worked out, it was to be 228 feet long, weigh 680,000 pounds, and be able to fly 6,000 miles at an average speed of 633 miles per hour.

The best news was that it was expected to cut transatlantic plane fares 10 to 15 percent.

There was another innovation in transport, the ground effect machine, which was more remarkable, perhaps, than any of the others. It had all the splendid attributes of the airplane, boat, and automobile wrapped up in one vehicle.

Lockheed's supersonic transport with "weather vision" nose that lowers 15 degrees from normal supersonic flight position to provide excellent vision for takeoff, holding and landing;

Lockheed Aircraft Corporation.

2. *the HH-52A to the rescue.*

Scientifically, the facts on this ground effect machine are these. By directing air through jet nozzles toward any surface below—be it mud, cement, snow, ice, or water—a ground effect machine can create an air cushion for itself and ride on it. By lifting its nozzles and directing the flow of air to the rear, it can push itself forward at speeds of hundreds of miles an hour. Or it can hover motionless over any spot it chooses.

By the summer of 1962 the British had hoverboats in commercial operation. They began a ferry service across the Dee Estuary in Wales, with hoverboats that each carried twenty-four passengers. They followed that with a service by hovercraft between Portsmouth, England, and the Isle of Wight, a ten-minute run that cost ten shillings, $1.40. In April, 1966, they inaugurated crosschannel service to Calais, France.

An American concern commenced testing a twelve-ton, 55-foot-long hoverboat on Long Island Sound in 1964, and the Soviet Union started construction of a twenty-ton hoverboat that was to tote fifty passengers, three on each side of the aisle, do seventy-five miles an hour, and have a range of 250 miles between ports. A report in *Pravda* on January 5, 1964, stated that, "The new ship, still without a name, will be able to reach areas now inaccessible by river transportation."

The size of these ground effect vessels was practically unlimited. Marine experts said that 40,000-ton ocean liners may come skimming over the Atlantic, 20 feet above the waves, at a speed of 100 knots instead of the customary 30 to 35. They were on the drawingboards in Britain.

Airmen were very interested in the ground effect because it permitted a plane to remain stationary in the air. The U.S. Army and U.S. Air Force were jointly experimenting with a ground effect plane that was shaped like a flying saucer, was to be capable of speeds up to 400 miles an hour, and would be able to rise straight up to 20,000 feet.

The possibilities of ground effect machines for land travel were, if anything, more exciting. Several American companies were exploring cars that skimmed above the ground on air cushions, and the U.S. Army was working on a ground effect version of the jeep. It was the *Caraboa*, it carried two men, and it could do forty miles an hour. The Army tested it in 1964 over Potomac ice floes, Florida swamps, and the Long Island surf with much success.

What about nuclear-powered travel by automobiles, trains, and airplanes? The answer is not in the foreseeable future.

Although atomic power can do a lot for surface ships and submarines, it is unlikely to be of help in land or air transport. Too dangerous, the scientists say. One crash of a nuclear-powered airplane could be as lethal as an H-bomb explosion.

Atoms for space travel? That's another matter.

This, too, was exciting. In Washington, D.C., there was new appreciation of the vital importance of transportation to the future of the American nation. In March, 1966, President Lyndon B. Johnson proposed to Congress that it establish a cabinet-level Department of Transportation to plan and coordinate an efficient, countrywide transportation system. It was to be the fifth-biggest department in the Federal Government with a budget of almost $5,000,000,000 and 100,000 employees—all to see that people and things move better inside and outside the United States.

XIV

The Widening Horizon

SHORTLY AFTER the midway mark in the twentieth century, man broke the shackles that bound him to his one small planet, and the space age began.

It almost had commenced some 450 years before.

Valid records prove that an audacious Chinese named Wan Hoo experimented with rocket travel early in the sixteenth century. According to these records, Wan lashed two giant kites to a great frame that he'd constructed, fastened forty-seven big gunpowder rockets to it to provide propulsion, and put a saddle in the center for himself. He mounted the saddle and had each of forty-seven torchbearers light one of the rockets.

When the smoke had cleared and the roar subsided, it was evident that Wan had gone traveling, but to where no one was ever able to discover. Every shred of Wan Hoo and his contraption had disappeared.

Chronologically, the history of space travel can be traced back still farther, to the invention of the rocket itself. This first major milestone on the road to the stars was reached in China about A.D. 232. That year, Ogodai, the third son of Genghis Khan, lay siege with his Mongol hordes to the city of Kaifeng, capital of Honan Province, and the desperate Chinese defended themselves with "arrows of flying fire." They were the first rockets—projectiles shot through the air by igniting combustible chemicals packed inside them.

Europe was quick, and happy, to adopt these projectiles as weapons for its wars. The capture of the island of Chioggia, south of Venice, in 1397 was due to them. A rocket fired off by the Venetian fleet hit a tower ashore and set the Chioggian fortifications ablaze.

After cannon became practical in 1600 or thereabouts, rockets faded away as weapons of war. People just used them for fireworks displays. Then the British wars in India started. At the Battle of Seringapatam in 1792, the soldiers of the Sultan of Mysore cut loose at the British cavalry with rockets. The British were routed and rockets came right back into military fashion.

A brainy British artillerist, Colonel William Congreve, now became interested in them and developed a new type with a range up to 2,000 yards. The chemicals he used were soaked in alcohol, making a paste which was so explosive that it had to be stuffed into the rocket under water to reduce the danger of an accidental blast. The rocket had to dry for four months before it could be utilized.

The British employed these new rockets against Copenhagen during the Napoleonic Wars. They burned down half the Danish city with them in 1807 and the Congreve invention became a standard weapon of the British Navy. The rockets Americans sing about in *"The Star Spangled Banner"* were Congreve rockets fired in the British naval assault on Fort McHenry in the War of 1812. They produced a lot more red glare there than physical damage, incidentally.

Rockets were soon again to go out of style as weapons; they didn't have the range or the accuracy of cannon. But their development meant that rocketry was out of the kindergarten and the first technological step had been taken toward the moon.

Some brave geniuses had, meanwhile, been providing man with the scientific basis for space travel. Vital questions of distance, time, and space mechanics had to be answered, and answered they were regardless of ecclesiastical opposition.

For nearly 2,000 years before the seventeenth century, philosophers and priests insisted that man, and therefore the earth, was the center of the universe; that the sun, moon, planets, and stars were set in revolving glass spheres, because the sphere was the most perfect form imaginable, and that, consequently, space was finite; that the physical laws which applied on earth did not hold true in the heavens; and that any attempt to challenge the veracity of such a view of the universe was heresy punishable by death.

Nicolaus Copernicus, a Polish astronomer, offered the first stiff challenge to this view in the sixteenth century by asserting that the world revolved around the sun, not vice versa—and thereby drew down the wrath of the Inquisition.

In 1584 an Italian monk, Giordano Bruno, had the temerity to theorize that while the earth was revolving around the sun, the sun was also in motion. Bruno visualized an infinite universe with innumerable planetary systems whirling through space. For this he too was burned at the stake.

Next, Tycho Brahe of Denmark, while not subscribing to Copernicus' disturbing suggestion, proposed one equally upsetting in 1598: that comets might move not in circles but in ellipses. Such an idea was obviously a crack in the so-called spherical, crystalline perfection of God's work.

Eleven years later, the German mathematician, Johannes Kepler, proved mathematically that the planets moved around the sun and, furthermore, that they moved not in perfect circles but in ellipses. The stultifying theory of spheres was collapsing.

The Italian Galileo Galilei—magnificent as a mathematician, physicist, and astronomer—discovered a new star in "the sphere of the stars" in 1604. That, added to the finding of another new star by Brahe in 1572, bespoke changeability in the heavens and exploded the outermost sphere concept. Soon after, Galileo invented an astronomical telescope, and in 1610 he published a booklet on some of the discoveries he had made with it. They were momentous. The moon, he wrote, seemed to have mountains, seas, and rivers; furthermore, the planet Jupiter had moons circling *it*. These were observations that could (and did) lead men to wonder whether life might not exist on planets other than the earth.

Following that, Galileo openly, valiantly, espoused the Copernican doctrine of a sun-centered universe.

His was great scientific wisdom, and, so far as the Inquisition was concerned, appalling heresy. In a tragic episode, Galileo was tried for his "crime" by ten cardinals, and compelled to kneel down before them and recant publicly the doctrine that the earth moved around the sun.

But he didn't recant inside himself. As he rose from his knees, legend has it that he murmured, *"E pur si muove"* (Nevertheless, it does move).

Then came England's Isaac Newton, one of the greatest thinkers of all time. He was born in 1642, the year that Galileo, blind and miserable, died.

Superb mathematician, natural philosopher, and human being, Newton capitalized on the findings of Copernicus, Galileo, and the others to establish a series of scientific laws that helped to explain the universe—and motion in space—to man.

He proved that it was possible to deduce from terrestial phenomena the laws that applied in space. Exhibit A was gravity. The same forces that made the apple drop on Newton's head caused the moon to revolve around the earth, a principle that had to be taken into consideration in many ways for space travel.

Newton also proved that for every action there was an equal and opposite reaction. This is commonly referred to as the Third Law of Motion, and few scientific concepts have ever carried men so far.

A graphic illustration of the workings of this Newtonian law could be a boy diving forward from a canoe into the water. He shoves the canoe backward. If no friction is involved, and the canoe and the boy are of the same weight, they will move at identical speeds—in opposite directions—away from the point at which the dive begins.

Or, to cite the excellent example of the English scientist Arthur C. Clarke, picture yourself standing on a railroad flatcar which is loaded with bricks. You can pick up a brick and heave it over one end of the car. If there is no friction to retard motion, the flatcar will begin to move along the rails in the direction opposite to that in which the brick is thrown. As you pitch other bricks away behind you, the flatcar will become lighter and go faster.

"It does not matter in the least," Clarke points out, "what happens to the bricks after they have left the hand of the thrower: all the recoil or thrust is produced in the act of throwing itself. The method of propulsion is, therefore, *independent of any external medium.*"

Here, in essence, is the reason why space travel is possible. Many laymen erroneously think that rocket power works by pushing against the air. It isn't so. Rocket power performs best in a frictionless environment where there is no air to provide resistance to forward motion. The rocket is propelled by the forces of gases being "thrown" backward from it, not by the gases pushing against the air behind it.

By the early nineteenth century, a few space scientists were seriously testing the possibilities of rocket travel. In Paris, Claude-Fortune Ruggieri, a well-known maker of fireworks, sent mice and rats aloft in rockets during the 1830's. At burnout the rodents' capsules were ejected and floated back to earth by parachute. These tests were so successful that Ruggieri scheduled a flight with a human passenger, a small boy who'd volunteered his services. The French authorities thought this was carrying matters too far, though, and the gendarmes intervened.

Modern rocketry came into being at the close of the nineteenth century. A Russian schoolteacher, Konstantin Edouardovitch Tsiolkovsky, launched it.

Born in 1857, the son of a woodsman, Tsiolkovsky was deafened by scarlet fever at the age of eleven and couldn't go to school anymore. He educated himself and at twenty this brilliant young man was teaching school in the little town of Kaluga. By the time he was twenty-three, he had devised, completely on his own, ways of measuring the speed of light. The fact that, unbeknownst to him, these techniques had been developed a number of years earlier by other scientists did not diminish the luster of his achievement.

At the outset of his career, Tsiolkovsky was chiefly interested in dirigibles, but by 1895 he had started to focus on the problems of space flight. Again, moving without knowledge of what any other scientists were doing, he worked out a theory for a rocket engine that could overcome the gravitational pull of the earth and function in the void of outer space. It was to operate on the Newtonian "reaction" principle, and to power it he had a capital new idea: liquid fuel.

Previously, rockets had always derived their power from the simple gunpowder and other dry chemicals with very limited thrust. Liquid fuel was vastly more powerful.

Tsiolkovsky conceived of rockets with more than one stage—a series of connected rockets that fired one after another. He thought it might be possible, too, to make a rocket over into a space station that could continually circle the earth and serve as a research laboratory.

Yet for all Tsiolkovsky's greatness, his pioneering ideas went largely to waste. Outside of Russia few heard of them, and inside Russia nobody did anything tangible about them. His ideas stayed on paper.

It was left to a sickly, secretive, suspicious American genius to use liquid fuel in an actual rocket. He was Robert Hutchings Goddard, he was born in Worcester, Massachusetts, in 1882, and one October afternoon when he was seventeen years old he had a vision of a space craft, spinning, rising up into the air. He carried that vision with him for the remainder of his painful, tuberculosis-racked life.

Before his thirty-second birthday he had been awarded his first rocket patents. During World War I, he did research on rockets, and in 1920 the Smithsonian Institution published a paper in which he summed up the work he had done on high-altitude projectiles. It would be possible to build a rocket to reach the moon, he said. If a charge of flash powder was packed into the nose, men watching from the earth through telescopes might be able to see it hit the moon.

Like Tsiolkovsky, Goddard was attracted by the thrust that seemed possible with liquid fuels. From 1920 to his death in 1945, liquid-fueled rockets held most of his attention. His efforts were marked by far more failures than successes, but one of the most important milestones in space flight was set up by him. At the farm of a relative in Auburn, Massachusetts, at 2:30 o'clock on the cold, bright afternoon of March 16, 1926, he successfully launched the world's first liquid-fueled rocket.

Essentially, what he'd designed and built was a two-part rocket. The engine and nozzle formed the nose, placed there in hopes of adding to the rocket's stability. For some distance beneath this section the body of the rocket consisted of two slender pipes, separated to make room for the engine's blast. They carried the gasoline and liquid oxygen fuel up to the engine from the tank unit at the tail. The rocket was 10 feet long, but in appearance it was mostly emptiness.

It rose 41 feet, burned for 2½ seconds, and came down 184 feet from the launching stand, flying at an average speed of sixty miles per hour.

While he continued to carry out a careful, workmanlike research program, Goddard was hampered by his disease, his obsessive fear of having his ideas stolen or eclipsed, and especially by his lack of funds. His secretiveness did not encourage other people to help him; only rarely did he speak freely in front of anyone other than his immediate family and his staff. Happily for him, one of the men with whom he felt safe was Charles Lindbergh. Lindbergh was deeply impressed with his research and enlisted the support for it of Harry Guggenheim, the copper magnate and aviation enthusiast, who subsequently supplied much of the cash spent by Goddard in his projects.

Enough money was forthcoming from Guggenheim, and, for a period, from the Smithsonian Institution, to keep Goddard going. But just barely. Always he had to worry about his next dollar. At no point was there anything like a crash program for his high-altitude, liquid-fueled rockets. Perhaps if he had been willing to admit other scientists to his laboratory and work with them in a team, he might have generated enough scientific ardor to spur United States government interest in his projects. But he was not willing, and Washington scarcely gave his high-altitude research a side glance.

Despite his enforced skimping, his illness, and his insistence on going it alone, Goddard made giant advances. Not only did he establish the worth of liquid-fueled rockets, but he designed the first practical automatic steering apparatus for rockets, based on a small gyroscope. One of his rockets, making use of this system, ascended to 7,500 feet in 1935.

In the testimony of Dr. Wernher von Braun, the most famous of all German rocketeers, "Dr. Goddard was ahead of us all."

Dear Sir,

Already many years I work at the problem to pass over the atmosphere of our earth by means of a rocket. When I was now publishing the result of my examinations and calculations, I learned by the newspaper, that I am not alone in my inquiries and that you, dear Sir, have already done much important works at this sphere. In spite of my efforts, I did not succeed in getting your books about this object.

Therefore I beg you, dear Sir, to let them have me.—At once after coming out of my work I will be honoured to send it to you, for I think that only by the common work of scholars of all nation can be solved this great problem.

Yours very truly
Hermann Oberth
stud. math.
Heidelberg.
Kaiserstr. 48[1]
Germany

The letter was dated May 23, 1922, and it was addressed to Dr. Goddard in America. It was written from Germany by a twenty-eight-year-old Rumanian who was studying mathematics at the University of Heidelberg.

This Hermann Oberth and a group of his talented German disciples were to learn from Dr. Goddard and proceed to surpass him. His disciples were to develop the first reliable long-distance rocket. And they were to make of it an instrument of horrible, mass death: the V-2, otherwise known by Adolf Hitler's Nazi nomenclature, "Vengeance Weapon-2."

Overriding his innate suspiciousness, Dr. Goddard sent young Oberth his 1919 Smithsonian report. The following year, he received a ninety-two-page treatise that Oberth had written. Its title was, *The Rocket into Interplanetary Space,* and it was a *magnum opus.* Whereas Goddard didn't go much beyond the thought of lunar flights, Oberth showed mathematically that the moon needed merely to be a first step. Mars and other planets, he said, were in rocket-reach.

With almost incredible foresight, Dr. Goddard memoed the Smithsonian Institution in 1923:

I am not surprised that Germany has awakened to the importance and the development possibilities of the work, and I would not be surprised if it were only a matter of time before the research would become something in the nature of a race.

Oberth himself was primarily a theoretician. When he tried to build a high-altitude, liquid-fueled rocket in 1929 as a publicity stunt for a German science fiction movie called *The Girl in the Moon,* he failed, and despondently returned to the town of Mediash in Transylvania where he had a job as a mathematics teacher in the local high school. A year later, he came back to Germany and successfully tested a small liquid-fueled rocket motor, but that was as far as he got in terms of "hardware." The first liquid-fueled rocket to go up in Europe was built and fired by the German aeronautical engineer Johannes Winkler on March 14, 1931.

However, an assistant of Professor Oberth on the rocket motor project was an eighteen-year-old Prussian, tall, blond, and very handsome, who was very proficient with "hardware"—Wernher von Braun. He had begun his acquaintance with Oberth by volunteering to help him set up a space flight exhibit in a Berlin department store.

"I'm still in technical school and can't offer you anything more than spare time and enthusiasm, but isn't there something I can do to help," he had asked Oberth.

"Come right over," Oberth had said.

Von Braun was to go on with his studies and garner a doctorate in physics from the University of Berlin at the age of twenty-two with a thesis on the scientific love of his life: liquid-fueled rocket engines. And go on from there to lead, successively, the rocket programs of Nazi Germany and the United States.

The youthful Prussian and a few other Oberth disciples became the moving spirits of a Society for Space Travel whose German name was commonly shortened to VfR. The members had imagination, talent, everything but money. They were so short of research funds that they had to scrounge equipment, chemicals, tools, a place to conduct their experiments. One of the best of the scroungers and early space scientists, Rudolph Nebel, softsoaped the municipal authorities of Reinickendorf, a suburb of Berlin, into letting them use an abandoned ammunition depot. There they built a number of crude liquid-fueled projectiles, including the *Mirak I* which went as high as 1,200 feet and settled softly down to earth with the help of a parachute.

The Ordnance Department of the *Reischswehr* was intrigued by their work. To the *Reischswehr*, it sounded like a clever ruse for circumventing the Versailles Treaty. The treaty banned Germany from manufacturing long-range cannon, but it made no mention of long-range rockets. At a conference with von Braun, the *Reichswehr* offered to underwrite his group's expenses in building a long-range, liquid-fueled rocket provided it could be manufactured industrially. And provided that he and his associates agreed to work in total secrecy under military control.

Of the three top men in the group, two, Nebel and Klaus Riedel, would have nothing to do with the Army's proposition. Regardless of the financial strain, they preferred to work as civilians upon civilian space undertakings. Von Braun saw it differently and decided to go with the Army. It was the best way to raise money for rocket research, he said, and at the age of twenty, he took charge of the German Army's liquid-fueled-rocket project.

In a few years this increased from a minuscule operation to an enormous one. Interservice jealousy helped it grow. Von Braun did some work for the *Luftwaffe* on rocket-powered aircraft, and the air arm was so impressed with the results that it allocated 5,000,000 marks to him to expand his project. Not to be outdone, the Army appropriated 6,000,000 marks for the same purpose.

As headquarters for his work, von Braun chose Peenemünde, a remote island in the mouth of the Peene River on the Baltic coast, and he built an establishment there with a staff of thousands and the best obtainable facilities. Once World War II broke out in 1939, Hitler and his Nazis gave von Braun's activities still higher priority. Von Braun's rockets would be the secret weapons to win the war for him, the Nazi *Führer* hoped.

After many false starts, von Braun and the crack team of space scientists he'd assembled at Peenemünde brought out a fifteen-ton rocket, 46 feet long, with an engine that operated on a combination of liquid oxygen and alcohol. Its official German Army designation was the A-4; the V-2 title was for public consumption.

On October 3, 1942, it was successfully fired. The rocket

climbed more than 30 miles high into the sky and impacted 118 miles away into the Baltic Sea.

"Today the space-ship was born," Major General Walter R. Dornberger, a noted scientist who was the military commander at Peenemünde, exulted. And he was correct. But first the rocket had a bloody war mission to perform.

Ironically, the first Vengeance Weapon that the Nazis used, prior to the V-2, was derived in large part from the pioneering research of Dr. Goddard. It was a pilotless, jet aircraft—in effect, a flying bomb—called the V-1. The Nazis launched 20,000 of them against England in early 1944 and they did considerable damage until the British learned how to fend them off. Many of the basic principles of the V-1 were patented by Dr. Goddard in 1934. Goddard's patent—U.S. patent No. 1,980,266—was translated and reprinted verbatim in the German aviation magazine *Flugsport* in January, 1939. The Nazis had no compunctions about learning from "the decadent democracies."

Von Braun's V-2's were infinitely more dangerous, of course. They went so high and so fast that there was no defense against them. They reached an altitude of 60 miles—316,800 feet—and attained speeds of 3,000 miles an hour! From launching pad to London, 190 miles away, was five minutes. Londoners were dead, blown to limp pieces, before they heard the rocket that killed them approach.

Three thousand V-2's were fired by the Germans, and 1,230 of them hit the British capital before the Allied armies captured the German launching sites and halted the slaughter.

If the war had continued, the Nazis had more ambitious plans for von Braun's rocket. They were designing a new winged model of the V-2 that was to carry a human pilot and have sufficient range to bomb the United States. New York City was marked as the first American target for European-based destruction.

The savage rivalry that exploded after World War II between the United States and the Soviet Union, the two leading powers on earth, inevitably spilled over into space. Not that this corollary was fully bad.

Once they had defeated the Nazis, the U.S. Army and the Red

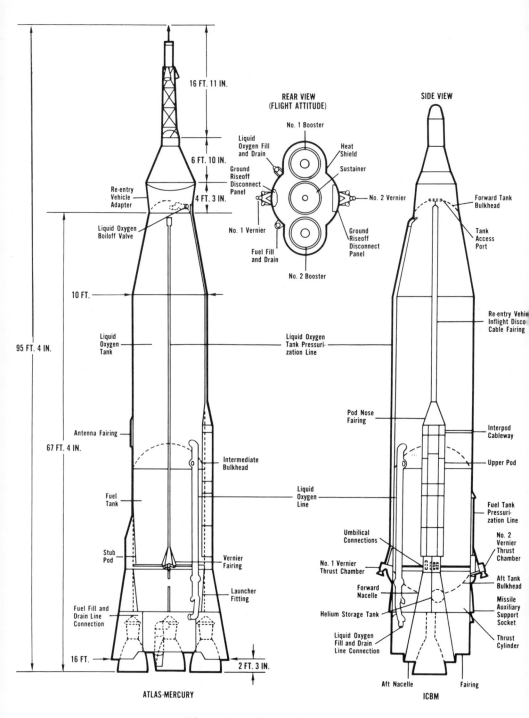

Three-view of standard Series D Atlas.

Army staged an amazing race across Germany to see which could grab off more German rocket experts. The U.S. Army won. It got von Braun and the vast majority of his tiptop Peenemünde crew. By choice they surrendered themselves, their V-2 working drawings, and sixteen shiploads of V-2 parts to the American forces.

Both nations centered their attention initially on the development of military rockets, trying to build ones that could go faster, farther, and kill more people. Steadily, they extended the scope of their rockets until both countries had intercontinental ballistic missiles with ranges up to 8,000 miles, ceilings 800 to 1,000 miles above the earth, speeds of more than 10,000 miles an hour, and the ability to transport thermonuclear warheads, each of which could kill millions of people at a blow. From pushbutton in Communist Russia to devastation of democratic America (or vice versa) might be less than thirty minutes.

The rockets that could deliver H-bombs could be put to other, better uses, though. And they were.

Early in the morning of Friday, October 4, 1957, fifteen years and one day after the first successful V-2 launching, the Russians provided the next monumental milestone of the space age. They put the first artificial satellite into orbit around the earth. *Sputnik* (Satellite) *I* was its name, it weighed 183.6 pounds, its first perigee was 142 miles from the earth, its first apogee was 588 miles up, and it circled the earth in 96.17 minutes at an average speed of 18,000 miles an hour. A report by Professor Yuri A. Pobedonostsev related that the first stage burned for a period of one to two minutes and raised the liquid-fueled carrier rocket directly up for approximately 5,280 feet where it veered off on a 45-degree angle and attained a speed of about 4,500 miles an hour. The second stage boosted the velocity to 12,000 miles an hour and brought *Sputnik I* some 625 miles away from the launching site where it took up a course parallel to the earth. In the third stage, *Sputnik I's* speed was increased to 18,000 miles per hour and it went into its permanent orbit 560 miles out from the earth.

The political, social, and scientific impact of this feat on the civilized world was immeasurable. Man, for the first time in his history, had burst out of his earthly environment and put a moon of his own up into the skies.

Sputnik I stayed in orbit until January 4, 1958. But not always alone. On November 3, 1957, the Soviets launched another satellite. This *Sputnik II* weighed 1,120 pounds. Along with scientific equipment for studying space, it carried the first animal to orbit the earth, a lively lady dog answering to the name of Laika, Russian for "Barker."

On January 31, 1958, the United States got into space. Dr. von Braun and his Peenemünde colleagues, who'd established a big rocket center for the U.S. Army at Huntsville, Alabama, put *Explorer I,* America's first satellite, into orbit. It weighed merely 18.13 pounds as compared to *Sputnik II*'s 1,120 pounds, but it showed that the United States was in the race. It also demonstrated the scientific versatility of the von Braun organization. Using an improved version of the V-2 as their carrier rocket, they built *Explorer I* in eighty-four days.

The Russians were to keep their lead for many years. Starting far earlier than the United States, they had developed more powerful propulsion systems that could lift much greater payloads. Consequently, they were able to run up an impressive series of firsts in space. On August 27, 1958, they sent up a research rocket from Soviet Central Asia that had a payload of 3,726.45 pounds and carried *two* dogs 280 miles out into space—and both dogs were recovered safely. On September 12, 1959, the Russians landed an 869-pound capsule, *Lunik I,* on the moon itself; it impacted in the neighborhood of the Sea of Serenity. Scarcely three weeks later, the Russians sent a *Lunik IV* into orbit around the moon. It radioed back to earth the first photographs of the far side of the moon.

On the morning of April 12, 1961, the Russians recorded another historic first. Twenty-seven-year-old Major Yuri A . Gagarin was launched into space in a five-ton satellite, *Vostok* (East) *I,* for a one-orbit, 108-minute flight to become the first human to travel through space. The "Columbus of the Cosmos," Premier Nikita S. Khrushchev phrased it. On August 6 and 7, 1961, a second Russian cosmonaut, Major Ghermain S. Titov orbited the earth seventeen times, and the world went even wilder over Russian astronautical prowess.

A year later, on August 11 and 12, 1962, the Russians doubled their achievements by putting two cosmonauts into space on successive days. Major Andrian G. Nikolayav made sixty-four orbits of the earth, and Lieutenant Colonel Pavel R. Popovich made forty-eight orbits. They were near enough to see each other's spacecraft.

To add a fine feminine touch to their space activities, the Russians put up a woman cosmonaut. On June 14, 1963, they launched Colonel Valery Bykovsky in *Vostok V* and followed him in two days with the world's first spacewoman, a blue-eyed blonde, Junior Lieutenant Valentina Tereshkova, in *Vostok VI*. The purpose of the joint flight, according to the twenty-six-year-old Valen-

North American Aviation, Inc., Columbus Division.

Twin-engine turboprop, OV-10A, designed to fill the performance gap between jets and helicopters.

tina, was the "simultaneous observation of the reactions of a man and a woman" to space travel. Miss Tereshkova managed forty-eight-plus orbits while Colonel Bykovsky went around the world eighty-one times. He stayed up four days, twenty-three hours, six minutes, and logged over 2,000,000 miles. Alas for fairy tale endings, romance did not flourish in space. Miss Tereshkova fell in love with Major Nikolayav instead. They were married and had a pretty girl baby in 1964 whom they named Yelena. A future cosmonaut, they predicted.

The United States was not going to let the Soviet Union get too far ahead of it in space, if it could help it. Less than a month after

Major Gagarin's epochal orbit, Commander Alan B. Shepard zoomed 116 miles out into space from Cape Kennedy, Florida, and made a 302-mile-flight over the Atlantic in the spacecraft *Freedom VII*. That was on May 5, 1961, and on July 21, Captain Virgil I. Grissom followed suit in *Liberty Bell VII*. Both of these were sub-orbital flights. Then, on February 21, 1962, Lieutenant Colonel John H. Glenn, Jr., a tall, forty-one-year-old Marine with a glorious smile, took off in the spacecraft *Friendship VII*. At a little after 9:47 A.M. Eastern Standard Time, a big Atlas ICBM rocket with the *Friendship VII* on its nose lifted itself from its pad on a thundering streak of flame. Five minutes, one and four-tenths seconds later, Colonel Glenn was in orbit, one-hundred miles up, speeding along at a speed of 25,730 feet per second, the first American space traveler. He found weightlessness to be "a very pleasant sensation," and looking out the window of his capsule a joy. "Oh, that view is treMENdous!," he exclaimed as he glanced down at "the sun on white clouds, patches of blue water beneath the great chunks of Florida and the southeastern United States." Three times Glenn circled the world, flying the capsule himself by manual controls in place of the automatic controls, performing various experiments, enjoying his several sunsets, and curiously studying the "fireflies" that seemed to surround *Friendship VII* at sunrise. He descended into the earth's atmosphere through temperatures as high as 9,500 degrees Fahrenheit, almost those of the sun, and landed his capsule safely by parachute in the Atlantic.

Other Americans followed hard on Glenn's space heels. Lieutenant Commander M. Scott Carpenter rocketed up on May 24, 1962, in *Aurora VII* and orbited the earth three times. He had a very hot time of it when the temperature controls on his space suit went awry. His body heat rose alarmingly, and he was drenched in torrents of perspiration. He had a little difficulty eating, too. The cookies he'd brought with him crumbled and flew out of their bags around the gravityless cabin "like a swarm of bees." Nevertheless, he savored his trip through space as much as Glenn did. As he sat on a raft in the sea, waiting to be picked up, he felt, Carpenter said, "that space was so fascinating and that a flight through it was so thrilling and so overwhelming that I only wish I could get up the next morning and go through the whole thing over again. I wanted

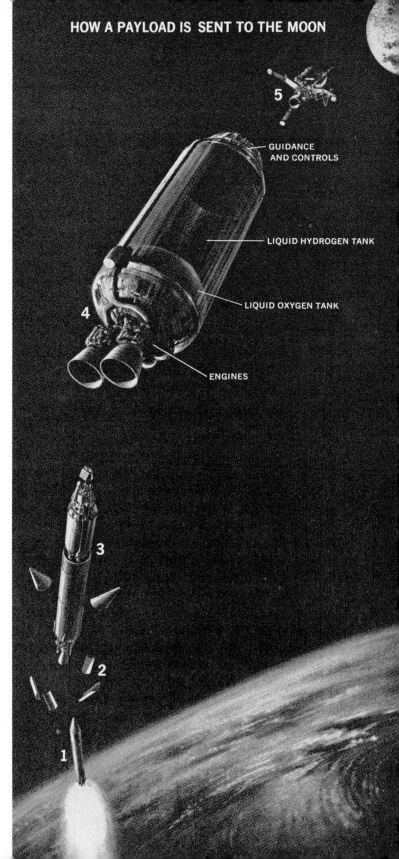

HOW A PAYLOAD IS SENT TO THE MOON

GUIDANCE AND CONTROLS

LIQUID HYDROGEN TANK

LIQUID OXYGEN TANK

ENGINES

1. Atlas starts Centaur and its payload on their flight.

2. Shortly before Atlas and Centaur have separated, insulation panels and then nose fairings have been jettisoned.

3. Atlas separates and Centaur and payload start their phase of journey.

4. Centaur has completed firing and separated from payload.

5. Payload continues along its orbit to the moon.

General Dynamics

to be weightless again, and see the sunsets and sunrises, and watch the stars drop through the luminous layer. . . ." Commander Walter M. Schirra, Jr., went up on October 3, 1962, in *Sigma VII*, orbited the earth six times, and returned as enthusiastic as the others.

A thirty-six-year-old U.S. Air Force pilot, Major Leroy Gordon Cooper, ascended from Cape Kennedy in the capsule *Faith VII* on May 15, 1962, and did twenty-two orbits. Of all the early space flights, Cooper's was the most harrowing, and, perhaps, the most significant. It demonstrated that man is more important than a machine even in a totally automated spaceship—that he is, in fact, indispensable.

"Gordo" Cooper's blast-off was nearly perfect and his first eighteen orbits passed off as smoothly and uneventfully as a ferry ride across San Francisco's Golden Bay. He carried out prescribed experiments, shot still and television pictures, discharged flashing orbs to check the visibility of objects in space, radioed messages of greeting to many of the one-hundred countries over which he soared, ate heartily, and had a comfortable 7½ hours sleep.

Halfway through the nineteenth orbit, a small green light on his control board lit up. The automatic system which was supposed to align the capsule and set off the retrorockets for reentry into the atmosphere, had failed. Cooper had to align the capsule manually and fire off the retro-rockets himself.

The least error could have demolished *Faith VII*, but Cooper didn't make any. As the precise moment approached for reentry, his fellow astronaut, Colonel Glenn, who was on a Navy ship in the Pacific, checked off the retro-rocket countdown with him by radio in an ideal exhibition of team work. With Glenn's help, Cooper steered his capsule back into the atmosphere and down to the target area in the Pacific, as he'd forecast, "right on the old bazoo," a short 7,000 yards from his recovery ship, the U.S. Navy aircraft carrier *Kearsage*.

"One of the victories for the human spirit," the late President Kennedy said.

On October 13, 1964, the Soviet Union put three men into orbit together in a 7½-ton spacecraft, the *Voskhod* (Sunrise). Blasting off from the Soviet cosmodrome at Baikonur, northwest of the Aral Sea, thirty-seven-year-old Colonel Vladamir M. Komarov, and two civilians, thirty-eight-year-old Konstantin P. Feoktistov, a space scientist, and Dr. Boris B. Yegerov, a twenty-seven-year-old physician, circled the earth sixteen times in twenty-four hours and seventeen minutes. Their bullet-shaped craft was so advanced that they didn't have to wear the usual bulky, unwieldy space suits. Dressed in ordinary gray sweatshirts, they lounged around their cabin in a pleasant 72-degree temperature, and they were able to eat tasty chicken fillets, tangy boneless Caspian fish called *plotva,* and vitamin-enriched candy without having to force them through the mouthpiece of a space helmet.

On March 18, 1965, the Soviet Union exceeded all its previous feats. At ten o'clock that morning, Lieutenant Colonel Aleksei A. Leonov left his two-man spacecraft *Voskhod II* as it orbited the earth, to float in space, the first man ever to do so. He remained outside the cabin for ten minutes, attached by a thin lifeline.

"I felt absolutely free, like a bird, as though I had wings," he rhapsodized.

The race into space was now to become two-sided, and close. In June, 1965, Major Edward H. White II went for a twenty-minute stroll in space while he and his fellow American Major James A. McDivitt passed four days in orbit.

"I felt red, white and blue all over," Major White exulted.

The following December 15, four Americans achieved a new, magnificent feat. Wally Schirra, a Navy captain by now, and Major Thomas Stafford, circling 185 miles above the earth at a speed of nearly five miles a second, maneuvered their *Gemini VI* spacecraft to within six feet of the *Gemini VII,* with Lieutenant Colonel Frank Borman and Commander James Lovell, Jr., in it, for men's first rendezvous in space.

"We have company tonight," Colonel Borman happily radioed the earth.

Borman and Lovell went on to set another spectacular record, staying up for 206 orbits—thirteen days, eighteen hours, and thirty-five minutes in space.

Three months later, a pair of American astronauts were to do something still more spectacular. On March 16, 1966, Neil A. Armstrong and Major David R. Scott in *Gemini VIII* made the first docking ever achieved in space. One hundred and eighty-five miles above the shores of Brazil, they locked onto an *Agena* target space-craft.

"Flight, we are docked. And he's really a smoothie," Armstrong messaged the Manned Spacecraft Center in Houston, Texas. For thirty minutes the two spacecraft flew together. Then . . .

The control system on the *Gemini VII* suddenly went crazy. Only by superb piloting skill were the two astronauts able to cut loose from the *Agena,* stop their craft from tumbling head over heels, and bring it down to a safe landing in the Pacific.

Yet theirs was a vital step up. The American moon project was contingent upon the docking of an *Apollo* mother ship with a lunar landing craft, and the *Gemini VIII* flight proved it could be done.

The United States had to its credit another space achievement. In August, 1962, it propelled an unmanned craft, *Mariner II,* on a 36,000,000-mile trip into space so accurately that, 3½ months later, it passed within 21,000 miles of Venus and was able to radio back the first close-up reports on the planet's atmosphere. The Soviet Union achieved a semi-hard landing on the moon in February, 1966. Its *Luna IX* dropped into a small crater near the Ocean of Storms and sent back the first television pictures ever taken on the moon's surface. And the United States went the Soviet one better in June, 1966. Its *Surveyor* made the first soft landing ever attained on the moon, gently alighting right at its lunar destination and quickly transmitting thousands of TV pictures. Its findings and those of *Luna IX* indicated that lunar explorers no longer have to fear drowning in a choking sea of dust. Apparently, the moon's crust is similar to the earth's, enough so certainly to bear the weight of a spacecraft.

The earth, the moon and the planets were coming close.

Undeniably, the space competition was urging each nation on to greater heights. In the United States, the aerospace industry had gotten to be the largest employer in the land with 1,253,000 workers and a payroll of more than nine billion dollars a year. In Russia, the aerospace industry had grown proportionately. In both countries, distinguished scientists were working on new and incredibly brawny sources of power for space exploration. Nuclear reactors able to drive spaceships millions of miles to the farthermost corners of the solar system were being designed, and research was well advanced on fuels more efficient than the atom, such as ion rays and plasma.

All mankind was benefiting. As Dr. von Braun had predicted, the time was nearing when travel to the moon would be a matter of routine; when "there would be a permanent base on the moon with a couple dozen people living there all year round," shuttling back and forth at regular intervals for vacations on earth. And the moon was only the first stop. According to Dr. von Braun, manned expeditions to Mars could be expected by 1983. "Our astronauts," he said, "should be able to travel the 35,000,000 miles from the earth to the 'Red Planet' in a little over two months, less time than it took the Pilgrims to sail the Atlantic."

So, in the historic countdown for space, the signal was, "All systems go."

It has been a long, long journey since the era, hundreds of thousands of years ago, when manlike creatures were plodding on foot through the trackless jungles and deserts, primeval forests and plains, of Europe, Africa, and the west of Asia; since the day when some man finally summoned up the courage to build himself a raft and travel downriver by paddle power.

To get here, man has invented a myriad of different means of transport. Determinedly he has adapted every known source of power—his own sinews, the wind, beasts, steam, electricity, internally combusted gasoline, split atoms—to his transportation needs, and, ceaselessly, he has worked to better his technology, moving up from the roller and the primitive wheel to chariots, coaches, trains, and automobiles; from logs, rafts, and dugout canoes to sailing ships, steamships, submarines, nuclear-powered vessels, and hovercraft; from the feathered glider and the smoke-filled balloon to the motorized box kite, the propeller-driven airliner, the swept-wing jet and the rocket ship. He has exhibited peerless talent, ingenuity, and versatility, expecially in recent years. It is often forgotten that for many millennia the horse was the fastest "vehicle" in the world. Nothing could keep up with its thirty-five miles per hour. Not until the steam locomotive arrived in the 1830's was the "hay barrier" broken. And it was to be 130 more years after that before any real speeds were achieved. When the legendary railroad engineer Casey Jones came roaring down the tracks and smashed into a halted train at Vaughan, Mississippi, on April 25, 1900, he was doing only seventy miles per hour. The first military airplanes purchased by the United States in 1910 had contract clauses demanding a speed of "at least forty miles per hour," that's all. Seventeen years later in 1927, Lindbergh, flying the Atlantic, barely averaged 107 miles per hour, and at the start of World War II in 1939 the fastest fighter couldn't go much more than 350 miles an hour. Twenty-three more years, though, and Colonel Glenn was doing 17,500 miles an hour.

Farther and farther, man has gone on his journey until he has reached virtually every spot on the surface of the globe (although he has yet to explore the bottom of most of his oceans), and steadfastly he has improved the efficiency, utility, and comfort of his means of transport.

National Aeronautics and Space Administration

Few activities of man have contributed as much to the progress of his civilization as these means of transport. Since the morning of history, the life of every human being has been affected by transportation. Transportation has made possible trade, exploration, travel. It has introduced the peoples of the world to each other, and shortened the distances between them. It has brought about some of the most romantic moments in the annals that men have lived and written. As much as any other one thing, transportation has helped to take man from his primeval mire and lift him higher and higher, economically, socially, and culturally.

One can see how far man has gone by looking around the world today. At stone age cultures in Australia still without the wheel. At Outer Mongolia where distances are measured in yak-days. At sleds hauled by reindeer in the Arctic, at dugout canoes on the Amazon, at reed skiffs on the Nile, and at a spaceship standing skyward on its ephemeral vapor trail.

One can see how far man has yet to go by looking up at the stars. As he has had to travel everywhere else, man must now travel to outer space. He must conquer distance and always go a little farther than he ever has before.

And he will.

Bibliography

BOOKS

Allen, Frederick Lewis, *Only Yesterday*. New York, Harper, 1931.
———— *Since Yesterday*. New York, Harper, 1939.
American Heritage, ed., *The American Heritage History of Flight*, Alvin M. Joseph, ed. in charge. New York, American Heritage, 1962.
Anderson, Rudolph E., *The Story of the American Automobile*. Washington, Public Affairs Press, 1950.
Anderson, Ruth Mary Clementi, *The Roads of England*. London, Benn, 1932.
Armstrong, Warren, *Atlantic Highway*. New York, Day, 1962.
Arrian, *Arrian's Life of Alexander The Great*, trans. by Aubrey de Selincourt. Baltimore, Penguin, 1958.
Ashton, T. S., *The Industrial Revolution 1760–1830*. New York, Oxford University Press, 1960.
Automobile Manufacturers Association, Inc., *Automobiles of America*. Detroit, Wayne State University Press, 1962.
Barger, E. L., and others, *Tractors and Their Power Units*. New York, Wiley, 1952.
Bates, Lindon, *The Russian Road to China*. Boston, Houghton Mifflin, 1910.
Beach, Captain Edward L., U.S.N., *Around the World Submerged*. New York, Holt, Rinehart & Winston, 1962.
Beatty, Charles, *De Lesseps of Suez*. New York, Harper, 1957.
Beckmann, Martin, *Studies in the Economics of Transportation*. New Haven, Yale University Press, 1956, c. 1955.
Beebe, Lucius, and Clegg, Charles, *Hear the Train Blow*. New York, Dutton, 1952.
Beebe, Lucius, *High Iron*. New York, Appleton-Century, 1943.
Berg, Gosta, *Sledges and Wheeled Vehicles: Ethnological Studies from the Viewpoint of Sweden*. Stockholm; Copenhagen, Fritze; Levin & Munksgaard, 1935.

295

Bergaust, Erik, *Reaching for the Stars.* Garden City, New York, Doubleday, 1960.

Bibby, Geoffrey, *Four Thousand Years Ago.* New York, Knopf, 1962, c. 1961.

Bigham, Truman Cicero, *Transportation: Principles and Problems,* 2nd ed. New York, McGraw-Hill, 1952.

Bird, Anthony, *The Motor Car 1765–1914.* London, Batsford, 1960.

Bishop, Joseph Bucklin, *The Panama Gateway.* New York, Scribner, 1913.

Bisset, James Gordon Partridge, *Tramps and Ladies: My Early Years in Steamers.* New York, Criterion, 1959.

Black, Archibald, *The Story of Tunnels.* New York, McGraw-Hill, 1937.

Blackman, Raymond V. B., *The Modern World Book of Ships.* London, Low, 1951.

Blair, Clay, Jr., *The Atomic Submarine and Admiral Rickover.* New York, Holt, 1954.

Bligh, William, *The Mutiny on Board H.M.S. Bounty.* New York, New American Library, 1962.

Boardman, Fon W., Jr., *Roads.* New York, Walck, 1958.

Bobbe, Dorothie, *DeWitt Clinton.* New York, Minton, Balch, 1933.

Botkin, B. A., and Harlow, Alvin F., eds., *A Treasury of Railroad Folklore.* New York, Crown, 1953.

Boulton, William H., *The Pageant of Transport Through the Ages.* London, Silow, Marston, 1931.

Boyd, Thomas Alvin, *Professional Amateur: The Biography of Charles F. Kettering.* New York, Dutton, 1957.

Breasted, James Henry, *Ancient Records of Egypt* (5 vols.). Chicago, University of Chicago Press, 1906–1907.

——— *A History of Egypt from the Earliest Times to the Persian Conquest,* 2nd ed., rev. London, Hodder & Stoughton, 1951.

Brittain, Robert, *Rivers, Man and Myths.* Garden City, New York, Doubleday, 1958.

Buchanan, Lamont, *Ships of Steam.* New York, McGraw-Hill, 1956.

Buley, Roscoe Carlyle, *The Old Northwest Pioneer Period, 1815–1840.* Indianapolis, Indiana Historical Society, 1950.

Burton, Elizabeth, *The Pageant of Stuart England.* New York, Scribner, 1962.

Canby, Courtlandt, *A History of Flight.* New York, Hawthorn, 1963.

——— *A History of Ships and Seafaring.* New York, Hawthorn, 1963.

Carpenter, M. Scott, and others, *We Seven.* New York, Simon & Schuster, 1962.

Carse, Robert, *The Moonrakers,* New York, Harper, 1961.

Casson, Lionel, *The Ancient Mariners.* New York, Macmillan, 1959.

Chalmers, Harvey, III, in collaboration with John H. Flandreau, *The Birth of the Erie Canal.* New York, Bookman Associates, 1960.

Chapelle, Howard I., *The History of American Sailing Ships*. New York, Norton, 1935.

Charlesworth, Martin Percival, *Trade Routes and Commerce of the Roman Empire*. Cambridge, England, Cambridge University Press, 1924.

Chi, Ch'ao-ting, *Key Economic Areas in Chinese History*. London, Allen, 1936.

Childe, V. Gordon, *What Happened in History*. London, Penguin, 1942.

Chinitz, Benjamin, *Freight and the Metropolis*. Cambridge, Mass., Harvard University Press, 1960.

Chrysler, Walter P., in collaboration with Boyden Sparks, *Life of an American Workman*. New York, Dodd, Mead, 1937.

Churchill, Winston S., *The World Crisis,* Vol. I. New York, Scribner, 1923.

Clark, Arthur H., *The Clipper Ship Era*. New York, Putnam, 1910.

Clark, Sir George, *The Seventeenth Century*. New York, Oxford University Press, 1961.

Clarke, Arthur C., *The Exploration of Space,* rev. ed. New York, Harper, 1959.

Clementson, George B., *The Road Rights and Liabilities of Wheelmen*. Chicago, Callaghan, 1895.

Clymer, Floyd, *Henry's Wonderful Model T*. New York, McGraw-Hill, 1955.

——— *Those Wonderful Old Automobiles*. New York, McGraw-Hill, 1953.

——— *Treasury of Early American Automobiles*. New York, McGraw-Hill, 1950.

Cochrane, Elizabeth, *Nellie Bly's Book: Around the World in Seventy-Two Days*. New York, Pictorial Weeklies, 1890.

Collinder, Per Arne, *A History of Marine Navigation,* trans. by Maurice Michael. London, Batsford, 1954.

Columbus, Christopher, *Journal of First Voyage to America*. New York, Albert & Charles Boni, 1924.

Commager, Henry Steele, and Nevins, Allan, eds., *The Heritage of America*. Boston, Little, Brown, 1951.

Compère, Tom, ed., *The Air Force Blue Book* (2 vols.). New York, Military Publishing, 1959, 1960.

——— *The Army Blue Book*. New York, Military Publishing, 1960.

——— *The Navy Blue Book*. New York, Military Publishing, 1960.

Cooper, Frederick Stephen, *A Handbook of Sailing Barges*. New York, de Graff, 1955.

Cottrell, Leonard, *The Anvil of Civilization*. New York, New American Library, 1957.

——— *The Bull of Minos*. London, Evans, 1953.

Cox, Donald W., *The Space Race*. Philadelphia, Chilton, 1962.

Creel, Herrlee Glessner, *The Birth of China*. New York, Ungar, 1937.

Cross, Wilbur, *Challengers of the Deep*. New York, Sloane, 1959.

Cutler, Carl C., *Greyhounds of the Sea*. Annapolis, United States Naval Institute, 1960.

Daggett, Stuart, *Principles of Inland Transportation*, 4th ed. New York, Harper, 1955.

Daniels, Jonathan, *The Devil's Backbone*. New York, McGraw-Hill, 1962.

Darwin, Charles R., *The Voyage of The Beagle*. New York, Harper, 1959.

Dawson, Philip, *Electric Traction on Railways*. London, "The Electrician," 1909.

de Camp, L. Sprague, *The Ancient Engineers*. Garden City, New York, Doubleday, 1963.

—— *The Heroic Age of American Invention*. Garden City, New York, Doubleday, 1961.

De Voto, Bernard A., *The Course of Empire*. Boston, Houghton Mifflin, 1952.

Dickens, Charles, *American Notes*. New York, Scribner, 1910.

Dodds, John W., *The Age of Paradox*. London, Gollancz, 1953.

Dollfus, Charles, *The Orion Book of Balloons,* trans. from French *Les Ballons* by Carter Mason. New York, Orion, 1961, c. 1960.

Donovan, Frank, *Wheels for a Nation*. New York, Crowell, 1965.

Dorion, Edith McEwen, and Wilson, W. N., *Trails West, and Men Who Made Them*. New York, Whittlesey House, 1955.

Duke, Neville, and Lanchbery, Edward, eds., *The Saga of Flight*. New York, Day, 1961.

Dulles, Foster Rhea, *Eastward Ho!* London, Lane, 1931.

Dunbar, Seymour, *A History of Travel in America*. Indianapolis, Bobbs-Merrill, 1915.

Duncan, Herbert Osbaldeston, *The World on Wheels*. Paris, Duncan, 1926.

Durant, John, and Durant, Alice, *Pictorial History of American Ships*. New York, Barnes, 1953.

Duryea, J. Frank, *America's First Automobile*. Springfield, Mass., Macaulay, 1942.

Earle, Alice Morse, *Colonial Dames and Good Wives*. New York, Ungar, 1962.

East, Gordon, *A Historical Geography of Europe,* 3rd ed., rev. London, Methuen, 1948.

Eaton, Jeanette, *The Story of Transportation*. New York, Harper, 1927.

Eggenhofer, Nick, *Wagons, Mules and Men*. New York, Hastings House, 1961.

Eliot, Charles W., ed., *The Harvard Classics*, Vol. 9, Cicero's *Letters*; Vol. 13, Virgil's *Aeneid*; Vol. 33, *Voyages and Travels*; Vol. 49, *Epic and Saga*. New York, Collier, 1909–1910.

Epstein, Samuel, and Beryl Williams, *The Rocket Pioneers*. New York, Messner, 1955.

Erman, Adolph, *A Handbook of Egyptian Religion,* trans. by Agnes S. Griffith. London, Constable, 1907.

—— *Life in Ancient Egypt,* trans. by H. M. Tirard. New York, Macmillan, 1894.

———— *The Literature of the Ancient Egyptians*, trans. by M. Blackman. London, Methuen, 1927.

Eyre, Frank, and Hadfield, E. C. R., *English Rivers and Canals*. London, Collins, 1947.

Fabre, Maurice, *A History of Land Transportation*. New York, Hawthorn, 1963.

Fa-Heen, *The Travels of Fa-Hsien (399–414 A.D.)*, trans. by H. A. Giles. Cambridge, England, Cambridge University Press, 1923.

Fair, Marvin Luke, and Ernest W. Williams, Jr., *Economics of Transportation* (rev. ed.). New York, Harper, 1959.

Fiske, John, *The Critical Period of American History 1783–1789*. Boston, Houghton Mifflin, 1888.

———— *Old Virginia and Her Neighbors* (2 vols.). Boston, Houghton Mifflin, 1900.

Fleming, Alice, *Wheels*. Philadelphia, Lippincott, 1960.

Forbes, R. J., *Notes on the History of Ancient Roads and Their Construction*. Amsterdam, N.V. Noord Hollandsche Ultgevers—M.J., 1934.

Ford, Henry, in collaboration with Samuel Crowther, *My Life and Work*. Garden City, New York, Garden City Publishing, 1922.

Frank, Tenney, *An Economic History of Rome*. Baltimore, Johns Hopkins, 1927.

Frankfort, Henri, *Birth of Civilization in the Near East*. New York, Doubleday, 1956.

Franklin, Benjamin, *Autobiography of Benjamin Franklin*. New York, Pocket Books.

Frederick, John H., *Commercial Air Transportation*, 5th ed. Homewood, Illinois, Irwin, 1961.

Freuchen, Peter, *Book of the Seven Seas*. New York, Messner, 1957.

Garbutt, Paul E., *A Survey of Railway Development and Practice*. London, Stockwell, 1939.

Gartmann, Heinz, *Rings Around the World*, trans. by Alan G. Readett. New York, Morrow, 1959.

Gest, Alexander Purves, *Our Debt to Greece and Rome: Engineering*. New York, Longmans, 1930.

Gibson, Charles E., *The Story of the Ship*. New York, Schuman, 1948.

Gilmore, Harlan Welch, *Transportation and the Growth of Cities*. Glencoe, Illinois, Free Press of Glencoe, 1953.

Glines, Carroll V., and Moseley, Wendell F., *Grand Old Lady*. Cleveland, Pennington, 1959.

Glover, T. R., *The Ancient World*. New York, Macmillan, 1935.

Goethe, J. W., *Italian Journey (1786–1788)*. New York, Pantheon, 1962.

Great Britain, Ministry of Transport and Civil Aviation, and the Central Office of Information, *Seafarers and Their Ships*. New York, Philosophical Library, 1956.

Grossman, William L., *Fundamentals of Transportation*. New York, Simmons-Boardman, 1959.

Gurney, Gene, *The War in the Air*. New York, Crown, 1962.

Gwyther, John, *Captain Cook and the South Pacific*. Boston, Houghton Mifflin, 1955.

Hadley, Arthur T., *Railroad Transportation: Its History and Its Laws*. New York, Putnam, 1885.

Halliburton, Richard, *The Flying Carpet*. Indianapolis, Bobbs-Merrill, 1932.

Hamilton, Edith, *Mythology*. New York, New American Library, 1961.

Harlow, Alvin F., *Steelways of New England*. New York, Creative Age, 1946.

Hart, Albert Bushnell, ed., *American History Told by Contemporaries*, Vols. I-IV. New York, Macmillan, 1900.

Haskin, Frederick J., *The Panama Canal*. New York, Doubleday, Page, 1914.

Havighurst, Walter E., *The Long Ships Passing*. New York, Macmillan, 1942.

Hawks, Ellison, *The Book of the "De Luxe" Ford (10 h.p.)*. London, Gregg, 1935.

—— *The Book of the Warship*. London, Harrap, 1933.

—— *The Romance of the Merchant Ship*. London, Harrap, 1931.

—— *The Romance of Transport*. New York, Crowell, 1931.

Hedin, Sven Anders, *The Silk Road*. New York, Dutton, 1938.

Heer, Friedrich, *The Medieval World*. Cleveland, World, 1962.

Heilperin, Michael Angelo, *The Trade of Nations*, 2nd ed., enl. New York, Knopf, 1952.

Henry, Robert Selph, *Trains*, Midcentury ed. Indianapolis, Bobbs-Merrill, 1949.

Herodotus, *The History of Herodotus*, trans. by George Rawlinson. New York, Tudor, 1956.

Hesiod, "Works and Days" in *Collected Works*, trans. by Richmond Lattimore. Ann Arbor, University of Michigan Press, 1959.

Highet, Gilbert, *The Migration of Ideas*. New York, Oxford University Press, 1959.

Hill, Ralph Nading, *Sidewheeler Saga*. New York, Rinehart, 1953.

Hoehling, A. A., *They Sail into Oblivion*. New York, Yoseloff, 1959.

Holbrook, Stewart Hall, *Machines of Plenty*. New York, Macmillan, 1955.

—— *The Old Post Road*. New York, McGraw-Hill, 1962.

—— *The Story of American Railroads*. New York, Crown, 1947.

Homer, *The Complete Works of Homer*, trans. by Andrew Lang, Walter Leaf, Ernest Myers, S. H. Butcher, and Andrew Lang. New York, Modern Library.

Horace, *Satires and Epistles of Horace*, trans. by Smith Palmer Bovie. Chicago, University of Chicago Press, 1959.

Howard, Robert West, *The Great Iron Trail*. New York, Putnam, 1962.

Howell, James, *The Familiar Letters of James Howell* (2 vols.). Boston, Houghton Mifflin, 1907.

———— *Instructions for Forreine Travell*. Westminster, Constable, 1895.

Hughes, Thomas, *Tom Brown's Schooldays*. New York, Dutton, 1952.

Hugill, Stan, comp. & ed., *Shanties from the Seven Seas*. New York, Dutton, 1961.

Hulbert, Archer Butler, *The Cumberland Road*. Cleveland, Clark, 1904.

———— *The Great American Canals*. Cleveland, Clark, 1904.

Jackman, William T., *The Development of Transportation in Modern England*, 2nd ed., rev. London, Cass, 1962.

Jenkins, Rhys, *Power Locomotion on the Highway*. London, Cate, 1896.

Johnson, Emory Richard, *Elements of Transportation*. New York, Appleton, 1909.

Kelly, Charles J., Jr., *The Sky's the Limit*. New York, Coward-McCann, 1963.

Kelly, Fred C., ed., *Miracle at Kitty Hawk: The Letters of Wilbur and Orville Wright*. New York, Farrar, Straus & Giroux, 1951.

———— *The Wright Brothers*. New York, Harcourt, Brace, 1943.

Kennedy, William S., *Wonders and Curiosities of the Railway*. Chicago, Griggs, 1884.

Ker, William Paton, *The Dark Ages*. London, Nelson, 1955.

Kidner, Roger W., *The First Hundred Road Motors*. South Godstone, Surrey, Oakwood, 1950.

Kipling, Rudyard, *From Sea to Sea: Letters of Travel* (2 vols.). New York, Doubleday & McClure, 1899.

Kitto, H. D. F., *The Greeks*. London, Penguin, 1954.

Knight, Frank, *The Sea Story*. New York, St. Martin's, 1958.

Kramer, Samuel Noah, *From the Tablets of Sumer*. Indian Hills, Colorado, Falcon's Wing, 1956.

———— *History Begins at Sumer*. New York, Doubleday, 1959.

Kyner, James H., as told to Daniel Hawthorne, *End of Track*. Lincoln, University of Nebraska Press, 1960.

Lamb, Harold, *The Crusades*. Garden City, New York, Doubleday, 1931.

Langdon, William C., *Everyday Things in American Life, 1607–1776*. New York, Scribner, 1937.

———— *Everyday Things in American Life, 1776–1876*. New York, Scribner, 1941.

Larsen, Egon, *A History of Invention*. New York, Roy, 1961.

Lee, Charles E., *The Evolution of Railways*, 2nd ed., rev. and enl. London, The Railway Gazette, 1943.

Lee, Norman E., *Travel and Transport Through the Ages*, 2nd ed., rev. Cambridge, England, Cambridge University Press, 1956.

Lee, W. Storrs, *The Strength to Move a Mountain*. New York, Putnam, 1958.

Leech, Margaret, *In the Days of McKinley*. New York, Harper, 1959.

Lehman, Milton, *This High Man*. New York, Farrar, Straus, & Giroux, 1963.

de Lesseps, Ferdinand, *Recollections of Forty Years*. New York, Appleton, 1888.

Leuchtenburg, William E., *The Perils of Prosperity 1914–32*. Chicago, University of Chicago Press, 1958.

Lewis, Naphtali, and Reinhold, Meyer, eds., *Roman Civilization: Selected Readings* (2 vols.). New York, Columbia University Press, 1959.

Ley, Willy, *Rockets, Missiles and Space Travel*. New York, Viking, 1961.

Li Chih Ch'ang, *The Travels of an Alchemist*, trans. by Arthur Waley. London, Routledge, 1931.

Lief, Alfred, *The Firestone Story*. New York, McGraw-Hill, 1951.

———— *Harvey Firestone, Free Man of Enterprise*. New York, McGraw-Hill, 1951.

Lindbergh, Charles A., *The Spirit of St. Louis*. New York, Scribner, 1953.

Lindsay, William S., *History of Merchant Shipping and Ancient Commerce* (4 vols.). London, 1874–76.

Lissner, Ivar, *The Living Past*, trans. by J. Maxwell Brownjohn. New York, Putnam, 1962.

———— *The Silent Past*, trans. by J. Maxwell Brownjohn. New York, Putnam, 1957.

Locklin, David Philip, *Economics of Transportation*, 5th ed. Homewood, Illinois, Irwin, 1960.

Lomax, Alan, *Folk Songs of North America*. Garden City, New York, Doubleday, 1960.

Lord, Walter, *A Night to Remember*. New York, Holt, 1955.

Ludwig, Emil, *The Mediterranean*. New York, McGraw-Hill, 1942.

Mahn-Lot, Marianne, *Columbus*. New York, Grove, 1961.

Mannix, Daniel P., in collaboration with Malcolm Cowley, *Black Cargoes: A History of the Atlantic Slave Trade, 1518–1865*. New York, Viking, 1962.

Marvin, W. L., *American Merchant Marine*. New York, Scribner, 1902.

Matthiessen, Peter, *Under the Mountain Wall: A Chronicle of Two Seasons in the Stone Age*. New York, Viking, 1962.

McBride, Harry Alexander, *Trains Rolling*. New York, Macmillan, 1953.

McCurdy, Edward, *The Notebooks of Leonardo da Vinci*. New York, Reynal & Hitchcock, 1939.

McKay, Richard C., *Some Famous Sailing Ships and Their Builder, Donald McKay*. New York, Putnam, 1928.

Means, James, ed., *Aeronautical Annuals*. Boston, 1895, 1896, 1897.

Merrill, George Edmands, *Crusaders and Captives*. Boston, DeWolfe, Fiske, 1890.

Middleton, P. Harvey, *Railways of Thirty Nations*. New York, Prentice-Hall, 1937.

Mills, J. Saxon, *The Panama Canal*. London, Nelson, 1914.

Montagu, Lady Mary (Pierrepont) Wortley, *Letters from the Right Honorable Lady Mary Wortley Montagu 1709 to 1762*. New York, Dutton, 1906.

Montross, Lynn, *War Through the Ages*, 3rd ed., rev. and enl. New York, Harper, 1960.

Moore, Byron, *The First Five Million Miles*. New York, Harper, 1955.

Morison, Samuel Eliot, *Admiral of the Ocean Seas*. Boston, Little, Brown, 1942.

———— *The Maritime History of Massachusetts*. Boston, Houghton Mifflin, 1961.

Morris, Richard B., ed., *Encyclopedia of American History*. New York, Harper, 1961.

Morse, Hosea Ballou, *The Trade and Administration of the Chinese Empire*. London, Longmans, 1908.

Morton, Frederick, *The Rothschilds*. New York, Atheneum, 1962.

Neider, Charles, ed., *The Travels of Mark Twain*. New York, Coward-McCann, 1961.

Nevins, Allan, *Ford: The Times, The Man, The Company*. New York, Scribner, 1954.

———— and Frank Ernest Hill, *Ford: Expansion and Challenge, 1915–1933*. New York, Scribner, 1957.

Nishimura, Shinji, *Ancient Rafts of Japan*. Tokyo, The Society of Naval Architects, 1925.

Niven, John, Canby, Courtland, and Welsh, Vernon, eds., *Dynamic America*. New York, General Dynamics Corp. & Doubleday, 1960.

Nolan, William F., *Barney Oldfield*. New York, Putnam, 1961.

Oliphant, Mrs., *The Makers of Florence*. New York, Burt.

———— *The Makers of Venice*. New York, Burt.

Outhwaite, Leonard, *The Atlantic*. New York, Coward-McCann, 1957.

Painter, Sidney, *A History of the Middle Ages, 284–1500*. New York, Knopf, 1958.

Palmer, Arthur Judson, *Riding High; The Story of the Bicycle*. New York, Dutton, 1956.

Pangborn, J. G., *The World's Railway*. New York, Winchell, 1894–1896.

Parsons, W. B., *Engineers and Engineering in the Renaissance*. Baltimore, Wilkins, 1939.

Partridge, Bellamy, *Fill 'er Up!* New York, McGraw-Hill, 1952.

Payne, Robert, *The Canal Builders*. New York, Macmillan, 1959.

Pendlebury, John D. S., *The Archaeology of Crete*. London, Methuen, 1939.

Penrose, Boise, *Travel and Discovery in the Renaissance*. New York, Atheneum, 1962.

Perry, John, *American Ferryboats*. New York, Funk, 1957.

Piccard, Jacques, and Dietz, Robert S., *Seven Miles Down*. New York, Putnam, 1961.

Piggott, Stuart, ed., *The Dawn of Civilization*. New York, McGraw-Hill, 1961.

Pliny, The Elder, *Historia Naturalis* (10 vols.), trans. by H. Rackham, W. H. S. Jones, and D. E. Eichholz. Cambridge, Mass., Harvard University Press, 1938–62.

Polo, Marco, *The Travels of Marco Polo*, trans. by Aldo Ricci. New York, Viking, 1931.

Pound, Arthur, *The Turning Wheel: The Story of General Motors Through Twenty-five Years, 1908–1933*. Garden City, New York, Doubleday, Doran, 1934.

Power, Eileen, *Medieval People*, 10th ed. New York, Barnes & Noble, 1963.

Powicke, Sir F. M., *Ways of Medieval Life and Thought*. London, Odhams, 1950.

Pratt, Edwin A., *A History of Inland Transport and Communication in England*. New York, Dutton, 1912.

Quigley, Carrol, *The Evolution of Civilization*. New York, Macmillan, 1961.

Rae, John B., *American Automobile Manufacturers*. Philadelphia, Chilton, 1959.

Ricci, Matthew, *China in the 16th Century: The Journals of Matthew Ricci 1583–1610*, trans. by Louis J. Gallagher. New York, Random House, 1953.

Robbins, Michael, *The Railway Age*. London, Routledge & Paul, 1962.

Robinson, Donald, *The Day I Was Proudest to Be an American*. Garden City, New York, Doubleday, 1958.

—————— *The Face of Disaster*. Garden City, New York, Doubleday, 1959.

—————— *The 100 Most Important People in the World Today*. Boston, Little, Brown, 1952.

Robinson, John, and Dow, George F., *Sailing Ships of New England 1607–1907*. Westminster, Maryland, Eckenrode, 1953.

Robinson, William, ed., *Yachting, The Science of Sailing*. New York, Scribner, 1960.

Rocheleau, W. F., *Great American Industries*, Vol. IV, *Transportation*. Chicago, Flanagan, 1914.

Rolfe, Douglas, and Dawydoff, Alexis, *Airplanes of the World*. New York, Simon & Schuster, 1954.

Rolt, L. T. C., *The Inland Waterways of England*. London, Allen, 1950.

Rugoff, Milton A., ed., *The Great Travelers* (2 vols.). New York, Simon & Schuster, 1960.

Saggs, H. W. F., *The Greatness That Was Babylon*. New York, Hawthorn, 1962.

St. Clair, Labert, *Transportation: Land, Air, Water*, rev. ed. New York, Dodd, Mead, 1942.

Saint-Exupery, Antoine de, *Wind, Sand and Stars*, trans. by Lewis Galantiere. New York, Harcourt, Brace, c. 1940.

Salmon, E. T., *A History of the Roman World From 30 B.C.–A.D. 138*, 2nd ed., rev. London, Methuen, 1950.

Sandstrom, Gosta E., *Tunnels*. New York, Holt, Rinehart & Winston, 1963.

Schreiber, Hermann, *Merchants, Pilgrims and Highwaymen*. New York, Putnam, 1962, c. 1961.

Schumer, Leslie A., *The Elements of Transport*. Sydney, Butterworth, 1955.

Scullard, H. H., *A History of the Roman World 753–146 B.C.*, 3rd ed. London, Methuen, 1961.

Sennett, A. R., *Carriages Without Horses Shall Go*. London, Whittaker, 1896.

Silverman, Jerry, *Folk Blues*. New York, Macmillan, 1958.

Simpson, George Gaylord, *Horses*. New York, Oxford University Press, 1951.

Singer, Charles, *A Short History of Scientific Ideas to 1900*. London, Oxford University Press, 1959.

—— Holmyard, E. J., and Hall, A. R., *A History of Technology* (5 vols.). New York, Oxford University Press, 1954–58.

Sloane, Eric, *The Seasons of America Past*. New York, Funk, 1958.

Smiles, Samuel, *Lives of the Engineers* (3 vols.). London, Murray, 1861–62.

—— and Brindley, James, *The Early Engineers*. London, Murray, 1864.

Smith, H. Shirley, *The World's Great Bridges*. New York, Harper, 1953.

Snow, Edward Rowe, *Women of the Sea*. New York, Dodd, Mead, 1962.

Sorensen, Charles E., in collaboration with S. T. Williamson, *My Forty Years with Ford*. New York, Norton, 1956.

Spectorsky, Auguste C., ed., *The Book of the Earth*. New York, Appleton-Century-Crofts, 1957.

—— *The Book of the Sea*. New York, Appleton-Century-Crofts, 1954.

Spratt, H. P., *Outline History of Transatlantic Steam Navigation*. London, Science Museum, 1950.

Stackpole, Edouard A., ed., *Those in Peril on the Sea*. New York, Dial, 1962.

Stanford, Don, *The Ile de France*. New York, Appleton-Century-Crofts, 1960.

Stanley, Arthur, ed., *The Golden Road*. London, Dent, 1938.

Steinbeck, John, *Travels with Charley*. New York, Viking, 1962.

Steinman, David B., and Watson, Sarah Ruth, *Bridges and Their Builders*. New York, Putnam, 1941.

Stern, Philip Van Doren, *Tin Lizzie*. New York, Simon & Schuster, 1955.

Stevenson, Robert Louis, *An Inland Voyage; Travels with a Donkey; The Amateur Emigrant*. London, Collins, 1956.

Stevers, Martin D., and Pendlebury, Captain Jonas, *Sea Lanes*. New York, Minton, Balch, 1935.

Stewart, George R., *The California Trail*. New York, McGraw-Hill, 1962.

Stillson, Blanche, *Wings*. Indianapolis, Bobbs-Merrill, 1954.

Stobart, John Clarke, *The Grandeur That Was Rome*, 4th ed., ed. & rev. by W. S. Maguiness and H. H. Scullard. New York, Hawthorn, 1962.

Stover, John F., *American Railroads*. Chicago, University of Chicago Press, 1961.

Strayer, Joseph R., and Munro, Dana C., *The Middle Ages 395–1500*. New York, Appleton-Century-Crofts, 1959.

Suggs, Robert C., *The Island Civilizations of Polynesia*. New York, New American Library, 1960.

Swain, Joseph Ward, *The Ancient World* (2 vols.). New York, Harper, 1950–62.

Sward, Keith, *The Legend of Henry Ford*. New York, Rinehart, 1948.

Swift, Jonathan, *Gulliver's Travels*. New York, Crown, 1947.

Sykes, Percy, *A History of Exploration*. New York, Harper, 1961.

Talbot, Frederick A., *The Railway Conquest of the World*. London, Heinemann, 1911.

Taylor, George Rogers, *The Transportation Revolution, 1815–1860*. New York, Rinehart, 1951.

Thackeray, William Makepeace, *From Cornhill to Cairo*. London, Dent, 1846.

Thoreau, Henry David, *Walden and Other Writings*. New York, Modern Library, 1950.

Thurston, Robert Henry, *A History of the Growth of the Steam Engine*, Centennial ed. Ithaca, New York, Cornell University Press, 1939.

Toland, John, *Ships in the Sky*. New York, Holt, 1957.

Torr, Cecil, *Ancient Ships*. London, Oxford University Press, 1894.

Toutain, Jules, *The Economic Life of the Ancient World*. New York, Knopf, 1930.

Toynbee, Arnold J., *A Study of History*. London, Oxford University Press, 1946.

Tunis, Edwin, *Wheels*. Cleveland, World, 1955.

Turner, Frederick J., *The Frontier in American History*. New York, Holt, 1920.

Twain, Mark, *Life on the Mississippi*. New York, Hill & Wang, 1961.

United States Coast Guard, *Coast Guard History*. Washington, 1958.

United States Department of Commerce, Bureau of Public Roads, *Highways in the United States*. Washington, 1954.

United States Public Roads Bureau, *Public Road Mileage and Revenues in the United States, 1914*. U.S. Agriculture Dept. Bulletin No. 390, 1917.

Vallentin, Antonina, *Leonardo da Vinci*, trans. by E. W. Dickes. New York, Viking, 1938.

Van Metre, Thurman William, *Transportation in the United States*. Chicago, The Foundation Press, 1939.

——— and Van Metre, Russel Gordon, *Trains, Tracks and Travel*. New York, Simmons-Boardman, 1956.

Van Thal, Herbert Maurice, ed., *Victoria's Subjects Travelled.* London, Barker, 1951.

Verne, Jules, *Space Novels by Jules Verne.* New York, Dover.

Vernon, Arthur, *The History and Romance of the Horse.* Boston, Waverly House, 1939.

Vitruvius, Pollio, *On Architecture* (2 vols.). London, Heinemann, 1931–34.

Von Hagen, Victor W., *Highway of the Sun.* New York, Duell, Sloan and Pearce, 1955.

———— *Realm of the Incas.* New York, New American Library, 1961.

Walker, George, *Haste, Post, Haste!* London, Harrap, 1938.

Wheeler, Sir Robert Eric Mortimer, *Rome Beyond the Imperial Frontiers.* London, Bell, 1954.

Whipple, Addison B. C., *Tall Ships and Great Captains.* New York, Harper, 1960.

Whitman, Roger B., *Motor-Car Principles.* New York, Appleton, 1909.

Wilson, B. G., and Day, J. R., *Famous Railways of the World.* London, Muller, 1957.

Wilson, Mitchell, *American Science and Invention.* New York, Simon & Schuster, 1954.

Wittfogel, Carl A., *Oriental Despotism.* New Haven, Yale University Press, 1963.

Woytinsky, Wladimir S., and Woytinsky, E. S., *World Commerce and Governments.* New York, Twentieth Century Fund, 1955.

Wright, Helen, and Rapport, Samuel, eds., *The Great Explorers.* New York, Harper, 1957.

Zehren, Erich, *The Crescent and the Bull,* trans. by James Cleugh. London, Sidgwick & Jackson, 1962.

MAGAZINES

Aerospace Industries Association of America, Inc., *Aerospace Facts and Figures 1962.* Washington, American Aviation Publications, 1962.

Air University Quarterly Review, Vol. II (Fall & Winter, 1959). "Air Force Nuclear Propulsion."

American Association of State Highway Officials, *Public Roads of the Past: 3500 B.C. to 1800 A.D.* Washington, American Association State Highway Officials, 1953.

———— *Historic American Highways.* Washington, American Association State Highway Officials, 1953.

American Transit Association, *The Urban Transportation Problem.* New York, American Electric Railway Association, 1932.

———— *Moving the Masses in Modern Cities.* New York, American Transit Association, 1940.

Automobile Manufacturers Association, Inc., *Automobile Facts and Figures.*

Detroit, Automobile Manufacturers Association, 1962, 1963, 1964, 1965.

———— *Motor Truck Facts 1965.* Detroit, Automobile Manufacturers Association, 1965.

Childe, I. G., "The First Waggons and Carts; from the Tigris to the Severn." *Prehistoric Soc. Proceedings* (London), Vol. 17, Pt. 2 (1951).

Colwell, M. W., "Worst Roads in America." *Outing,* Vol. 51 (Nov., 1907).

Dayton, T. S., "Motor Truck and the Farmers." *Harper's Weekly,* Vol. 57 (March 1, 1913).

Goodyear News, March, 1937.

Harper's Weekly, Vol. 41 (Sept. 18, 1897). "Opening of the Boston Subway."

Jenkins, C. F., "Transcontinental Highway." *Scientific American,* Vol. 106 (June 15, 1912).

Kelly, Fred C., "The Great Bicycle Craze." *American Heritage,* Vol. VIII, No. 1 (Dec., 1956).

Literary Digest, Vol. 44 (April 13, 1912). "Transcontinental Roads."

———— Vol. 45 (Oct. 12, 1912). "Ocean-to-Ocean Motor Highways."

———— Vol. 46 (Jan. 11, 1913). "Potent Facts About Motor Trucks."

———— Vol. 57 (June 8, 1918). "Our Crazy-quilt Road-system."

———— Vol. 103 (Oct. 26, 1929). "Our Next Job, Exporting Highways."

Pitcairn-Knowles, A., "Sailing on Terra Firma." *Badminton Magazine,* Vol. 27 (1908).

Pope, A. A., "Good Roads and the Nation's Prosperity." *Harper's Weekly,* Vol. 51 (Mar. 16, 1907).

Robinson, Donald, "Remember the Berlin Airlift." *The Reader's Digest* (Oct., 1961).

Scientific American, Vol. 103 (Nov. 12, 1910). "First Trackless Trolley in America."

———— Vol. 108 (April 19, 1913). "Good Roads Movement."

———— Vol. 134 (Feb., 1926). "Some Features of 1926 Motor Trucks."

———— Vol. 144 (Feb., 1931). "Diesel on the Highway."

Traffic World, Nov. 4, 1961. "Prophesy for 1990."

Wells, H. G., "Locomotion in the 20th Century." *Fortnightly Review,* Vol. 75 (April, 1901).

Wilson, J. "Good Roads Era." *Harper's Weekly,* Vol. 44 (Sept. 1, 1900).

Winton, Alexander, "Get a Horse." *Saturday Evening Post,* Vol. 202, No. 32 (Feb. 8, 1930).

World's Work, Vol. 59 (June, 1930). "New Highway Construction Record."

Index